THE FIRST AIR WAR
1914–1918

THE FIRST AIR WAR
1914–1918

Lee Kennett

THE FREE PRESS
A Division of Macmillan, Inc.
NEW YORK
Collier Macmillan Canada
TORONTO
Maxwell Macmillan International
NEW YORK   OXFORD   SINGAPORE   SYDNEY

The Free Press
A Division of Macmillan, Inc.
866 Third Avenue, New York, N. Y. 10022

Collier Macmillan Canada, Inc.
1200 Eglinton Avenue East
Suite 200
Don Mills, Ontario M3C 3N1

Printed in the United States of America

Printing number
1 2 3 4 5 6 7 8 9 10

Library of Congress Cataloging-in-Publication Data

Kennett, Lee B.
    The first air war, 1914–1918/Lee Kennett.
        p.   cm.
    Includes bibliographical references.
    ISBN 0–02–917301–9
    1. World War, 1914–1918—Aerial operations.   I. Title.
D600.K46   1991
940.4′4—dc20   90–43632
                                                              CIP

Pour Anne-Marie, qui est parue enfin.

Contents

To the Reader

Go into any large library and you will find at least one book on the events of April 21, 1918, the day the Red Baron fell; but you will find no book on aerial reconnaissance, that vital task of the World War I aviator. From the titles on the shelf you might conclude that the first air war was an Anglo-German duel; most likely you will find nothing on the French air force, the largest in the world in 1918, and there is even less chance of locating a book on the aerial effort of other belligerents. If you want to read about the impact of air power on the war at sea, you must look in another section of the library. The whole subject of the first air war is like some imperfectly explored country: there are areas that have been crisscrossed by several generations of historians; there are regions where only writers of dissertations and abstruse monographs have ventured, and others yet that remain *terra incognita*. My main purpose is therefore to achieve an overview in which all the parts of the picture are visible, with each given the prominence that the historical record indicates it merits.

As I have reviewed this first air war, I have also looked at the assumptions and the judgments that have been made about it and about its significance. Many of these are solidly anchored in fact; others have seemed to me simplistic, and still others grounded in little more than myth and wishful thinking. But I would like it understood that my goal is not to debunk or to discredit; even less would I wish to diminish the record of human valor and sacrifice in the pages that follow.

Acknowledgments

A historian who undertakes to write a book on a subject of this magnitude soon leaves behind the small area of his or her particular expertise. At that point one begins to call on the knowledge, the assistance, and sometimes simply the counsel of others. When I reached this stage it was my good fortune to hold the Lindbergh Professorship at the National Air and Space Museum. The appointment permitted me to work with a great wealth of materials, but most of all it put me in daily contact with the extraordinary group of aeronautical specialists on the Museum's staff. They were extremely generous with their time and expertise. Individually they helped me grasp such abtruse matters as monocoque construction, compression ratios, focal lengths, and early altimeters; collectively they were my richest source for the preparation of this book. Seven of them earned my special gratitude by reading and offering criticisms on portions of the text: Tim Wooldridge, Dom Pisano, Joanne Gernstein, Tom Dietz, Karl Schneide, Howard Wolko, and Don Lopez.

I also called on many others, both in the United States and abroad, and here I would like to thank all those who made a prompt and generous response: in Canada, Jean Pariseau; in France, Emmanuel Chadeau, Patrick Facon, Arnaud Teyssier and Gérard Fouilloux; in Italy, Ferruccio Botti and Andrea Curami; in Sweden, Klaus-Richard Böhme; in Mexico, Manuel Ruiz Romero; and in Greece, Konstantin Varfis and Paul Nicolaides. I am also indebted to a number of American colleagues: Robert Meyer, Jr., Despina White, Tim Nenninger, Charles Wynes, Frank Futrell, Rebecca Welch, James Hogue, Peter Grosz, Robin Higham, John Haag, and Warren Trest.

My research took me to a number of institutions that opened their holdings to me or helped me in other ways. I received a research grant to work in the United States Air Force Historical Research Center, Maxwell Air Force Base, and spent several very profitable weeks there. Dr. Lloyd Cornett, former head of the Research Center, extended every courtesy to me, as did his successor, Colonel Elliott V. Converse, III. I am also indebted to Dr. Horst Boog, Scientific Director of the West German Militärgeschichtliches Forschungsamt for his assistance to me in the course of my visits to Freiburg in 1986 and 1988; likewise I am grateful to Air Commodore Henry Probert, R.A.F. (Ret.), former Head of the Air Historical Branch, Ministry of Defence, and also to members of his staff, for assistance during my visit to London in 1988. General Lucien Robineau, Director of the Service Historique de l'Armée de l'Air, very much facilitated my use of French archival and printed materials held by his service, and I am most grateful for his help and that of his staff. Archivist Timothy Dubé gave me a cordial reception at the National Archives of Canada and helped make the days of research I spent there very rewarding ones.

I owe a final word of thanks for the assistance I received from the institution that has been my academic home for nearly three decades: the University of Georgia.

=1=

The Dawn of Air Power

I n May 1899, an extraordinary international conference opened at The Hague. The idea for a conference to promote "general peace and a possible reduction of excessive armaments" had come from the Russian government the previous year, and the response had been uniformly positive. Most of Europe was caught up in an arms race that was absorbing much of its attention and treasure. The Russian government hoped particularly for an agreement that would slow the growth of land armaments (it had learned that the fieldpieces its artillery had recently acquired at considerable expense were now rendered obsolete by advances in Germany and Austria). Other powers were concerned about new naval weapons such as the submarine and the impact it would have on war at sea, and there were other weapons whose use did not seem compatible with the customary laws of war.[1]

A new dimension of warfare was already on the horizon by 1899. One year before, a Polish scholar named Ivan Bliokh had published an influential study on modern warfare in which he predicted that "very soon balloons will be used to drop explosive substances." This prediction was accompanied by a warning: "It appears that we are very close to finding ourselves face to face with a danger before which the world cannot remain indifferent."[2]

The Russian government also acknowledged the danger, for in the proposals it circulated to other governments before the

1

Conference it included as point three "the prohibition of the discharge of any kind of projectile or explosive from balloons or by similar means." The intention of the Russians was to make the ban permanent, but when the assembled delegates took up point three it was an American delegate, Captain William Crozier, who proposed that the prohibition be temporary:

> The balloon, as we know it now, is not dirigible, it can carry but little; it is capable of hurling, only on points not exactly determined and over which it may pass by chance, indecisive quantities of explosives, which would fall, like useless hailstones, on both combatants and non-combatants alike. Under such conditions it is entirely suitable to forbid its use, but the prohibition should be temporary and not permanent. At a later stage in its development, if it be seen that its less desirable qualities still predominate, there will still be time to extend the prohibition.[3]

Captain Crozier moved that the ban be for a period of five years, at the end of which a second international conference could take up the whole question again. To the delegates, the captain held out the same glimmering possibility that has been evoked to justify every new weapon since the Gatling gun: by making war more efficient, it would make it less bloody and indiscriminate. Crozier said an effective air weapon might "localize at important points the destruction of life and property," and he felt it could "decrease the length of combat and consequently the evils of war." Such arguments carried the day. The delegations voted the five-year ban, and almost all the great powers ratified it.[4]

At the time of the First Hague Conference, every major army in Europe had for some time been making an ongoing investment in military aeronautics. To be sure, in 1899 the involvement was still modest, but that would soon change. Of all the powers, France had the longest record of interest, dating back to the French Revolution, when for a brief period the Revolutionary armies had included a corps of balloonists or *aérostiers*. There had been other periods of sporadic experimentation, and then in 1874 the French Army made what proved to be a permanent commitment. While overhauling its organization in the aftermath of the Franco-Prussian War, the Army created a communications subcommission charged with "aerostation," confiding to it matériel left over from the war and assigning it a base at Chalais-Meudon, not far from

Paris. In 1874 aerostation meant only one thing, free or tethered balloons carried aloft by hot air or hydrogen, most commonly the latter. These devices had been used to some effect in the late war, so that in the years following, military authorities in several countries carried out tests and demonstrations, though in most cases these were soon dropped. The French, who had the most extensive experience, were thus the first to create a permanent body for work in military aeronautics, while balloons of French manufacture, particularly those of Gabriel Yon, became a modest item of export. The British followed four years later with the creation of a balloon section under the Royal Engineers.[5]

The 1880s and 1890s saw a significant increase in military interest in the balloon; in 1884 alone ballooning units appeared in the armies of Russia, Germany, Italy, and Spain. In that era their chief use was in colonial campaigns; their employment was made easier by the introduction of portable cylinders for storing compressed hydrogen. The British took balloons to the Sudan and to South Africa, the Italians took them to Ethiopia, and the French used them in Indo-China and elsewhere. Their essential function everywhere was observation, and here they generally proved their value. The balloon section which the U.S. Army Signal Corps took to Cuba in 1898 was able to confirm the presence of the Spanish fleet in Santiago harbor, find a trail up San Juan Hill, and bring artillery fire to bear on Spanish positions. When it was used against primitive peoples the balloon promised other dividends. A British officer wrote in 1886 that the very sight of a balloon might go far in pacifying the rebellious Moslems of the Sudan:

> The realization by those fanatics that their camps and towns could by chemical means be fired in daylight by an unapproachable enemy, and on dark nights by an invisible agent would create the belief that we were assisted by supernatural powers and that Allah himself must surely befriend us.[6]

It was one thing to make an enemy fear that balloons would rain incendiary devices and explosives on him—the Boers in Pretoria seem to have feared that British balloons would do just that—and quite another to turn the balloon into an offensive weapon. A century after the first balloon took to the air (1783) several generations of inventors had devised nothing more effective than small bombs that could be released from a balloon when the wind carried it over an enemy position. The German aeronautical expert H. W. L. Mödebeck wrote in 1885 that "The value of the balloon as a weapon is still very much in doubt;" nor did he think the situation would change until the aerostat could become *lenkbar*, that is, steerable, or to use the term that would soon be on everyone's lips, dirigible.[7]

Even as Mödebeck wrote, the dirigible or airship was taking form. By 1884 at Chalais-Meudon a French officer named Charles Renard had already constructed a sausage-shaped balloon and suspended from it a scaffolding that contained an electric motor and a propeller. In August of that year, Renard had taken off in his dirigible, which he had named *La France*, and flown a four-mile circuit in 23 minutes. Renard then began the construction of an even larger airship and a more efficient power plant for it (the electric motor of *La France* had required a half-ton of batteries). The work did not go well; the search for the new motor was particularly frustrating. Renard had immersed himself completely in the project; when the succession of disappointments became unbearable, he took his own life. An equally sad fate was reserved for the self-taught Austrian engineer David Schwarz, who began construction of a dirigible in 1890. Schwarz had an advantage over Renard in that he had an efficient power plant in the internal combustion engine, which had been developed in the 1880s; then, too, he had at his disposal a new construction material, aluminum, which became plentiful with the introduction of the electrolytic process in 1886. Schwarz built and flew what was probably the first rigid dirigible, and embarked on a long search for government support in his work. He tried the Austrian government, then the Russian authorities, and then the Germans. When, in January 1897, Schwarz finally received a telegram from the German government agreeing to finance test flights, he fell dead from shock. Count Zeppelin, who had seen Schwarz's dirigible in flight, purchased the inventor's notes and drawings from his widow.[8]

In Germany, Count Ferdinand von Zeppelin had been occupied with dirigible design for years; his first proposal was presented to the King of Württemburg in May 1887. Other proposals to various German authorities followed, but the responses he received were cautious at best. The Count argued that his airships would be able to do many things, including taking men to the North Pole and "opening up the interior of Africa without great sacrifice," but his basic argument was that the airship would be useful in war. In principle the German military were eventually won over to this view, particularly after the French began extensive experiments with airships. In 1905 a German officer prepared a report acknowledging that the airship could be of significant value for reconnaissance, transport, and attacks on the enemy. But to be effective the new weapon would have to meet certain requirements: among other things it would have to stay in the air for many hours and cover hundreds of kilometers at a height of at least 1,500 meters. None of the Count's early dirigibles had been capable of anything approaching such performance.[9]

Meantime, research on the dirigible was continuing in France and Italy, and by the middle of the decade it seemed the greatest progress was being made in those countries, rather than in Germany. The Italian Army contributed to the building of the first civilian airship in Italy in 1905; in 1904 its Brigata Specialisti began studies for a military dirigible, which took to the air in 1908 as the Crocco-Ricaldoni No. 1. In France the army was sponsoring research at Chalais-Meudon, and inventors were busy in the private sector as well. Among these latter was Santos Dumont, who in 1902 went aloft in a dirigible, steered it around the Eiffel Tower, and returned safely to his starting point. Then there were the Lebaudy brothers, who had underwritten the development of a promising semi-rigid design in 1903. So impressed was the French Army with the Lebaudy system that it bought the firm's first dirigible in 1905. Before the year was out the specialists at Chalais-Meudon had begun a variety of tests with the new airship, including its use for reconnaissance, for directing artillery fire, and for bomb dropping.[10]

The five-year ban adopted at the First Hague Conference expired in 1904. The second conference, originally scheduled for that year, had to be postponed because of the Russo-Japanese War. When the Conference assembled in 1907, it was the French delegation that led the opposition to extending the ban; the French argued that it would be quite sufficient to impose on airships the same rules that had been adopted for land and sea forces, rules designed to shield non-combatants and their property during military operations. The delegates nevertheless agreed to propose the ban's extension to their governments; as it turned out, this was a fruitless gesture, for by 1914 only Great Britain had ratified the ban.[11]

It is tempting to speculate on what might have happened

had the ban been accepted by the powers. It might have had no impact whatever on the evolution of warfare—after all, the Hague Conference had banned the use of poison gas, with obvious lack of success. Yet the delegates to the Second Hague Conference did realize that their generation was taking a very fateful step in militarizing the skies, quite as fateful as that of militarizing space today. A British delegate spoke very eloquently of the need to step back from "the fatal precipice." Some lingering doubts remained about the legality and the morality of dropping bombs, particularly if it were done over a not clearly defined battlefield. Socialist and pacifist circles continued to denounce *Luftmilitarismus* and the dangers it presented to the populations of Europe. A perhaps more generalized feeling that the aerial weapon was improper, an *arme déloyale*, lingered on into 1914. When the first British civilians were killed by Zeppelin attacks, coroner's juries, duly convened, brought in indictments of "willful murder" against Kaiser William II of Germany.[12]

The years 1908 and 1909 were critical for flight generally, and particularly for military aeronautics. First and perhaps most spectacularly, 1908 finally saw the triumph of Count Zeppelin. On July 1 of that year his huge LZ-4—longer than a football field—rose from its mooring for a flight that captured headlines all over Europe. That day the great airship remained aloft for 12 hours, covering a distance of some 350 kilometers.

The airship had proved itself in Germany. Soon there were three types of dirigibles in the inventories of the German Army: the rigid, aluminum-framed Zeppelins, as the Count's creations were now commonly called, the non-rigid Parseval, and the semi-rigid "M" ship, built by the army's own aeronautical section, now known as the Airship Battalion. In 1909 Professor Johann Schütte offered the German Army yet a fourth design—a rigid dirigible with a framework of wood. The first Schütte-Lanz airship joined Germany's growing fleet at the end of 1912.[13]

Earlier, as if to presage Germany's lead in lighter-than-air craft, Major August von Parseval had also made a great improvement in the tethered observation balloon. The typical spherical balloon had a bad habit of bobbing and turning in a stiff wind, usually making its observer airsick in the process; if the wind blew hard enough, the balloon could even be driven to the ground. Parseval's kite balloon, however, looked somewhat like a fat sausage with a fin or vane attached to one end; correctly tethered, it rode the wind like a kite, and indeed it soon acquired the name *Drachen,* the German term for kite. The new balloon entered the German service in 1896 and was soon being marketed in many other countries.[14]

European navies were also beginning to eye the airship with considerable interest, impelled in part by the hope that it might help them combat two new weapons that would be encountered in any future war at sea: the naval mine and the submarine. As early as 1908 the French Navy named a commission to look into the role the dirigible might play at sea, and in Germany naval authorities were following closely the German Army's assessment of the Zeppelin and laying down performance requirements for a naval dirigible. Even Great Britain, the premier naval power of the day, could not afford to ignore the airship's potential. In 1909 the Admiralty began investing in its first dirigible, Rigid Naval Airship No. 1.[15]

The airplane too, came to the fore in the critical years 1908–9. One can date the formal beginnings of military aviation from February 10, 1908, when the U.S. Army's Signal Corps ordered a Wright airplane and arranged for the Wrights to give flight instruction to two officers. While Orville Wright gave lessons outside Washington, his brother Wilbur left for Europe on an extended publicity and sales trip. The Wrights' flying activities up to that time had not made a profound impression in Europe; the flights had not been public, and just how well they flew was unclear; their offers of sale to the various European powers had not been well received, partly because they were asking a very high price for a machine whose performance was open to some question. But Wilbur Wright began public demonstrations in France in August 1908, and ended all doubts about the flying ability of his machine; before the year was out he had flown two and a half hours at a stretch.[16]

The Wright machine was not the only airplane flying in France that summer: in July, Henry Farman had flown a distance of more than 20 kilometers in an airplane of his own design. Twelve months later another Frenchman, Louis Blériot, flew across the Channel in a plane he had created. One month after that, in August 1909, a spectacular week-long air meet was held in Reims. Over 40 aircraft participated, as did a number of aviators who were acquiring international reputations: Curtiss, Latham, Farman, Blériot, etc. The meet was unmarred by serious accident and some impressive records were set, including a long-distance flight of 180 kilometers. These successes were not lost on military observers. The German military attaché described some of the flights he witnessed as "astonishing"; he reported "the technique of flying has now passed the stage of sport or fruitless trials." The French Army was even more impressed; after the meet it bought five of the best planes exhibited. The Italians had already acted: early in 1909 the Ministry of War, the Ministry of the Navy, and a newly formed Club Aviatori pooled their resources to buy a Wright airplane and hire Wilbur Wright to come to Rome and teach two Italian officers to fly—one from the Navy, and one from the Army Engineers. In July 1910 the German government came to an agreement with the Albatros Company, which undertook to supply two airplanes and to train 10 officer-pilots. In Great Britain the army's formal commitment to aviation came with an order creating an Air Battalion of the Royal Engineers as of April 1, 1911. That same day, seven years later, the Royal Air Force was born.[17]

The trend established among the great powers was taken up by other countries, whose governments placed orders for airplanes, mostly in France, and designated a number of officers to be trained in flying. At the behest of their governments, Russians, Serbs, Swedes, and Rumanians went to France and enrolled in the flying schools of Blériot and Farman. In 1911 the Greek government invited a dozen French officers to advise it on the air service it was planning, and by April of 1912 it had enrolled 6 of its own officers at the Farman School in Etampes. In April 1913, President Victoriano Huerta of Mexico ordered no fewer than 30 graduates of the Escuela Militar de Aspirantes to be selected for flight training in France.[18]

By 1912, then, there was a generalized movement to acquire and develop aerial armaments in countries large and small, in the old world and the new. Was this movement simply a trend toward the new and the fashionable in armament, or was it traceable to a kind of national *amour-propre,* and an urge to "keep up with the Joneses," or perhaps outdo them? All of these considerations counted for something in the development of aerial armaments, but it is likely that the basic, driving compulsion—among the European powers especially—was military necessity, real or perceived. One has only to read the documents collected by the Luftwaffe's *Kriegswissenschaftliche Abteilung* for its study of German military aeronautics before 1914 to be struck by the influence developments in France had upon German military thinking. The brief flight of *La France* in 1884 led Major Buchholtz, head of the German Army's Balloon Detachment, to urge on his superiors research into dirigibles, an endeavor the War Ministry and the General Staff both endorsed as of "extraordinary value." The Germans were similarly sensitive to the progress the French were making in 1906 with the Lebaudy system. When the Chief of the German General Staff learned that the French government and the Lebaudy firm were placing large orders for balloon fabric with German textile firms, he alerted the Minister of War: "Judging by this there is no doubt that France is building more airships. This places us under an even greater obligation to carry through with the construction of our own airships, so as to overcome the lead France has gained over us in this field." A few weeks later the Reichstag accorded the War Minister the sum of 550,000 marks to enable the Airship Battalion to develop a semi-rigid dirigible; the "M" ship was the ultimate result.[19]

By 1912 the situation had changed completely; Germany then possessed a clear superiority in airships. In October of that year the Army's Chief of Staff wrote the War Minister that he was having bomb-dropping experiments stepped up: "In the new Z ships we possess an implement of war far superior to anything of the kind our opponents have; and it cannot be matched by them in any reasonable length of time if we work energetically to perfect it."[20]

If this advantage was a source of satisfaction in Berlin, it was a cause for concern in Paris and London. In Paris military and political leaders were particularly worried about the great dirigible facility the Germans had constructed at Frescaty, near Metz, and only a stone's throw from the French frontier, while their Russian allies were keenly aware of the sheds placed at Königsberg, Allenstein, Thorn, and Posen, not far from their own frontier with Germany. In London there was concern in government circles as early as 1909 over the possibility of a sudden, devastating Zeppelin raid against the ships of the Royal Navy as they rode at anchor; in May of that year the Home Fleet was even alerted. A blue ribbon committee looked into the new aerial armaments and reported it would be "possibly dangerous to ignore the risk of attacks from the air." Early in 1910 the Admiralty sponsored a study on the dangers to ports and naval facilities.[21]

In that same year the dirigible cast its long shadow over international law, bringing to a head an issue that had been simmering since the beginning of the century. Balloons had occasionally been carried from one country to another by wind currents. Then in 1908 Count Zeppelin had made a flight that took him over Switzerland, and the following year Blériot had flown from France to England. To whom did the air belong? The question had never been decided, and now it was becoming a matter of national security. As a writer in *Flight* magazine observed, "We may regard the advent of military ships of the air as, in a measure, obliterating present national frontiers in conducting military operations."[22]

The French jurist Paul Fauchille had suggested an answer in 1902: he proposed that there be freedom of the air in the same way there was freedom of the seas, with individual states having control of that portion of the atmosphere contiguous to them; thus the maritime three-mile limit would have its parallel in a "national" air zone up to a certain altitude, and the airspace above would be open to all. The French aviation authority Ferdinand Ferber agreed with this solution, suggesting that the national airspace go up to about 500 meters. In 1910 the French government called an international conference to resolve the issue. The Germans argued for an essentially "open skies" solution. The British delegation, headed by an admiral, insisted that above all it was "necessary to safeguard the interests and the sovereignty of the states." The conference broke up without reaching agreement, and within a matter of months many European governments had enacted laws regulating use of their airspace. "Forbidden zones" multiplied; when war came in 1914 one of the first acts of the belligerents was to strengthen the security of their airspace, in some cases prohibiting all flying save by their own military.[23]

Governments for the most part kept their fears to themselves; the discussions that went on in Paris rarely bore directly on military matters. But some politicians and any number of journalists decided it was best to alert the public to the new menace of air power. And the public reacted. Beginning in 1908, there was a series of "Zeppelin scares," or outbreaks of "Zeppelinitis," in France and more particularly in England. Along the French frontier with Germany there were frequent sightings of mysterious airships, and though the French authorities were rarely able to confirm the sightings, the population was convinced that the Zeppelins from Frescaty were systematically probing French frontier defenses. In England the publication of H. G. Wells' *War in the Air* helped set the stage, along with a much quoted estimate by a German official that Germany's airship fleet was capable of transporting 350,000 men from Calais to Dover in one night. A story circulated widely that a Zeppelin attack on England would coincide with the sudden appearance of 50,000 German soldiers who were already in the country, disguised as tourists. In Parliament the government was asked if it were true that there were 50,000 Mauser rifles and seven million rounds of ammunition concealed "in a cellar within a quarter-mile of Charing Cross." From time to time incidents would rekindle the public's concern: in September 1912, a German dirigible hovered over units of the Royal Navy which were then in Danish waters; in April 1913 a brand new Zeppelin lost its way and came down in Lunéville, France. Officials on both sides were courteous and correct, and the Zeppelin was allowed to depart again after paying a customs fine, but a reporter present noted that "the attitude of the people was hostile." There were further outbreaks of Zeppelinitis when war came, and in 1915 one of the phantom airships was even reported in upstate New York.[24]

If there was a Zeppelin scare, there was also a "Zeppelin craze"—that's what Admiral Alfred von Tirpitz called the infatuation with the great airships that developed in Germany. Just how profound that infatuation was became clear as early as 1908. A series of record-breaking flights by the LZ-4 that summer electrified the entire country. Then, one day in August, a sudden squall tore the ship loose from its anchorage at Echterdingen; it bounded into the air, then fell to earth where it was completely consumed by fire. In a spontaneous gesture of sympathy and generosity the German people gave over 6 million marks so that Count Zeppelin could carry on his work.

With the twentieth century also came a renewed interest in another form of aerostat. Balloon ascensions, long a feature of festivals and fairs, had generally been carried out by professionals. But now there was a burst of interest in "sport ballooning" with free balloons, particularly among the well-to-do. The movement spread across Europe and America; aficionados formed Aero Clubs, acquired balloons, and learned to use them. Soon meets and races were organized, leading to the creation of an international competition by New York publisher James Gordon Bennett.

The first was held in 1906, and thereafter the annual competition for the Gordon Bennett trophy drew great public interest.[25]

Infatuation with the airplane was even more widespread. A year after the "Miracle of Echterdingen," the sponsors of the Reims air show were astounded by the appearance of a million spectators; subsequent meets, from Lisbon to Kiev, evoked a similar response. Newspaper editors soon learned that there was an avid readership for anything concerning aeronautics. Specialized journals and magazines sprang up to feed the popular taste. A new popular hero emerged in the intrepid airman. The names of pilots such as Pégoud, Nesterov, Olieslagers, and von Hiddessen were often in the newspapers and even more often on the lips of schoolboys—and their fame would continue into the war, where they would become the first "aces." A writer in one of the early aeronautical journals explained that all of Europe was succumbing to a new disease:

> Aeronitis is a pleasant and decidedly infectious ailment which makes its victims "flighty" mentally and physically. At times it has a pathologic, at times a psychologic foundation. It has already affected thousands, it will get to the rest of the world in time.[26]

For the immense majority of Europeans, flying could be a spectator sport at best. In France, which was presumably the most "air-minded" country, in 1914 there were perhaps a thousand Frenchmen with pilot's licenses in a population of 40 million. One year earlier, Frederick Janes had estimated that there were 2,000 airplanes in the entire world. While the number who could know the thrill of flight first-hand was small, it contained a high concentration of the rich and the influential, and their enthusiasm for flying had considerable repercussions. At the beginning of the twentieth century what organized groups there were dedicated to aeronautics usually had in their membership a heavy concentration of naturalists, physicists, engineers, and not a few genteel eccentrics. Much of their preoccupation was theoretical; they gathered to listen to erudite papers on the flight of the bat and the use of varnished silk for balloon envelopes. The new generation of devotees cared less for the stuffily scientific approach; like the "balloonatics," they wanted to fly and they wanted to encourage others to fly. They were people like Winston Churchill, who got his license in 1912, and C.S. Rolls, co-founder of the Rolls-Royce firm, who, like others, followed the progression from the automobile to the airplane. In Italy there was the prominent parliamentarian Carlos Montù, and in Germany Prince Heinrich of Prussia, brother to the Kaiser, who learned to fly in 1910. In France there was a whole constellation of prominent figures, among them Emile Raymond, a respected member of the French Senate who would die in 1915 when his observation plane was shot down in no man's land.[27]

Those who flew made up an international fraternity of sorts, and flying itself promised easier and more rapid contacts between nations; consequently there were those who felt that the airplane and the dirigible could contribute significantly to international peace and understanding. Yet, inexorably, aeronautics in the years 1908–14 took on an increasingly nationalistic and martial connotation. It was an age of strong national feeling, and one of keen competition in the military sphere. Given their high visibility, the airplane and the airship were ideal symbols of national strength and pride.

By 1908, there was already a subtle conflict within the flying fraternity between aeronautics as an international sport on the one hand, and a national resource on the other. In that same year the trend toward the national perspective became visible with the formation of the Air Fleet League in Germany and the National Air League in France, both of which preached the message of national self-sufficiency and preparedness in the air. The Aerial League of the British Empire, organized in January 1909, took as its mission the task of convincing the British people of the "vital importance to the British Empire of aerial supremacy, upon which its commerce, communications, defense, and its very existence must largely depend."[28]

It was inevitable that when a country achieved this fabled "supremacy," its government, its media, and its people derived a certain satisfaction from its position of leadership. The French boasted of their advances in aircraft and in engine design. The German government heaped honors on Count Zeppelin after his string of triumphs beginning in 1908. "Thereafter," notes historian Jürgen Eichler, "in newspaper articles, in popular science publications, and in the offerings of *Trivialliteratur*, the Zeppelin airship with its imposing dimensions was especially extolled as a symbol of the German spirit of invention and of German greatness, and it was glorified as a kind of wonder weapon that Germany's enemies could not match." And even a responsible military organ like the *Militärwochenblatt* asked its readers: "What other people can produce an airship anywhere comparable to our Zeppelin cruisers?"[29]

On the other hand a clear national deficiency—for example, a reliance on imported motors and airframes—was keenly felt. European authorities declined to acquire Wright airplanes in part because they hoped to come up with locally created aircraft, the British with the designs of J. N. Dunne, and the Germans with that of W. S. Hoffmann, in which the Kaiser took a special interest. The Bavarian government, which had its own air service, spent a considerable amount of money on the machine of a Lieutenant Wildt, so that it would not be dependent on aircraft of Prussian origin. Prizes and other incentives were offered to engineers and designers, and as soon as they could, governments limited their procurement to domestically produced matériel.[30]

In most countries the public was keenly interested in aerial armament. As the president of the Aero Club d'Italia put it, "public opinion has correctly seen in and through aeronautics a whole great new field of possibilities on behalf of defense." The "miracle of Echterdingen" was not forgotten. In 1910 the London *Morning Post* launched a public subscription to the "National Airship Fund," whose goal was to acquire a dirigible and offer it to the British military. In 1911 it was the turn of the Paris journal *Auto,* which led a campaign to buy airplanes for the French air service. The authorities could only give their blessing to these undertakings, since they increased the nation's armaments without imposing further burdens on the budget. The year 1912 saw the movement at its peak. That summer there was a drive to fill the coffers of the Austrian Air Fleet Fund. In Germany Prince Heinrich, "the flying Hohenzollern," presided over a *Nationalflugspende* that raised over 7 million marks for aerial armament; the French opened a national subscription which eventually brought in over 6 million francs, enough to purchase over 100 airplanes and pay for the training of 75 pilots.[31]

The Italians launched a similar campaign with great fanfare under the watchword *Dati ali al'Italia,* "Give Wings to Italy." The King gave 100,000 lire, the Ministry of Education turned over 180,000 contributed by schoolchildren, and the Ministry of Foreign Affairs produced 740,000 lire collected from Italians living abroad. The total raised was 3.5 million lire. The Greek Air Service came into being that same year, largely through popular donations, including 20,000 gold francs sent by Greeks in the United States; in an elaborate ceremony presided over by Prime Minister Elefterios Venizelos, each of the four airplanes in the new air fleet was christened. The fund drives continued in 1913. With the Tsar's blessing a Committee for the Expansion of the Air Fleet issued a public appeal, and in Italy the air service received two dirigibles named *La Città di Ferrara* and *La Città di Milano,* the citizens of those cities having raised the money to buy them. Also in 1913 neutral Switzerland set up an air service, its citizens having contributed enough money to order six airplanes from Germany.[32]

The public was also an enthusiastic supporter of the many contests organized for airmen and the prizes offered for certain feats, such as being the first to fly non-stop from one city to another. By 1911 a number of these had clearly military overtones. The Prinz Heinrichflug in Germany was essentially an exercise in tactical and strategic intelligence gathering, and while open to both civilian and military airmen (German only), it was the military which always came off best. The *Aeroplanturnier* held in Gotha in August 1912 also revolved around the use of the airplane in war, with bombing exercises and simulated attacks on airships. The Michelin Prize or "Aéro-Cible," organized that same year by the French tire manufacturers, was essentially a contest in bombing accuracy. André Michelin made it clear that his brother and he had not created the competition for essentially sporting purposes, but "out of the desire to see France keep supremacy in the air."[33]

One has the impression that in all of these activities—promoting aerial armament, raising money, and organizing various contests and prizes—there was a fairly smooth and consistent cooperation among three groups—governments that wanted to enhance their military stature at little or no cost, flying enthusiasts who wanted to promote both civilian and military aeronautics, and manufacturers and suppliers glad to have their business expand. In France one finds Colonel Roques, head of the French Air Service, active in organizing the Michelin bombing contest, while Captain Ferber, one of the French Army's best aeronautics experts, is "detached" for duty with the National Air League; the League's military committee is in turn helping with the publication of an army airman's treatise on aerial observation. When the Swiss Army begins thinking about acquiring aerial armament in 1912, its first step is to ask the Swiss Aero Club for its ideas on the subject. In

Italy Major Maurizio Moris, head of the Club Aviatori, is also head of the army's Aeronautical Section, while Carlo Montù, President of the Aero Club d'Italia, is also chief of the civilian airmen who volunteer to serve with the Italian Army in its campaign in Libya. In Germany the Lanz prize is sponsored by industrialist Karl Lanz, a leading figure within the Mannheim Luftflottenverein and the German Air Fleet League, and a financial backer of the Schütte-Lanz dirigible.[34]

One clear result of this spirit of cooperation was the arrangement that would place civilian airmen and their planes at the disposal of the government in time of war. Such a system already existed in several countries in the case of cars and trucks; their owners received a small subsidy, and in return their vehicles could be taken for government use in time of need. There were a few dirigibles in private hands; the largest number were owned by the German Delag firm, operators of a Zeppelin air service which carried some 34,000 passengers between various German cities from 1910 to 1914. The company received government support to maintain its airships and sheds, both of which figured in the German Army's mobilization plans. For the owners of airplanes, the German government used a different arrangement that was imitated in a number of other countries: the Deutsche Freiwillige Fliegerkorps was an organization of civilian airmen under the aegis of the German Aero Club. Its members volunteered to serve in the corps for three years, during which time they and their planes might be mobilized in the event of national emergency. In peacetime the volunteers pledged to participate in military exercises 10 days each year and to follow certain courses of instruction. In exchange they got a subvention for maintaining their airplanes, and 40 marks for every day of military service. When Germany mobilized in 1914, an immediate call went out for these volunteers; they responded, and at least one served with sufficient distinction to attain the status of ace.[35]

Civilian volunteers made it possible for armies to test the usefulness of airplanes in the field even before they acquired their own aircraft; thus in 1910 civilian aviators agreed to participate in the British Army's maneuvers on Salisbury Plain, carrying out the Army's first reconnaissance by airplane; the next year, civilian pilots provided the same service during the maneuvers of the Austro-Hungarian Army. The maneuvers themselves proved decisive in establishing the military value of both the airplane and the dirigible. The success in the French Army's Picardy maneuvers of 1910 led to an organizational change that gave the airmen more autonomy. In the Italian maneuvers of 1911 the "red" and "blue" armies were each provided with five airplanes, while the general directing the whole exercise followed the movements of the contending forces by means of a dirigible; the King of Italy went up in the airship to see for himself the perspective it provided. Each year saw a larger aerial contingent at the various maneuvers, and with each exercise ground commanders acquired more understanding of the new arm and how to use it. The understanding did not always come easily. At the French maneuvers of 1911 one general lined up his escadrille of airplanes in the van of his forces, even in front of the infantry.[36]

The various maneuvers confirmed the value of the airplane for observation purposes, but also indicated where improvements should be made. The French found that a single-seat airplane had to fly twice as much for its pilot to bring back the same amount of information supplied when the airplane carried both pilot and observer. When the U.S. Army first used airplanes in small-scale maneuvers in 1912, it was found that while the information obtained by the planes "was much more accurate and full than that gathered by the cavalry patrols on either side," the aerial observers had no rapid and easy means of relaying their information to ground commanders. The message-dropping technique was primitive and slow, so an enterprising airman named Benjamin Foulois landed in order to telegraph the "Blue" commander that his flank was being threatened. Before he could get his message off, he and his plane were surrounded by "Red" forces. The solution, everyone agreed, was the wireless, but it would have to be adapted for use in airplanes.[37]

But there were any number of questions for which maneuvers provided no clear answer. How low could an airplane fly without becoming vulnerable to the small-arms fire of enemy troops? During maneuvers the airplane's approach had been announced by the noise of its engine. Would it be the same over a real battlefield? Only war could supply the answers. Beginning in 1911 there was a series of small wars in which new weapons were used, among them the airplane and the airship: the Italians fought the Turks in a brief war in Libya in 1911–12, the French used airplanes to help put down an uprising in Morocco in 1912, the Mexicans introduced airplanes into their Revolution of 1910, and in 1912–

13 the Balkans were convulsed by two brief wars—the first lost by Turkey, the second by Bulgaria. The Libyan and Balkan conflicts were the object of special interest among the European general staffs; military attachés filed elaborate reports and so did observers despatched to the fighting fronts.

In the fall of 1911 the Italian Army took nine airplanes, two drachen balloons, and two dirigibles to Libya, and immediately began to claim a number of "firsts" in aerial warfare. On October 23 the airmen flew their first reconnaissance mission, on November 1 they dropped the first bombs on enemy positions, and shortly thereafter they had the first aviator wounded in action—Carlo Montù, the leader of the corps of civilian volunteer pilots, who was struck by a Turkish bullet. A photographic section accompanied the air component to Libya; the Italians took a considerable number of aerial photographs and also shot some of the first motion picture film taken from the air. Italian airmen also carried out extensive field trials of wireless communications, and Guglielmo Marconi himself came to Libya to help with the work. An Italian airplane with a small receiving set was able to pick up a ground signal, which the Italians claimed as another first (wireless transmission from air to ground had already been accomplished, most notably by the Russians).[38]

The Italians had the air to themselves, since the Turks at this point had no air service. Still, the air campaign was not without its difficulties. The dirigibles gave trouble, both they and their sheds being buffeted by heavy winds. The airships did not get into action until March; from then until October they flew 127 sorties, which involved reconnaissances in depth and experimenting with several types of bombs. A French observer, Lieutenant Marzac, reported that the effect of the bombs was minimal; those released from the dirigibles either did not explode or missed their target. Those dropped by airplanes were so small (about five pounds or so) that they had no effect. A reporter from the *Berliner Tageblatt* probably summed up the view of most observers when he wrote that dirigibles and airplanes had provided the Italians with excellent observation, but had been a disappointment as offensive weapons. The Italians did not see it that way. An officer named Giulio Douhet announced after the war ended late in 1912: "A new weapon has come forth, the sky has become a new battlefield."[39]

The fighting in the Balkans involved air forces on both sides, though these were rudimentary at best. A good proportion of the pilots were foreign: German, French, British, and even an American or two. The airplanes they flew were whatever could be purchased on the market, a great variety of types, some of which were outmoded and many of which were poorly maintained. When the Rumanians created their first *grupul aviati* or air unit in 1912, it was composed of seven airplanes of three different types.[40]

There was very little offensive use of aircraft. The French sent the Rumanians three Morane monoplanes equipped with Hotchkiss guns, but they do not seem to have been used. The foreign pilots who flew for the various belligerents sometimes refused to drop bombs. A French pilot who worked for the Bulgarians would drop nothing more harmful than leaflets, explaining, "We had agreed to fly with or without officer observers, but we had not agreed to become active belligerents and kill people we had nothing against." The same pilot revealed that these distinctions meant nothing to the Turks, who had sent word by wireless that they would summarily execute any enemy airmen, Bulgarian or not, who fell into their hands.[41]

Reporters who covered the war were particularly interested in the use of airplanes. A *New York Times* correspondent wrote that "the average man's first question is as to the result of the use of the airplane in a big war." Most journalists who covered the fighting seemed disappointed that the war in the air had not been more decisive; "war has not been revolutionized," wrote one. Professional military assessment was more measured. There was more convincing evidence that aerial reconnaissance was of great benefit in learning the enemy's disposition and movements. The *Militärwochenblatt* published an account, complete with sketches, of how in March and April of 1913 the Turks had obtained through aerial observation a very clear picture of the enemy forces, down to the movements of divisions, and learned of an enemy attack shaping up. On the other hand, the accounts from the Balkans echoed those from Libya indicating the vulnerability of airplanes to small-arms fire at altitudes of under 1000 meters. As a consequence, by 1914 the infantry training manuals of most European armies contained instructions on firing at aerial targets, while in the various air services the armored plane was much talked about. The French displayed three armored models in 1914.[42]

The Second Balkan War ended in July 1913, leaving the general staffs of the great powers little time to draw lessons from the conflict and apply them to their own armies: within twelve months the great storm broke over Europe, engulfing the major powers one after the other. The outbreak of the Great War thus brought to an end three decades of peacetime development that were extremely important for the subsequent history of military aeronautics, so important that later we will need to evoke the prewar experience when treating various aspects of wartime aviation. For the present it might be well to offer a brief sketch of military aeronautics as it stood on the eve of the Great War, at the same time correcting some misconceptions about the prewar experience that have tended to linger.

First of all, by 1914 the embryonic and experimental stage in the development of the air weapon was ending. The typical air service had come of age in several ways: it was recognized as having a mission and function in warfare; it had achieved a viable organizational structure, whose basic element in most cases was a six-airplane unit (as in the French *escadrille* and the German *Fliegerabteilung*); its increased importance and its specialized functions were transforming it from an appendage to the engineers, to an autonomous arm, achieved by the creation of the Royal Flying Corps (April 1912), the Direction de l'Aéronautique Militaire in France (April 1914), and the Corpo Aeronautico Militare in Italy (January 1915). The Italian Air Service acquired "equal status with all the other arms and corps of the Army." Its organization, which was fairly typical, contained two separate *Comandi*, one for airplanes and tethered observation balloons, the other for dirigibles; within its purview were also schools, laboratories, construction and research facilities, and various depots.[43]

It is sometimes suggested that the air services were the Cinderellas of the various military establishments, disdained, neglected, and at best tolerated by the older services and the army's high command. Judging from the materials surviving in the French and German archives, this was emphatically not the case in those countries, especially after 1910–11. The progress and the promise of the air arm are followed closely in the highest military circles; from 1912 onwards the needs of the air services are the object of the same progressive expansion programs used in the older services, save that the expansion was accelerated; thus the French Air Service was scheduled to add 100 aircraft in 1913, a second 100 in 1914, and 600 more in 1915.[44]

At the outbreak of war in 1914 there were well over 1,000 military aircraft in the flying units, schools, and depots of the various powers, large and small; five years earlier there had been none. Germany began the war with 232 airplanes that were *einsatz-bereit* or ready for use in the field. Russia, the second-ranked power in aircraft, had 190; France fielded 162, grouped into 21 escadrilles; the other major powers—Great Britain, Italy, and Austria-Hungary—each possessed somewhere between 50 and 100. Belgium had 16, and each of the Balkan countries had a handful. The United States Army, which had been the first to acquire an airplane, carried in its inventories a grand total of 8. Airships were less widely distributed among the powers: Germany led with 12; France and Italy, the only other countries with any significant strength here, had 6 and 4 respectively.

Many of the aircraft carried on army inventories in 1914 were specifically designed by their builders to meet government specifications and standards of performance, which had been issued as early as 1911. Though some writers have stressed the initiative of early airmen in experimenting with weaponry "on their own," a considerable amount of officially sponsored research was done in this field, though its orientation varied from one country to the next. The French, for example, were particularly interested in a method of destroying German dirigibles, and they groomed the airplane for this role, devising for it such armament as incendiary flechettes. For the Italians a major antagonist would be the Austro-Hungarian Navy; consequently they pushed the development of the airborne torpedo, and valued the dirigible as a means of striking the Austrian naval base at Pola, just across the Adriatic.

It has often been said that there was little realistic conception of how air power might be used—what air forces like to call doctrine. This is true, but it is also understandable. The air weapon was after all distinctive, indeed unique. Of all the "new" weapons of the Great War, it alone had no predecessor and no precedent. The tank, after all, had been preceded by the chariot—indeed the French still use the same word, *char,* for both; and the submarine and the dreadnought, however innovative, were nonetheless ships. And as there was some precedent for these weapons there was also some precedent for their role and their employment.[45]

But the earliest air strategists and tacticians had no such stock to draw upon. Not surprisingly, they often drew inspiration from that other essentially alien element in which men had learned to wage war—the sea. They were often led astray. Ferdinand Ferber, a highly respected figure in French military aviation, believed that air supremacy could be maintained in the same way as supremacy on the seas: once the enemy's aircraft had been driven from the skies, constant patrols over airfields and aircraft factories would keep his planes on the ground. And a number of early airmen who speculated on war in the air—Henry H. Arnold among them—spoke of large, heavily armored aerial "cruisers" and "destroyers," yet no such plane appeared. And if the airmen themselves could not read the future, generals on the ground could scarcely be expected to.[46]

If the airplane and its mission were still hard to define, that was not the case of the airman of 1914. By 1911 the French and the Germans both had realized that a military airman needed more thorough training than the civilian aviator, and they introduced training programs accordingly. It was also known by 1914 that the airmen needed mental and physical qualities beyond those required for general military service, though just what these qualities were was unclear before the war—and not entirely clear after it was over. And the airman's distinctive image and personality were emerging. In the public eye, at least, the aviator was—indeed, he had to be—brave. This view had its origin in the rapidly rising number of fatal flying accidents: In Germany there were 13 in 1911, but 43 in 1913, each one of them reported in the press. Considering the rapid increase in the number of people flying from one year to the next, the actual casualty rate may not have gone up all that much—as some observers pointed out at the time. But as an editorial writer in the London *Times* noted during the First Balkan War, where thousands died anonymously on the ground, while the death of each flyer was noted, the airplane was "still a novelty, picturesque and full of possibilities that loom the larger because the imagination, not knowledge, defines them."[47]

The repercussions on the air services were significant. In many cases only single men were accepted for the flying service and all airmen continued to be volunteers. And a number of people, civilian and military, stopped flying. As for those who remained, they were now "intrepid airmen"—the adjective had become linked to the noun. When they flew off to war in that summer of 1914 they were already a distinctive caste, a military fraternity like no other—and so they would remain.[48]

=2=

The Eyes of the Army

Journalists visiting the Western Front in World War I rarely failed to comment on the line of observation balloons suspended along the front. Actually there were two lines of kite balloons, Caquots on the Allied side and Drachens paralleling the German lines. By 1918 there might be as many as 300 strung along the front, in some sectors sparsely distributed; in others, as in the Somme in 1916, so closely spaced that their cables became entangled. Pilots nursing crippled airplanes back to their lines took the balloons as beacons; infantry replacements moving up knew when they saw them that their trip was almost over. To the veterans in the lines the balloons were a familiar presence. French *poilus* never called them anything but "sausages"; the Drachen, with its vaguely penile shape, was referred to in the German trenches as *das Mädchens Traum*, the maiden's dream. The meandering balloon lines were peculiar to the Great War. In preceding conflicts—the Balkan Wars, for example—the occasional observation balloon was still a novelty to be commented on. By 1939 what few balloon companies remained in the armies of Europe were living their last days: there was no place for them in the age of Blitzkrieg warfare.

The idea of using the balloon to observe a battlefield was as old as the device itself, indeed a book-length treatise on military aerostats appeared in Germany within a year of the first manned ascension. The emergence of the dirigible and then the airplane could only serve to heighten the interest in aerial reconnaissance, while at the same time evidence was beginning to accumulate

23

that the customary methods of reconnoitering and intelligence-gathering might not work in future wars. Military observers who watched the fighting in the Russo-Japanese War described the battlefields there as having the appearance of a desert, with men and weapons elaborately concealed. A Russian infantry officer wrote an account of the fighting in which he said the chief characteristic of the battlefields was "the invisibility of the enemy." And this desert was swept by a fire that was deadly to infantry patrols, roving bodies of cavalry, and staff officers looking for a prominence from which they could train their binoculars on the field.[1]

But no one knew for sure what form the fighting would take if a major conflagration broke out in Europe. In positional warfare between heavily entrenched armies the balloon would probably be of value, as it had been in the Russo-Japanese War. But in a war of vast and rapid movement aerial observation might better be left to airplanes and dirigibles, for the balloon units with their cumbersome horse-drawn ground elements had no better mobility than heavy artillery. Then too, a tethered, hydrogen-filled balloon made a large, stationary, and highly inflammable target; in 1911 a British Army report warned of "the eventual inability of balloons to keep the air in the face of hostile aeroplanes and improved artillery." The French had similar misgivings; that same year they abolished their balloon units, save for a handful which were attached to various fortresses. When the British and French armies took the field in August 1914, they were not accompanied by balloons. Most of the other powers had acquired at least a few German Drachens, but were unsure what use they would make of them. As for the Germans, they mobilized ten *Feldluftschifferabteilungen,* which gave a good account of themselves in the opening campaign.[2]

It was not until later in the fall of 1914, when the opposing armies had gone to earth along a continuous front, that the observation balloon came into its own. The British Army borrowed balloons from the Royal Navy, while the French brought into the field the old spherical aerostats they had consigned to fortress duty. Quickly recognizing the superiority of the Drachen, the French set about copying it in October. But a young French engineer, Albert Caquot, was able to improve on the German device; a whole series of Caquots appeared, culminating with the Type R, which held 1,000 cubic meters of hydrogen and could take an observer up nearly 5,000 feet. The French became the chief

suppliers for the Allies, producing some 4,000 balloons of various
types by the time of the Armistice; the Germans built nearly 2,000
Drachens. The Italians experimented with both Drachens and
Caquots before introducing a balloon of their own, the Avorio-
Prassone or A. P., which some specialists claimed was the best
of all the designs. The Italians also used their balloons at higher
altitudes than was the practice on the Western Front—in large
part because the mountainous terrain tended to limit the observer's
view. An Italian A. P. model holding 1,200 cubic meters of hydrogen could take an observer to 7,000 feet.[3]

At a height of about 4,000 feet, a balloon provided its observer
(or observers, for there were sometimes two) with a matchless
view of the battle zone and enabled him to collect data that no
one else could supply. Under good conditions he could see at
least 15 miles beyond the enemy's front lines; while an observer
in an airplane could obtain the same view, the man in the balloon
had several advantages over him. First of all, the observer suspended in his basket was in constant voice contact with the ground,
thanks to the telephone line incorporated into the balloon's cable.
Often, vibration and the movement of the balloon basket were
so slight that its occupant could use high-magnification binoculars
of up to 20-power—something the airplane observer could not
do. Then, too, the man in the airplane could get only a brief
look at an objective as he passed; the man in the balloon could
keep it under constant surveillance from dawn to dusk, and by
1918 there was nighttime surveillance as well.[4]

When the army launched an attack, the balloon observer
was called on to gauge the effect of the preliminary bombardment
and the state of the enemy's defenses. He was to track the infantry's
progression as best he could, and report on obstacles it had encountered, and on the enemy's preparations for a counterattack. But
even when the sector was quiet there was much to do. From the
balloon it was possible to count the number of trains that arrived
at a railhead behind the enemy's lines, and it was also possible
to gauge the direction and intensity of road traffic. And the balloon
observer soon became so familiar with his sector that he would
notice the smallest telltale changes, such as freshly turned earth.
He could take oblique photographs of the enemy positions in
front of him, and these, spliced with others taken from neighboring
balloons, yielded very useful panoramas of the enemy complex.
And sometimes the observer was ordered to scrutinize friendly

positions as well, and advise on how well they were concealed from enemy aerial observation—for by the end of 1914 camouflage had become a major new element in warfare.

But the essence of the balloon observer's work was with the artillery. It was not that he spent more time working with the big guns than anything else—though that was often the case. It was that the artillery piece was the most important weapon of the war, the one that dominated the great battles and determined their outcome. This came as something of a technological surprise to many of the generals of 1914, who had not fully appreciated the artillery's quantum leap over the preceding decades, in range, accuracy, rapidity of fire, and general destructiveness. Yet soon the generals were doing all they could to enhance further the power of the new queen of battles, bringing onto the battlefield mortars and superheavy artillery traditionally reserved for sieges, and adapting for their use great naval rifles with their high accuracy and flat trajectories. By early 1916 the Germans were able to concentrate an elaborate "orchestra" of several thousand guns to play upon Verdun and its environs, with each type of weapon assigned its category of objective. In the first day's bombardment a million shells were fired; the reverberations carried a hundred miles.[5]

The gunners in World War I batteries almost never saw their targets. They directed their fire where they were told to direct it, often by an observer aloft in a balloon or in an observation plane. In a sense the observers wielded enormous destructive power though they were usually following a prescribed firing plan, "registering," for example—that is, helping a battery get on target with a few trial rounds in preparation for a later systematic bombardment. Balloon observers often worked with several batteries at once, and conversely two observers might combine their efforts to help put a large gun on its objective: one observer in the approximate line of flight of the shell would indicate if it fell to right or left of the target while the second observer with a more lateral view would report whether the shot was long or short. Observers and artillerymen were aided in their work by a map of the sector with a grid overlay and coordinates. In the German system each square kilometer was given a number, then divided into twenty-five squares with coordinates (A-2, B-5, etc.), and then each of these was in turn divided into four blocks designated a, b, c, and d. If an observer wanted to report the location of an enemy battery he had only to indicate "1022 B3 d" to fix it within an area 100 meters square.[6]

The balloon observer who directed the flight of so many artillery shells occasionally found he had them directed at him; indeed, in the early months of the war, enemy artillery fire was the balloonist's chief hazard. To reduce that hazard the balloon line was generally fixed about three miles from the enemy's most forward positions; even so, some of the more accurate big guns at the front—the German 240 mm, for example—would sometimes undertake "balloon shoots." An adroit observer could usually spot the gun that was firing at him; once he identified it, as soon as he saw a muzzle flash indicating another shot was coming his way, he would order the balloon to be rapidly raised or lowered, knowing that he had perhaps forty seconds to move before the round arrived.

Inevitably, the observation balloon became a tempting target for enemy aircraft once they were armed. The French began to have trouble as early as October 1915, when they lost two balloons which were apparently ignited by German pilots firing flare pistols. The Germans, too, began to lose balloons, and for a time they limited ascensions to 1,500 feet. The balloonist was ill-equipped to defend himself; even if he were armed his own balloon blocked much of his field of fire. This did not prevent some observers from firing at their attackers, and in April 1917 a French balloonist named Peletier was credited with downing an attacking Albatros with a shot from his Winchester. Allied balloon units in the Balkans were so harrassed by German aircraft that they took to sending up balloons containing a dummy observer and several hundred pounds of explosive which could be detonated electrically from the ground. They blew at least one attacker out of the sky by this means; the British report on the affair said the enemy airplane "folded up like a book."[7]

One sensible solution was to protect the balloon with anti-aircraft fire, and this was done. As a second safeguard, the French at the end of 1915 began to provide the observer with a parachute, and the practice became general. It was not as good a solution as it might seem, for the parachutes of the day were not wholly reliable (the French model would not open about one time in a hundred), and though the parachute was suspended for instant use and the observer was already harnessed to it, it was hard for him to evacuate the basket cleanly and quickly with 20,000 cubic feet of hydrogen igniting over his head. The parachute fouled all too frequently; or it might open cleanly, only to have the burning mass of the balloon fall on it. The parachute was to be used *in extremis,* and only then. Some observer training centers offered their students a "free" parachute drop as part of their training, but the offer was invariably declined. At the front parachutes were frequently tested with bags of sand as ballast, but a non-emergency jump by an observer—what the British called a "joy jump"—was not a common thing.[8]

For the balance of the war enemy airplanes remained a grave threat to observation balloons. Max Erhardt, who was a balloonist on both the Eastern and Western Fronts, claimed "the great majority" of balloons were lost through aircraft attacks, and the figures for German losses in 1918 bear him out: some 315 Drachens fell to enemy aircraft, and only 35 to artillery fire. Some pilots specialized in destroying balloons, sometimes with an utter disregard for their own safety. When the Belgian ace Willi Coppens found his guns jammed as he was attacking a German balloon he succeeded in tearing its envelope open with one of his wings, after which he managed to fly his badly damaged machine back home. An Italian lieutenant named Ancillotti succeeded in flying *through* an enemy balloon in December 1917, and returned to his base with balloon fabric still draped over his wings. Aside from these individual efforts, we should also note the campaigns planned by the authorities to deprive the enemy artillery of its eyes: thus, on May 22, 1916, French aircraft armed with air-to-air rockets succeeded in destroying five Drachens, effectively blinding the German artillery in a portion of the Verdun sector.[9]

In an active sector of the front the balloonists did not have an easy time of it. The Belgian Air Service, which kept six balloons aloft on the northern end of the Allied line, recorded that from May 17 to June 30, 1918, it observed Allied artillery fire 154 times and located and reported enemy batteries on 141 occasions. While engaged in that work it had five balloons attacked and burned by enemy aircraft, and another four attacked without serious damage. Fourteen balloons were hit by shrapnel, two had their cables severed by shell fragments, and eight others were shelled by enemy guns without result. Observers had to take to their parachutes 20 times.[10]

Added to the threats from the enemy were the dangers that nature posed for the balloonist. At least two French balloons were struck and destroyed by lightning; sometimes electrical charges would build up in the balloon and pass down the cable to the winch (the Avorio-Prassone had a wooden valve rather than a metal one to lessen the danger of a fatal spark). The cables holding the balloons were only of eight or nine millimeter thickness, for anything thicker would add too much weight. Cables broke when shrapnel hit them or when an airplane collided with them; even a strong wind could sometimes snap them. A cable break was worse news for an Allied balloonist than for a German one, since the prevailing winds on the Western Front blew from west to east, and while the balloonist could open the valve to bring his balloon down, it took time. The other solution was the parachute. May 5, 1916, was a particularly stormy day in Northern France. A strong squall tore loose 24 French balloons and 21 of them passed over the German lines. Sixteen observers parachuted safely; the others died in the attempt.[11]

The strains of such an existence would eventually tell. Joseph Branche, who was a French *aérostier*, wrote that "a long and very tiring day of observation combined with an unexpected attack by an airplane and followed by a parachute descent" could sometimes be too much for an observer. He couldn't bring himself to climb back into the basket. And yet there were veteran *aérostiers* who logged 2,000 hours in the air. Most balloon observers were officers, and an officer with a background in the artillery was considered an ideal choice. One has the impression that the balloon observers were an older, more settled group than the buoyant youths who generally seemed to people the air services. Few balloonists bothered to write memoirs, and few received much by way of distinction or recognition for their work. This is certainly true of the Italian balloonists, about whom there is a good bit of documentation: not one of them received the Medaglia di Oro, the country's highest decoration for valor, although two airplane observers received them. In 1917 the French aviation publicist Jacques Mortane proposed that a balloon observer who parachuted five times be given the same recognition as the airman who downed five enemy planes. Nothing came of the proposal.[12]

Within the air service the balloon observers led an existence apart. They almost never worked in cooperation with airplanes, and aviators felt little kinship with them. One pilot who consented to go up in a balloon said it seemed "unnatural" to be at such an altitude without the sound of a motor; another aviator put the difference this way: "balloons float, they don't fly." Given the strong ties between the observation balloon and the cannon, it might have made better sense to make the balloons a part of the artillery rather than of the air service; the British considered the idea briefly but rejected it.[13]

There was a mild rivalry between the men in the balloon baskets and the men who flew in observation planes. German aviators sometimes referred to the balloonists as their "puffed-up competitors." Though the airplane was a relative newcomer to the European armies, by 1914 it had already attracted far more attention than the balloon. From 1910 on military authorities tested its information-gathering abilities in annual maneuvers; there was much discussion in professional military journals, and by 1912 book-length treatises on reconnaissance by airplane had appeared in Germany, France, and Russia. There was a consensus reflected in military manuals that airplanes could best gather information behind the battlefronts rather than on the battlefields themselves, where ground fire would force them so high they could not follow the details of the fighting. In the Italian manual on *Servizio di Guerra,* issued in the fall of 1914, the task of "exploration" was to be shared by two new elements, airmen and cyclists, and the traditional reconnaissance arm, the cavalry.[14]

When the war began and the airplanes were sent out on their reconnaissance missions—virtually their only missions in 1914—there were the inevitable mistakes and shortcomings of a service untried in war. In many cases the observers had been trained for their job, but in the excitement of those first days of war they tended to exaggerate the importance of their discoveries: a supply column became a column of troops, a regiment became a brigade, and the like. There were errors in identifying the nationality of troops, though on the dust-clogged and tree-lined roads of Northern France that was understandable. Sometimes the errors were comical. It was reported that in the early days of the war a German observer brought back information that in one British position the men were "thoroughly disorganized and running about their post in blind panic." He had actually flown over a group of Tommies playing soccer.[15]

In those early and hectic days of the war a large number of observers' reports never reached the appropriate authorities. Some messages that were dropped in weighted bags either lodged in trees or were lost in undergrowth; others, though retrieved, were not forwarded. The airman's information was sometimes regarded by army authorities with skepticism, especially if it contradicted indications coming from cavalry patrols, prisoner interrogations, and other traditional sources. General Joffre acknowledged that "at the beginning of the campaign, some intelligence of the highest importance was not exploited because little credence was given to it." Among other instances Joffre cited the case of a French observer who had recognized Kaiser Wilhelm II and his staff travelling in open cars near Nancy. When he reported what he had seen everyone laughed at him. Such episodes often figure in accounts of the air war as evidence of the jealousy and hostility of the older arms. But in fact the caution with which early airmen's reports were received was often prescribed by the high command. The Italian *Servizio di Guèrra* of 1914 warned that aerial observation was "a technique still in the course of development," and the information it provided should be considered in the nature of a "general indication."[16]

In general, however, during those first hectic weeks of war the airmen proved themselves as gatherers of information. The weather was one reason for this success, for August and the first half of September provided day after day of perfect flying weather, with a minimum of wind and clouds. Then, too, most air units were able to follow the rapid movements of those first weeks, thanks to the mobility that had been built into their ground elements. From August 15 until September 9 the *Fliegerabteilung* of the German Third Army Corps changed airfields 18 times and during that time was grounded by bad weather only two days.[17]

Thanks to the airmen the armies no longer moved so blindly, and their commanders had a better idea of where the enemy was. German observation planes played a significant role in the east, where their reports, coupled with interceptions of Russian radio transmissions, set the stage for the victory at Tannenberg. Field Marshal von Hindenburg acknowledged his debt to the German Air Service: "Without the airmen no Tannenberg." The Russians too had their aerial observers. A French aviator named Alphonse Poirée, who happened to be in Russia when the war broke out, volunteered his Farman airplane and his services as pilot. As early as August 2, he brought back "valuable" information to General Samsonov's army. Poirée may also have carried out the first aerial bombing of the war, for during his first flight he threw down a 42-millimeter projectile. And the medal Poirée received, the Cross of Saint George, Fourth Class, was the first of a deluge of decorations for the airmen of the Great War. In the west the Royal Flying Corps had its role in the survival of the British Expeditionary Force, particularly when the B. E. F. was imperilled at Mons, though there is now some doubt as to whether the British Army "was twice in thirty days saved by a single observer." As for the French, airmen's reports gave their commanders a clearer picture of the German armies sweeping south early in September (some of the reports, hastily scribbled in midair, survive in the archives of the French Air Force). Thanks in part to the knowledge they contained, General Joffre could say to his staff on the evening of September 4, "Gentlemen, we will fight on the Marne." The Battle of the Marne was a testimony to the value of aerial reconnaissance and also to the perils of being without it. The German Second Reserve Corps had no *Fliegerabteilung* of its own, but had to rely on the airplanes of the neighboring Fourth Army Corps; these failed to reconnoitre adequately to the west, precisely where the French Sixth Army was moving to the attack.[18]

Most generals went out of their way to praise the contributions of the airmen in those opening weeks of the war. In his despatch of September 7, Sir John French said of the Royal Flying Corps squadrons, "they have furnished me with the most complete and accurate information which has been of incalculable value in the conduct of the operations." But the surest gauge of the value accorded to aerial reconnaissance lay in the efforts everywhere to strengthen the air component. The French, who had started the war with some 20 escadrilles, decided in October 1914 to increase the number to 50. They also abandoned a number of airplane types because they were not well-designed for observation, and concentrated on producing those that were—the Voisin and the Farman. The Germans launched an expansion program, spurred on by the clamor of corps commanders who did not have air units.[19]

When the Western Front solidified into a vast complex of earthworks, the tasks of the observation units changed. Earlier the airplane had been given the job of finding the enemy and following his movements; now he was immobilized just on the other side of no-man's land. The airplane had also been allotted the role of messenger, replacing the galloping courier in transmitting messages from one general to another, but with positional warfare the telephone was a better messenger. On the other hand "tactical" tasks, those performed in the immediate vicinity of the battle zones, increased considerably.

First and foremost of these was working with the artillery, a technique that had been experimented with well before the war. The French artillery had acted to acquire planes as early as 1909, and indeed for a time the French Air Service had been under its wing; in 1912 a unit of the Italian Air Service was assigned to work exclusively in developing spotting techniques. Similar experiments were going on in other countries, and with the coming of the war these efforts accelerated. The French got spectacular confirmation of the dividends airplane-artillery collaboration could pay during the Battle of the Marne. On September 8 the crew of a French observation plane spotted a concentration of enemy field pieces and were able to direct French artillery fire on it. The German caissons began to explode in spectacular fashion, and when the firing ended the German Sixteenth Army Corps had lost half of its artillery.[20]

The next day General Joffre announced a change in the direction of the French air effort. Henceforth the number of planes sent out on various reconnaissances was to be reduced to a minimum, so that the greatest number of aircraft possible could be assigned to work with the artillery. Ideally Joffre wanted each artillery regiment to have its own airplane; all other missions, liaison, bomb dropping, etc. were to be carried out only after the artillery's needs had been met. Joffre prescribed that the pilots be paired with batteries and work with them day after day, and his hope was that by working together steadily they could overcome the difficulties inherent in their cooperation. The chief of these was imperfect communications, and in 1914 airmen and artillerymen were encouraged to work out their own system of signals (later these were prohibited and a standard set of codes was imposed).[21]

In the early days of the war, when an air observer spotted a target, he could have the pilot land near the battery with which he was working and tell the artillerymen what he had found and where, or he could drop a note with sketch or map indications. When the battery was firing on an objective and he needed to correct its fire, he might have the pilot maneuver the plane in a certain fashion, or release flares or smoke grenades of various colors, or empty boxes of talc into the slipstream. Within a matter of months after the war broke out these methods were replaced by wireless telegraphy. The earliest sets were cranky and unreliable, and at first two planes could not transmit simultaneously if anywhere near to each other; in such cases they had to be given specified blocks of time in which to send their messages. The Italians found transmissions of their Marconi sets scrambled by those of the Austrian Telefunkens. German observers complained that the Russians jammed their transmissions intentionally.

Eventually these problems were resolved and the observer could tap out messages in Morse code with the expectation they would be received by the ground station. By late 1915 the wireless transmitters had become a fixture on observation planes flying on the Western and Italian fronts. A German observer in the Somme noted "now we can get hits regularly; before they were just accidents." For the balance of the war the airborne observer could transmit by wireless but he still could not receive. In addition to the additional weight and the technical challenges the wireless receiver represented, it was almost impossible for the observer to hear its signal against the roar of the engine and the wind noise of an open cockpit. (However, the Germans began trying wireless reception in 1917; by the end of the war it was in limited use in several air services.) The usual procedure was for the observer to unreel a trailing antenna of a hundred feet or so, tap out a prearranged message in Morse—in the British system the letter "R," which meant "are you receiving my signal?" and wait for a response from the ground receiver, who was often located in the battery the observer was to work with. Ground signals were smokebombs, flares, signal lamps, or most often "panels": cloth rectangles that could be arranged in various configurations. In the Italian system of 1917 the panels could be used to signal "yes," "no," "battery ready," "am suspending fire," "land," and "I don't understand."[22]

In a typical "shoot," as the British called it, the observer would have the pilot place the plane where he could see the battery and he would send down an order to fire. When he saw the muzzle flash he would signal the pilot—often by a tap on the head—to take him where he could see the fall of shot. The observer would calculate the flight time of the shells fired and watch the target for their impact. He would then send the battery another signal from his considerable repertory, indicating in "clock code" where the shot had fallen in relation to the target. The artillerymen below would make corrections while the observation plane returned to a position where the observer could see the next rounds fired.

At best the "shoot" was tedious and time-consuming work; when visibility was poor or communications with the battery intermittent, or many batteries firing at once, it was exhausting. Far greater effort was required than for balloon-directed shoots, and the result was often less satisfactory. Yet the airplane was indispensable. It could go up on windy days, when the balloon was obliged to remain in its "bed." Then too, the airplane could work at ranges and against targets far beyond the view of the balloon observer. Counter-battery work for example, firing at enemy batteries, was largely done with airplanes, particularly if the enemy guns were large ones, located well behind the enemy's lines. When a sector was active, "shoots" became the chief work of air units charged with observation. In the summer of 1916 British corps squadrons in France were devoting about two-thirds of their resources to cooperation with the artillery.[23]

The day-to-day work of a German observation unit can be seen in the daily log of Feldflieger-Abteilung (A) 263, prepared by one of its officers and based on the unit's *Kriegstagebuch* or war diary. The "dawn patrol" was a tradition the Italians had started in the Libyan War, and by 1914 there was also an evening patrol, a second sweep of the enemy positions. These were usually the unit's first and last flights of the day, with the early patrol taking off in pre-dawn darkness and the evening plane returning just as night was falling. Artillery work figures prominently, except in the winter months of inactivity.[24]

Reconnaissance tasks took much of the units' time—*Nahaufklärung*, or short-range reconnaissance, and *Fernaufklärung*, deeper probes sometimes involving flights of several hundred kilometers (eventually, special long-range reconnaissance units appeared in most air services, equipped with aircraft specifically built for high-altitude, long-distance flights). Interspersed with these activities were bombing, leaflet-dropping and other tasks. There was some night-flying on clear nights with sufficient moonlight and starlight for some visibility. Night reconnaissances were useful in gauging port and railyard activity; enemy forces in the field were also often betrayed by their bivouac fires. There were occasional night-time artillery shoots directed from the air. The Germans had a 380-millimeter naval cannon concealed near Lille, which they used to shell the rail junction at St. Omer, 30 miles away. The gun lay hidden under its camouflage by day, and fired only at night, with help from an aerial observer.[25]

Reconnaissance airplanes were often chosen for depositing spies behind enemy lines. This too was usually night work, and required the pilot to land in enemy territory. The landing place had already been carefully scouted by day, but the operation was always a risky one. If the airmen were caught they could be shot as accomplices in espionage, or so it was said (two American airmen caught when their motor would not start were indeed put on trial by the German authorities; the Americans hired a German attorney who got them off). The risks to the airmen could be reduced if the agent were parachuted into enemy territory. William Wedgwood Benn, who flew such missions in Italy, recalled that in order to avoid the problem of an agent who hesitated or refused to jump, he was placed in a cockpit in which both the seat and the floor were hinged. When the pilot reached the drop site he pulled a lanyard and the agent dropped out the bottom of the plane.[26]

For the fundamental task of keeping the enemy under observation, the airplane was the indispensable complement to the kite balloon. The fortified fronts constituted a barrier, a "crust," to use the common term, which no cavalry patrol could slip through. Then too, behind the lines was a vast communications zone many miles in depth, and developments there—the laying of railway track, the creation of depots—often signalled the enemy's intentions. Only the airplane observer could see those developments. Closer to the front, the combined information from balloon and airplane observation could also reveal the enemy's plans. German air reconnaissance supplied clues to the British Somme offensive of July 1916 as early as February, and confirmed it by further detective work in April, May, and June. In the spring of 1918 the Italian Air Service detected significant changes in the disposition of the Austrian artillery along the Piave River. In one sector the number of guns spotted increased from 700 in April to 1,800 in June; moreover the orientation of the guns changed. Originally they were arranged and sighted defensively, to put down a curtain of fire along the river where Italian troops might attempt a crossing; but by June the enemy's guns were sighted to place their barrage on the Italian side of the stream. This change, along with other information, announced an impending Austrian offensive.[27]

The observer would see much more than he could remember, so in the early days considerable emphasis was placed on rapid sketching; but very quickly the sketch was replaced by the photograph. There is a persistent myth that in the beginning of the war aerial observers took photos with their own cameras, because the hidebound and niggardly authorities had neglected to furnish any. This seems to have been the case only with the British, and even there the oversight was corrected by February 1915 with the introduction of the "A" camera. Aerial photography was already a half-century old in 1914, and its military applications had been extensively investigated. The French, Spanish, and Italian armies had taken cameras into the field in colonial campaigns, but Germany probably had the most effective aerial photography service throughout the war, thanks in part to the skills of the optical firms in Jena; the technical challenges of high-altitude photography had been met there by 1914. The German Air Service had 100 aerial cameras on hand when hostilities began. The automatic or serial camera—one that would take pictures at intervals as the airplane flew along—had also made its appearance. One of these devices developed by Giulio Douhet was in use in the French and Italian Air Services when the war broke out.[28]

Positional warfare gave the cameraman the time he needed in his work, and as the war continued the role of photography increased. It largely replaced visual observation in long-distance missions, as reconnaissance craft sought the security of higher altitudes. Above 10,000 feet the observer's ability to see anything of military value was very limited, while by the end of the war aerial cameras could take photographs at 15,000 feet which would, when blown up, make recognizable such details as footprints in sand. Eventually the photographic service could supply vertical, oblique, and even stereoscopic photos (the obliques were most popular in high command levels because they could be understood by the non-specialist). Battlefield photography grew tremendously, serving as the basis for highly detailed maps of the enemy's positions and also for the artillery's firing plan when attacks were being prepared. Hardly had the artillery bombardment ended before planes were photographing the results. The infantry, too, was supplied with photographs of its objectives. By 1916 the Italian Army was distributing them down to division and even brigade headquarters; by the end of the war they were being passed out in the trenches. Vast sections of the enemy line were systematically put on film. Enemy artillery emplacements were photographed at least once a week, and sometimes once a day. During four years of war the British took a half-million pictures. The Germans calculated after the war that if all the aerial photographs they had made were laid out, they would cover an area six times larger than Germany.[29]

But the observer's own view of things still retained its value, especially in rapidly evolving situations; in the second half of the war he was increasingly called on to work with the footsoldier in the infantry contact patrol. Infantry units in battle were often cut off from contact with the rear by the destruction of telephone lines; when that occurred there were other expedients, such as runners and pigeons. When even the expedients failed, the unit was isolated, sometimes with unfortunate results. More than once army headquarters knew that the ground ahead of a regiment was not occupied, but there was no way to order its advance. Sometimes the infantry had advanced further than headquarters thought it had; thus, in the notorious case of the "Trench of the Tents" in September 1915, French artillery poured its fire into positions held by French infantry. It took 18 hours to get the firing stopped.[30]

The contact patrol plane was charged with following and reporting on the infantry's progress or lack of it—work which often brought the aircraft down to an altitude of 1,000 feet or less. There were sporadic experiments with this sort of aerial surveillance in 1915, but it took another year before the contact patrol became a regular function. The observation plane thus became a participant of sorts in the land battle; a British airman described it as "the most fascinating of all duties carried out by reconnaissance squadrons." It was also frustrating work, chiefly because the infantrymen below often refused to identify themselves by laying out panels, flashing lights, etc., for fear of calling the enemy's attention to themselves. Or occasionally they would mistake the low-flying contact plane for an attacking enemy and meet it with a volley of small-arms fire. Despite these and other problems, the contact patrol became a standard component in infantry attacks.[31]

The crew of an observation plane working in the vicinity of the battlefield ran a number of risks. The pilot had to vary his path and change his altitude as he flew back and forth; otherwise, an enemy antiaircraft battery would be able to predict his course and send a shell up to meet him. At the same time both pilot and observer had to keep an eye out for enemy fighters. Were this not enough, the plane often flew in airspace being traversed by artillery shells. A large shell passing nearby could shake the plane with the turbulence it created; occasionally a projectile would pass harmlessly through the fabric of a wing. One British airman recalled the situation in the battle of the Somme:

> The vast amount of ammunition passing through the air posed a safety problem for the aviators, who would frequently see salvoes pass near them. In fact, more crews were lost by being hit by our own shells than were lost to enemy action in this battle.[32]

Enemy aircraft also sought out the observation plane; it was the preferred prey of the fighter, which began to emerge in 1915. Encumbered with the weight of two airmen, a wireless transmitter, and perhaps a camera strapped on the side of the fuselage, the observation plane was at a severe disadvantage. A French instructor told American observation crews training in France: "Your planes will be slower, less maneuverable. Do not hesitate to run." And when an observation crew came to grief and had to ride a crippled plane down to the battlefield, their death ride was witnessed by thousands. "It was always the same," wrote a soldier who saw many such episodes. "We knew that they were both still alive up there, but that they were going to die in fifteen seconds, in ten seconds, in five seconds. . . . We could never take our eyes from that long streak of smoke in the sky."[33]

Yet the work had its rewards. Not only could the aerial observer follow the unfolding of a battle as no one else could, he would sometimes influence its outcome. It was said that two men in a ten-thousand-dollar airplane could save a billion-dollar army. Sometimes the airmen were summoned to describe the situation and answer questions before a roomfull of generals. Hindenburg and Ludendorff closely quizzed their aviators at the time of Tannenberg. On other occasions generals climbed into observation planes and asked to be shown a portion of the battle zone. General Cadorna on the Italian Front and General Sarrailh in Macedonia both followed this practice. Occasionally the aerial observer himself made decisions normally reserved to higher authority. If a Royal Flying Corps observer saw a fleeting target that he thought was important, he could send down an "LL" call, directing onto the target the fire of every battery in the corps. At such times a second-lieutenant held the powers of a major-general commanding the corps artillery.[34]

The aerial observer was right in believing that he contributed something vital to the course of the war. The various belligerents went to extraordinary lengths to place him where he could serve as the eyes of the army. In addition to the hundreds of airplanes and kite balloons, they used the dirigible where they could. Nor did their efforts stop there. The French and the Germans sometimes used man-carrying kites, and in 1917 the Austrians developed a *Fesselschraubenflieger,* a kind of captive helicopter held by three cables (Dr. Theodor von Karman was one of its designers). But of all the vehicles, old and new, that were put into use, the airplane was the most important; what is more, it may have been more important in the observation role than in any other. In the words of the R.A.F.'s official historians, "Its first duty was reconnaissance. All its other and later uses were consequences of this central purpose, and were forced on it by the hard logic of events."[35]

=3=

The Emergence of
the Bomber

Though reconnaissance was the official function, the "central purpose," of the airplane in 1914, any number of reports in those first weeks of war indicate it was being converted to another, more offensive use, as airmen pelted enemy troops below with any projectile they could find. Among aviators there has long been a belief that it was the flyers themselves who thus introduced aerial bombing, quite contrary to the wishes of their earthbound superiors. Major-General Benjamin Foulois told an oral history interviewer in the 1950s "we always had ideas about using the airplanes as offensive weapons, which was contrary, of course, to military policy at the time." The first part of the General's assertion rings true, but the reference to policy calls for some elaboration. In any event, aerial bombing was hardly a daring new concept for the military of 1914, since the press and the public had been talking about it for years.[1]

In truth, aerial bombing had a significant "prehistory," if we can call it that, one that helped make it a function of air power that the literate civilian could already appreciate when the war broke out, even if the European military could not. In Britain, Wells' *War in the Air* appeared in 1908, and the emergence of the German dirigible fleet shortly afterward gave substance to his visions. As the airship and the airplane became realities, the journalist joined the novelist in forecasting the nature of the war to come. In both Europe and America newspaper editors and

41

writers in popular reviews posed such questions as "Can the Panama Canal be Destroyed from the Air?" In France one could read *How We Will Bomb Berlin with our Escadrilles of Aeroplanes as Soon as the War Begins*. Its author described a sudden raid on Paris by a fleet of 20 Zeppelins which produced "unspeakable horrors"; but a riposte by French bombing planes obliterated "the principal landmarks of Berlin, ministries, public administrations, stores, banks, newspaper offices, etc."[2]

In these scenarios the hazards and the difficulties of the new method of warfare were ignored or glossed over. The dirigibles and the airplanes were never hampered in their flights by adverse weather; they found their way straight to their objectives and, once there, they dropped their bombs unerringly. The attack usually had a double consequence: material destruction to the point of obliteration, and the moral collapse of those who endured the bombing; the image of hysterical mobs surging through the ruined streets was often evoked. Some of these same notions had been circulating among airmen as well; as far back as the 1880s, H. W. L. Modebeck had insisted on the emotional impact of aerial bombing: "Receiving blows from above no doubt generates a feeling of depression." Yet it is likely that political and military observers of the post-1900 era were in some fashion influenced by the apocalyptic visions in the reviews and the tabloids. It is significant that where aerial bombing occurred in the wars before 1914, observers and commentators almost invariably looked for signs of demoralization and panic—and almost always claimed to have found them. The outbreaks of "Zeppelinitis" in Britain and France in the years before 1914 were carefully chronicled by the German press, and exaggerated in the process. In German political and military circles the dread the Zeppelins apparently inspired must have seemed a confirmation of the moral or psychological power that novelists and journalists had attributed to the air weapon.[3]

This notion of psychological power persisted in one form or another throughout the war, while the belief in the enhanced material destruction the aerial bomb could achieve tended to linger as well. "Throughout the war," an R.A.F. officer recalled, "staffs who were under no illusions as to the weight of shells required for a given operation, appeared to think that some magic in the air would enable them to gain decisive results with one-hundredth the part of the necessary weights, provided it was in the forms of aircraft bombs." Even after the war, proponents of air power,

Giulio Douhet among them, tended to over-estimate the destructive effect of the aerial bomb. Early notions of bombing accuracy were also overoptimistic, as the experience of the war soon revealed. It is not unusual to expect too much of a new and untried weapon, but in the case of the bomber the expectations were so unrealistically high in some quarters that the disappointments which came were sometimes bitter. There may be a tinge of disillusionment in some of the postwar assessments of aerial bombing. General Felice Porro wrote that despite great sacrifices the bombing units of the Italian Air Service had only "modest possibilities for action." The author of a Luftwaffe treatise on bombers published in 1937 wrote that because of "inadequacies in matériel," it had not been possible to use the airplane in "a decisive, autonomous air war."[4]

By 1912 the offensive use of the dirigible and the airplane had begun to draw some interest among military authorities. The 1912 *grandes maneouvres* of the French Army involved the extensive use of both airships and airplanes; the compiler of the General Staff report on the maneuvers found that in addition to their reconnaissance roles, the airship and the airplane had a potential for "real offensive power." In the secret report following the German Army's *Kaisermanöver* that same year, the possibilities of aerial bombing were treated in some detail; they seemed so promising that the report urged the arming of all reconnaissance planes with bombs so they could attack suitable targets they encountered. Among those targets the report listed bivouacs and other military concentrations, rail yards, and even moving trains.[5]

Some political and military figures went far beyond these official appreciations of the air weapon. Early in 1912 an "air-minded" member of the British Parliament named E. Joynson Hicks published an article in the *National Review* which carried the ringing title, "Command of the Air." Among other things, he confided to his readers: "It is now known that bombs and bullets can be discharged from aeroplanes over hostile armies with considerable effect—quite sufficient to expedite a retreat and probably, to prevent a junction of forces." This judgment, which could have been based on nothing more substantial than the extremely limited experience in the Libyan War, was at the very least premature. But Joynson Hicks laid before his readers even more sweeping notions. While analysts on the general staffs pondered how air power might contribute to future land battles, Joynson Hicks and others were wondering what the airplane and the dirigible might contribute far beyond the battlefields, and in the last years before 1914 they sketched out a strategic role for the bomber, in which three distinct types of objectives could be identified.[6]

There were first of all targets whose destruction would deprive the enemy of important material resources, or at least deprive him of ready access to them. The great Krupp plant at Essen and the British arsenal at Woolwich were world-famous and came most immediately to mind. Then there were major weapons which the bomber could surprise and destroy at their home bases; there were, for example, the German dirigibles in their sheds, and the British Home Fleet at its moorings. In other cases it would be easier to make the resources inaccessible rather than destroy them. A British army in France would have a long and vulnerable lifeline, and this could be cut at the Channel ports; by the same token bombing the Kiel Canal would reduce the mobility of the German fleet, and destroying the Rhine bridges would halt the trains necessary for the supply of any German army in France.

There were other inviting targets for the far-ranging bombing planes and dirigibles. In a speech to the National Defense Association in 1909, Lord Montague of Beaulieu raised the spectre of a Britain paralyzed and helpless after a sudden air strike at her "nerve centers:" government buildings, the Houses of Parliament, the central railway stations, the central telephone and telegraph offices, and the stock exchange. In 1911, this same theme was taken up by a Lieutenant Poutrin in an article in the newly launched *Revue Générale de l'Aéronautique Militaire*. Poutrin described a hypothetical air attack in which 500 German planes, each carrying 300 kilograms of bombs, departed Metz just after the presentation of a German declaration of war and appeared over Paris three hours later. By attacking key ministries and transport and communications centers they shut down the essential public services, thereby rendering the country incapable of mobilization. The article had considerable repercussions in France. André Michelin was so struck by it that he decided to further the knowledge of aerial bombing through his international Aéro-Cible competition.[7]

The third category of objective was the population itself, or more properly its morale. Lieutenant Poutrin wrote that even if an air attack on Paris did little by way of material damage, its psychological impact on Parisians would be "immense." The American aviator Riley E. Scott, West Point graduate and winner of the 1912 Michelin bombing competition, felt an air attack of modest proportions against New York City would be devastating: "No great accuracy would be needed in the congested areas, and the loss of life from fire, high-explosive bombs, and panic would be appalling." In other scenarios the distracted population would turn upon its own rulers, forcing them to capitulate in order to end the reign of terror overhead. Though this sort of air offensive raised serious moral questions, it was also the most tantalizing. It seemed to offer—for a relatively small commitment in weaponry—not just the defeat of the enemy, but his collapse. In Imperial Germany particularly, in those last years before the storm, more students of warfare than a few must have asked themselves this question: "If the mere rumor of Zeppelin flights over London can produce hysteria, what would be the effect if one day the Zeppelins really did appear over the city and sow it with high explosives?"[8]

By 1912 the speculations on the military value of the airplane and the dirigible were accompanied by a wide variety of tests and trials. Officially sponsored bombing trials were under way in France, and in Germany, and in a number of other countries. In May 1913 the French Air Service was testing no fewer than five different types of bombsights, while in Britain the Naval Wing of the Royal Flying Corps had made "considerable progress in trials with bombs, bomb release gear, and bombsights." In Italy important experiments were under way to determine if an airplane could successfully release a heavy bombload without risk (it was widely held that the sudden loss of weight might destabilize the plane and cause it to crash). In July 1913, Captain Alessandro Guidoni of the Italian Navy dropped a 220-pound bomb without ill effect to his Farman; in February 1914, flying a two-engined airplane, he successfully released an 800-pound torpedo.[9]

The essential ingredient for aerial bombing was of course the bomber itself, a machine that could take considerable loads aloft and carry them for some distance. At first only the dirigible could do this; many of the early airplanes had such feeble lifting capacities that air services fixed maximum weights for their aviators; yet in 1914 the bombing plane existed in archetype, and curiously enough it was developed simultaneously in two countries which had not been in the van of aeronautical developments.

Beginning about 1910 both the Italian Giovanni Caproni and the Russian Igor Sikorsky begun work on large airplanes with exceptional range and carrying capacity. Since the chief limitation on the airplane's performance was its low-horsepower engine, both men began designing multiengine aircraft, though some engineers felt the idea was unworkable. Caproni was putting the final touches on his three-engined plane when the war broke out (it first flew in October 1914). By that time Sikorsky had built a series of airplanes, leading to the four-engined Ilya Muromets of 1914. To dramatize the plane's ability to fly long distances, in the summer of 1914 Sikorsky flew his giant plane from Moscow to Kiev and back, a distance of 1,400 miles; the machine stayed aloft for as much as eight hours at a time. Late in 1914 Sikorsky's planes became the nucleus of a special bombing and long-distance reconnaissance unit known as the Squadron of Flying Ships. In August 1915, three months after Italy's entrance into the war, the first Caproni bombers joined the Twenty-First Squadriglia of the Italian Air Service.[10]

But aerial bombing did not await the appearance of the first bombing planes; it started virtually with the war itself. Of all the powers, Germany had placed greatest confidence in the offensive potential of the dirigible. The secret *Dienstvorschrift* or service regulations of 1913 did not place much confidence in the bombing abilities of the airplane, since it could not place its small bombload with any accuracy from an altitude greater than 800 meters; yet the airplane needed to fly higher than that to be safe from ground fire. To the dirigibles, therefore, were allotted the tasks of strategic reconnaissance and bombing. And of course the British and French anticipated dirigible attacks immediately (there was another outbreak of Zeppelinitis when war was declared). But in Berlin there were some worries about the vulnerability of the great airships, so in August they were committed sparingly to the fighting on the Western Front—wisely so, for the German Army lost three Zeppelins within the space of a month, all of them to ground fire (the Z-6 during a bombing attack in Belgium, the Z-7 while making a reconnaissance in Alsace, and the Z-8 brought down by French artillery after bombing Badonvillers). Stunned by the loss, the German High Command virtually halted dirigible operations for a brief period.[11]

The French, too, learned that the daytime skies over the Western Front were no place for their airships, though their great-

est enemy proved to be their own ground forces. French soldiers
had heard so much about the German Zeppelins that they opened
fire on any airship they saw. On August 9 they fired at the *Conté*
for 10 minutes, putting 1,300 bullet holes in it and damaging it
so seriously that it barely made it back to its base. On August
24 French troops near Reims fired on the *Dupuy-de-Lôme*. They
put thousands of bullets into it, killing one of the officers on
board and doing such extensive damage that the airship had to be
scrapped. Thereafter the rest of the French dirigible force was
grounded by the high command and did not take to the air again
until April 1915.[12]

The brief, spectacular forays of the great airships caught
public attention in those first weeks of war, but it was the airplane
that made aerial bombing an everyday reality. In August and
September millions of soldiers were moving over the roads of
Europe; for airmen on reconnaissance the massive columns of
enemy troops below them were a target impossible to resist, so
they attacked them on their own initiative, with whatever weapons
they could devise. Official sanction for these efforts came very
quickly. General Joffre gave bombing his blessing in a note to
his army commanders on September 27. Late in October the
Royal Flying Corps issued a memorandum calling for all pilots
doing reconnaissance to carry bombs; soon after, the commander
of the German Air Service issued orders for similar arming of
all planes departing on a *Feindflug* or flight over enemy-held territory. The war diary of Feldfliegerabteilung (A)263 records that
on November 12, 1914, bomb racks were fitted to the unit's aircraft
and that they began bombing operations the very next day.[13]

Bomb production had not begun in state arsenals, which
were still carrying out tests and trials; but private arms producers
had already begun manufacture, and they put their products at
the disposal of the belligerents. The French Air Service had a
number of Swedish Aasen bombs left over from stock it had acquired for use in Morocco; the Germans and Austrians used bombs
manufactured by the Carbonit firm, while the Italians had at their
disposal Cipelli and Bontempelli bombs. To supplement these,
artillery shells of the 75–120-mm range were converted into bombs
by the addition of tail fins (large stocks of munitions for obsolete
cannon were disposed of in this way).

The early bombing activity was of necessity random and spontaneous, with little by way of official guidance and instructions.

Initially the airmen were delighted with the diversion that bombing offered from their reconnaissance work; it allowed them to take an active, offensive role in the fighting. "We took to bombing with enthusiasm," one R. F. C. officer recalled, "although we may now wonder what good we thought we were doing." Eventually the novelty wore off. The diarist of Feldfliegerabteilung (A)263 acknowledged in April 1915 that "the planes already had such a poor rate of climb that nobody carried bombs unless it was specifically ordered. Only Lieutenant von Bojanowsky never flies without the 10-kilogram bombs." And an R. F. C. note on bombing operations complained about "pilots who belittle the importance and utility of these operations."[14]

By early 1915 sufficient experience had been acquired for the first formal directives on bombing to appear. The French Air Service issued an *Instruction* on February 1, and the Royal Flying Corps brought out a note on "bomb dropping attacks" on the fifteenth. Neither document offered much by way of tactical guidelines. Both recognized the difficulty of achieving accuracy in bombing operations. The British recommended releasing bombs from an altitude of only 500 feet in order to achieve accuracy "within 50 yards." The French guidelines suggested extensive practice would help and promised a bombsight would soon be forthcoming. The list of recommended targets was extensive, and, significantly, few of the targets were on the enemy's front lines. The French recommended attacks on artillery positions and massed reserves as the sort of missions that would be of direct help in the ground fighting. Further back the most rewarding objectives were road and rail transport, barracks, and supply depots.[15]

The bomber very soon became an extension of the artillery, striking 30 or more miles behind the enemy's front lines, attacking targets beyond the range of the heaviest cannon. In some situations the bomber and the bomber alone could hit objectives well within artillery range but shielded from shellfire by the terrain—reserves sheltered in a ravine, for example. The Austrians and Italians soon learned that in the mountainous areas where they fought, troops and weapons placed on reverse slopes could be protected from the enemy's guns—but not from his bombers.

When a sector of the front became active, when one side or the other mounted an offensive, then the quantity of potential targets increased greatly: there were greater concentrations of artillery and a buildup in depots and reserves; the roads and particularly the rail lines became gorged with traffic. As early as the battle of Neuve Chapelle, in March 1915, the British arranged to send their bombers against objectives whose destruction would have maximum effect on the outcome of the land battle, most of these being railway stations or junctions. The effect, of course, would be a gradual one, slowing or cutting off the flow of men and munitions and thus gradually reducing the enemy's frontline strength. But sometimes the bombing of the enemy's supply lines would have an effect that was rapid and dramatic: at the battle of Messines Ridge in the summer of 1917, German bombers succeeded in destroying an entire British train loaded with munitions; as a result, the British artillery was obliged to cease its counterbattery work for three hours.[16]

The "bombers" the British used at Neuve-Chapelle were in fact ordinary observation aircraft that had been shifted from their usual task; they did their best, but their performance in this new role was often disappointing. It soon became apparent that there was enough bombing work to justify units specially trained for it, and that these would probably perform more creditably. The French were among the first to see this, bringing together three escadrilles to form Groupe de Bombardement No. 1 (G.B. 1) late in 1914. The new unit used Voisin pusher planes, which gave pilot and bombardier a good view and could carry 100 pounds or so of bombs. That September the German Air Service secretly formed a special bombing unit known under the code name *Brieftauben-Abteilung Ostende* (B.A.O.), meaning the Ostend Carrier Pigeon Detachment. The new unit was staffed with the best pilots of the German Air Service and was reserved for special bombing missions across the Channel.[17]

Such units, at the disposal of the army's high command, could be used against a wide variety of targets; the B. A. O., for example, began bombing Channel ports in December 1914. In the spring of 1915 G.B. 1 bombers raided the Badische Analin und Soda Fabrik, which was reputed to be the source for the chlorine gas the Germans began using on the battlefield that April; a little later the unit bombed the vast Mauser works at Oberndorf. The bombers also had their "special missions," usually clothed in secrecy. In October 1914, French military intelligence learned that Kaiser Wilhelm would be visiting the town of Thielt on November 1. Joffre sent orders to Escadrille V. 114 to attack the

Kaiser's cortege as it left the town (the mission was cancelled when the Kaiser changed his plans). Later the Allies tried without success to bomb the German Crown Prince at Stenay, and Prince Rupprecht of Bavaria at his headquarters. The Germans, for their part, tried to catch Tsar Nicholas with their bombers at least once.[18]

Many other tempting targets lay at the limit of the bomber's range or beyond it. The French attacked the dirigible hangar at Frescaty before the war was two weeks old; the R.N.A.S., with more success, bombed the dirigible shed at Düsseldorf in September and again in October and succeeded in destroying both the shed and the airship it contained; but the major dirigible bases were out of reach. For its part, the German B.A.O. was to bomb British coastal targets once the German Army took Calais. But the Army failed, and without Calais as base the B.A.O.'s planes did not have the range to strike effectively across the Channel. At the beginning of 1915 the German air service began a search for a more suitable bombing plane, which led to the Gothas of 1916. About the same time the R.N.A.S., which had a particular interest in long-range bombing, placed orders for a larger bomber that would eventually emerge as the Handley-Page 0/100. The French high command, much encouraged by the successful attacks on German industrial sites, approved plans for the development of a long-range bomber capable of carrying a greater bomb load, the so-called "Essen bomber."[19]

As the bomber was sent against an increasingly wider range of targets, the armaments industries were called on to provide a variety of aerial bombs to replace the earlier makeshift projectiles. Some of the early designs—the German A.P.K. and Carbonit projectiles, for example—were subject to wind drift; the Claude liquid-air bomb, used briefly by the French, was abandoned when it proved dangerous to air crews. But generally aerial bombs presented few problems beyond fitting them into production schedules. The metal case, the high explosive and the fuse were pretty much those of the artillery shell. The fragmentation bomb, widely used throughout the war, was generally a small projectile of 20 pounds or so, though larger ones were occasionally used. This type of bomb had a thick iron or steel container which would shatter into hundreds of fragments when the small bursting charge exploded. The fragmentation bomb was used against personnel and light structures, such as airplanes parked on a field. For the destruction of field fortifications and more resistant structures the blast effect of the explosive itself was more effective, so this was packed into a thin-walled metal container. Demolition bombs came in a variety of weights from about 40 pounds on up, with bombs weighing a ton introduced toward the end of the war. The third major type of bomb was the incendiary, whose flammable agent was usually a petroleum derivative.[20]

The various air services introduced bombsights, often a succession of them, in an effort to obtain greater accuracy. Initially the emphasis had been on practice, as if dropping bombs were an art akin to throwing darts; but even veteran bombardiers often got poor results. In the fighting at Festhubert and Aubines Ridge in the spring of 1915, the R.F.C. had tried to disrupt enemy rail traffic, but an after-action survey revealed that not a single bomb had scored a direct hit on its objective; a broader study of both French and British bombing results from March 1 to June 20, 1915, revealed that of 141 attempts to bomb railway stations, only 3 had been successful.[21]

The bombsights helped but little. Using them was a complicated procedure, sometimes involving the use of a stop-watch; accurate sighting depended on knowing the airplane's altitude, but early altimeters were notoriously inaccurate. There were bombardiers who preferred their own aiming methods. John Slessor recalled: "We had the C.F.S. bombsights, but most of us bombed by eye, aided by home-made arrangements of wires or marks on the leading edge or bracing wires." To the end of the war bombers found it extraordinarily difficult to hit a railway trestle or a train moving through a railway cut, the two most effective ways to cut a rail line. Thus, to drop bombs on a target was one thing, and to hit it was quite another, but this difference is often lost sight of in the official communiqués. The airmen sometimes made ironic references to the publicized version of their exploits. "In the war reports," wrote Jacques Mortane, "there were always passages which made one smile, such as the dropping of 10 bombs from 2,000 meters on 'military targets'."[22]

Despite these problems, bombing in support of the armies continued to develop. Now the bombers did not just attack targets they encountered; these were selected beforehand, often relying on intelligence reports. Early in 1915 French and British bomber crews would be given the objective, but each crew was free to choose the hour of its departure, the route it would take, and the altitude and direction from which it would bomb. By the end of the year bombing techniques had begun to crystalize. The French adopted the practice of always attacking the target downwind. This simplified aiming and reduced the time the bomber would be over the target and over any anti-aircraft guns that might be protecting it. And bombers now attacked in a formation of sorts; an R.F.C. note on bombing prepared at the end of 1915 revealed that "the go-as-you-please methods have been abandoned definitely both by the French and ourselves in favor of attacks carried out by swarms of aeroplanes."[23]

Bombing from formations increased the chances that at least some of the bombs would hit the objective, but it also presented the enemy's antiaircraft batteries with many targets at once and this meant that the individual planes had less chance of being hit than if they had attacked singly in "go as you please" fashion. For by the end of 1915 what the French called "the golden age" of aerial bombing—those first months of the war when the bombers could go and come essentially unmolested—was coming to an end. In August of 1914 the German Army had possessed only a score of antiaircraft guns, and the Allies had none at all; but soon this category of weapon began to multiply on both sides of the line—by April 1915 the Germans had 138 of them.[24]

The fighter began to emerge in that same year; at the beginning of 1915 the Morane scout, flown by such French airmen as Roland Garros, made a name for itself; later that year appeared the Fokker E type monoplane, with which Oswald Boelcke and Max Immelmann would begin their meteoric careers. The impact of improved air defenses was soon felt. In May, when the French sent 18 Voisin bombers against industrial targets in Ludwigshafen, only one bomber failed to return, and that because of engine failure; but when 18 planes were sent against Saarburg on August 20, 6 fell to German air defenses. In September the French High Command was forced to review its bombing policy; it decided to suspend the long-distance raids on German industrial targets and concentrate bombing activity on military objectives in the enemy's immediate rear.[25]

In 1916 the problems that the bomber faced grew steadily as the fighters and antiaircraft batteries multiplied. Ultimately there was only one solution: if the bombers were to continue to operate with acceptable losses, they would have to fly under cover of darkness (night flying had occasionally been practiced before the war). As early as December 1914, German reconnaissance units were night bombing on a random basis, simply to shake the Allied soldiers' morale; the first major night bombing raid by the German Air Service came in late January 1915, when the B.A.O. attacked the port of Dunkirk. The French began night raids in December of that year; then, in 1916, began a gradual conversion to night bombing by all the belligerents on the Western Front.

Day bombing did not entirely disappear, but what missions there were over the enemy lines generally did not involve deep penetrations of hostile airspace. According to General Keller, the Germans generally reserved daylight bombing for "days of heavy fighting when the artillery on both sides was fully committed." The French sometimes used day bombers as bait, hoping to bring out the enemy fighter force. On the Italian front some daylight bombing also persisted, though there was a move to convert long-distance operations to nighttime—notably the bombing "duel" the belligerents carried on back and forth across the Adriatic, the Austrians attacking port facilities at Venice, and the Italians bombing the Austrian naval base at Pola.[26]

Training bomber crews for night operations was challenging work, which according to General Keller "cost much in fatigue and also unfortunately in lives sacrificed." Some airmen who were excellent pilots in the daytime remained totally disoriented at night; for the first time the problem of nightblindness manifested itself. Night flying required navigational skills not required by day. In some units the flying was done when there was sufficient moonlight or starlight to make out something of the terrain below—perhaps one night in three. But as the war progressed the night flyers acquired considerable skill in navigating by the stars or by compass. "In the end," recalled General Keller, "with the exception of fog, the weather hardly played a role. In pitch-dark nights without moon or stars, and even in rain and snow, flights were made without incident." Whatever the degree of visibility, night bombers did not fly in formation, since the risk of collision seemed too great. The bombers departed singly, usually at five minute intervals.[27]

If we are to believe those who participated in them, night bombing missions were never humdrum affairs. Franz Schlenstedt recalled that a nighttime takeoff in a heavily laden bomber from a field that was usually too short "was, God knows, no easy matter." Once aloft, there were other risks. There were the enemy's guns and searchlights of course, but there was also the risk of mechanical breakdown. In the daytime a pilot worried about engine failure only when he was on the enemy side of the line; at night he had to worry about it all the time, for a "blind" emergency landing at night often ended in catastrophe. The final task was to find one's own flare-lit airfield or, barring that, one of the emergency fields. Late in the war the Germans developed a sort of aerial beacon that could be fired to a considerable height by a cannon; it was visible as far away as 60 miles, and a bomber that had lost its way could home in on its light. Some bombing units avoided the risks of night landings by timing their raids so they returned at first light. Squadron Leader C. P. O. Bartlett, who flew Sopwith 1½ Strutters for the R.N.A.S., recalled: "One took off down a parafin flare path, usually about two hours before dawn, and on return waited until sufficient light enabled one to see the ground clearly before landing."[28]

Bartlett's unit usually had as its targets "the docks and shipping at Ostend, the docks and submarine pens at Bruges, and the Mole and shipping alongside at Zeebrugge." Most night bombing missions were directed at targets more closely associated with the front. This was certainly true of the French Air Service, if we are to judge by a "note" on aerial bombing drafted late in December 1917. Under the rubric "Battlefield Bombing" three categories of targets were listed: airfields, railway stations, and cantonments and artillery parks. These were particularly worthwhile because they were missions of short duration that could be carried out several times in single night if necessary. They could be flown in "mediocre" weather, and the bombing could be done with relatively light aircraft and bombs. The "distant bombing" had to have as its goal targets related "to the supply of troops and matériel to the enemy's fighting front." These were listed, and they were almost all railway stations or junctions no more than 50 miles behind the enemy's first line.[29]

The French note dwelt at length on a third category of objectives under the heading "Industrial Bombardment." Here there was a major night target on which the French Air Service was expending considerable effort, and this was the Briey basin, located in Lorraine. By French estimate the Germans were drawing about three-quarters of their needs in iron ore from this small region, and shutting off that supply would severely affect the German war effort. The iron mines themselves were not viable targets, but the rail system by which the ore was moved was vulnerable. If the movement of ore trains through eight key stations could be interrupted, the French could achieve a "blockade" of the basin. The targets lent themselves to night bombing, and so the French Air Service mounted a long-term bombing campaign, even borrowing a *squadriglia* of Caproni bombers from the Italians.[30]

A fourth type of mission was described under "reprisal bombing," which was "frequently demanded by public opinion" in retaliation for damage the enemy inflicted on French towns. For the bomber had been drawn inexorably to the great cities, and by the end of 1917 attacks on them had become almost commonplace occurrences. The trend had begun virtually with the war itself. In 1914 the German government accused the French of having bombed Nuremburg even before the two countries had exchanged declarations of war. The French accused the Germans of an attack on Lunéville on August 6, and at the end of the month Paris was bombed for the first time by a single German Taube. Paris was only the first of many capitals to be bombed, often only in token fashion. The British, French, and Russians all managed to send bombers over Constantinople, and Allied planes also found their way to Sofia. In addition to London and Paris, the Germans struck Bucharest from the air and ultimately Petrograd as well, and looked into the possibility of bombing attacks on New York.[31]

Such raids were usually little more than symbolic, but they had considerable propaganda value. They made good headlines at home, while the enemy government was made to look powerless to its own people. A sustained bombing campaign against the enemy's population centers was quite another matter. Though such a campaign was bound to raise legal and moral issues, they could be dealt with. Most large cities contained too many military installations, arsenals, and the like to be considered "open" cities under the Hague rules for land warfare, and most experts would acknowledge, privately at least, that portions of their great cities were legitimate targets. No less a body than the World Peace Foundation had acknowledged in 1914 that the bombing of cities would be legal, however much it might offend "the world's sense of humanity."[32]

What mattered far more was whether a belligerent had the capacity to wage such a war, and whether in doing so it could deliver more blows than it would receive. The French authorities, whether military or political, showed considerable reluctance to get involved in this sort of warfare, chiefly because they would wage it on disadvantageous terms. With the German Army deep in northern France, most German cities were difficult to reach from French bases, while the German Air Service had Paris and many other French cities within easy reach. "We would need," says the note of December 18, 1917, "ten to twenty times more bombers than the enemy to produce on his cities (Karlsruhe, Frankfurt, Mainz) the same effect that he would have on Dunkirk, Nancy, or Bar-le-Duc." The wise course, then, was "not to let public opinion get carried away with the idea that reprisals are worthwhile unless we are sure that the morale of our civilians is ten or twenty times stronger than that of German civilians, for if a battle of this sort starts, that is the proportion in which the explosives will come."[33]

Managing public opinion on such an issue was not easy in wartime France; the authorities had their hands full with the calls for vengeance coming from both journalists and figures in public life. A writer in Le Figaro, stung by a recent nighttime Zeppelin raid on Paris, offered his readers this choice: "Either we resign ourselves to accepting more and more frequently the insults these Zeppelins show us, or we decide to carry to the other side of the Rhine all the horrors of the air war." And in the wake of the Zeppelin attack the French Air League, led by such figures as Georges Clemenceau, voted a resolution calling for the immediate creation of an air fleet armed and trained for the essential purpose of "carrying the war to the enemy."[34]

The Italian authorities found themselves in a similar situation. They had better bomber forces than the Austrians, but Austrian cities were not within easy range. Only by the most strenuous effort did the colorful Gabriele d'Annunzio make an appearance over Vienna. The towns and cities which were attainable were for the most part Italian in population and lay in areas the Italian government hoped to annex after the war. As General Porro wrote, that placed severe limitations on the Italian Air Service: "The Italianità of Venezia Giulia, Istria, Dalmazia, and the Trentino prevented us from making the cities our targets and limited the objectives to those of strictly military nature." On occasion these prohibitions could influence the military situation on the ground. In April 1916 Italian First Army intelligence learned Austrian troops were massed in certain towns in the Trentino;

the Commando Supremo refused to permit attacks on the towns because of their Italian populations.[35]

Of all the belligerents Germany was best placed to engage in this sort of strategic warfare; in her dirigibles she had an air fleet with unrivaled range and bomb-carrying capacity. Moreover, her position was geographically favorable, particularly vis-à-vis the Western Allies. Much of Germany was inaccessible to Allied planes; during the entire war no bomb fell on Berlin, though one intrepid French pilot did shower the city with leaflets. Within the German High Command there were a number of partisans of immediate raids into the heart of France and Britain. Helmuth von Moltke, chief of the German General Staff, argued as early as 1912 that the effect would be "extraordinary." Admiral Paul Behncke, deputy chief of the naval staff, urged that the Navy's dirigibles be sent against London, and his chief, Admiral Alfred von Tirpitz, was strongly tempted, though he felt "the indiscriminate dropping of bombs" was wrong, and that they were "repulsive when they hit and kill an old woman." Still, "if one could set fire to London in thirty places," Tirpitz reasoned, "then the repulsiveness would be lost sight of in the immensity of the effect."[36]

There had been plans for an aerial offensive on England by the combined forces of the dirigible fleet and the B.A.O. bombing unit, whose commander, Major Wilhelm Siegert, believed the bombing of London would provoke a crisis there that would end the war; but the plans could not be implemented. Then, too, the Kaiser had misgivings; not until May 1915 did he give a blanket authorization to bomb that portion of London which lay east of the Tower, including the arms center of Woolwich. In July the bombers got authorization to bomb any area of the city, providing they limited themselves to military targets. When the raids began, the *Heeresbericht,* the German Army's official bulletin on operations, duly indicated that the dirigibles had been sent to strike "military targets," and it often referred to the city as "Fortress London." Nighttime probes of the English coast by airships had actually begun early in 1915; on the night of January 9 the naval airships L 3 and L 4 had scattered bombs over Yarmouth and King's Lynn; but bad weather kept them from coming again until April. Then, on the night of May 31, the LZ 38 swept over the northeastern outskirts of London, releasing 600 pounds of high-explosive and incendiary bombs; these, strewn as the Zeppelin followed its course, killed seven people and started some small fires. The next raider did not appear over London until three months later.[37]

In all there were 54 airship raids, and though the last took place in 1918, the critical year was 1916. That autumn the Germans lost six airships within the space of three months, five of them sent down in flames by the British defenders, now more plentifully supplied with antiaircraft guns, searchlights, and night fighters firing incendiary bullets. For the embattled inhabitants of London the turning point came with the raid on the night of September 2–3. Sixteen German dirigibles of Zeppelin and Schütte-Lanz construction had started for England earlier that evening, and 13 of them reached the island. In London the sweeping searchlights and the antiaircraft fire had much of London's population watching the sky at about 2 A.M., when a British fighter pilot succeeded in igniting the SL-11. The great airship was at 11,000 feet when it was stricken. It began to glow from one end to the other as it started a long, slow descent that took a full two minutes. The entire ship became incandescent from the 1.5 million cubic feet of hydrogen she carried, bathing the whole metropolis with light and treating its inhabitants to a spectacle they would remember the rest of their lives; as the airship fell, cheers welled up from the entire city.[38]

At the end of the year the German Army gave up its airship campaign, passing its remaining dirigibles to the Navy. In the Navy the great airships still had their partisans; on the afternoon of October 19, 1917, 11 dirigibles started across the North Sea on what was to be the last big attack on Britain. High winds drove them away from London before they could do much damage and swept them over France, where more fighters and antiaircraft guns were waiting. Only seven of the airships made it back to Germany. Were this not disaster enough, on January 5, 1918, fire broke out in the Navy's dirigible sheds at Ahlhorn; within minutes five airships were destroyed. Of the 140 dirigibles the Germans used in the war, more than half were lost in action or succumbed to storms or accidental explosions. Douglas Robinson, who made a thorough study of the campaign against Britain, calculated that the airship crews that took part had heavier losses than any other combat organization in the German Army: their casualties were 40 percent.[39]

In the meantime the airship was faring no better among the other belligerents. The Italians lost the *Città di Ferrara* and the *Città di Jesi* in 1915, both being shot down during night bombing raids. In May 1916 the M-4 was lost in particularly tragic circumstances. The airship ran out of fuel battling headwinds after a nighttime bombing mission. Daybreak—and Austrian fighters—found it drifting helplessly over Gorizia. The Austrians signalled the ship's commander to take her down; when he refused they sent the M-4 and its crew down "wrapped in flames and glory." The loss of the M-4 was the beginning of a *série noire* for the Italians. On June 2 an airplane crashed into the M-5 and it was consumed by fire; on August 5 violent winds blew the M-7 out to sea, where it sank; on August 13 the P-6 was destroyed in its hangar by an aerial bomb. The French Army was scarcely more fortunate. It converted its airships to night-bombing operations beginning in 1915, and had two shot down that fall and lost another two over Verdun the following summer, briefly reducing the army's dirigible strength to one ship. In February 1917 the French Army, like its German counterpart, passed its airships on to the sea service.[40]

The eclipse of the airship did not mean the end of the bombing war against the cities. Late in 1916 the Germans took the first steps to create a new heavy bombing unit, which would be known under the acronym Kagohl 3; many of its airmen were veterans of the B. A. O.[41] As a result, in 1917 London faced a more serious threat than Zeppelins, with the appearance of large German bombers, the twin-engined G plane or *Grossflugzeug* (often called the Gotha, for one of its builders) and later the multiengined R plane or *Riesenflugzeug*, meaning giant airplane.

The German High Command saw the renewed bombing of London as one of two bodyblows to be delivered against Britain in February 1917; the other would be unleashing of 140 U-boats in unrestricted submarine warfare. Wholesale sinkings around the British Isles would have devastating effects on the British economy while the renewed bombing would simultaneously deliver a psychological shock to Britain's heart. The target of choice was central London, "particularly the government buildings around Downing Street, the Admiralty, the Bank of England and the press buildings in Fleet Street." Only when London was inaccessible would the bombers strike munitions factories and depots outside the city. And the bombers would attack London in the daytime, which would afford better bombing accuracy, but above all would make their operations "high-profile." Millions of Londoners would see the bombers fly over their city with impunity. This the German planes would be able to do in part because they would fly at an altitude of 16,000 feet, which would make them less vulnerable to antiaircraft fire; though the most advanced British fighters could reach that altitude, it would take them considerable time, and the planes of Kagohl 3 would meet them in close formation with mutually supporting fire.[42]

The first G plane raid did not take place until May 25, 1917, and the 22 attacking bombers could not attack London because it was shrouded by clouds; they released most of their bombs on Folkstone, killing 72 people and provoking a groundswell of indignation throughout Britain. Then, just before noon on June 13, a score of white Gotha bombers wheeled over London, strewing bombs across the city, including three which devastated the Liverpool Street Station; 16 bombers from Kagohl 3 repeated the raid on July 7, all 16 returning safely to their bases. In August the Germans' luck turned bad. That month a combination of strengthened British defenses and adverse weather cost Kagohl 3 a total of 22 planes; on some of the missions the loss rate approached 50 percent. In September the high command ordered a switch to night bombing, and for a time the tempo of raids actually increased; at the end of September the raiders appeared over London on six successive nights; then the attacks tapered off.[43]

If the Germans had hoped for a strong reaction to their bombing program that summer, they were not disappointed. The War Cabinet met in anxious sessions; at one of them Field Marshal Sir Douglas Haig, the Commander-in-Chief of the British forces in France, and Major-General Hugh Trenchard, commanding the R. F. C. in France, presented a pessimistic report on how Britain might counter the bombing attacks. They spoke of reprisals on German towns; though they were "repugnant to British ideas," the real reason they could not be used was the lack of "suitable machines." There were also gloomy statistics indicating war production was declining because factory workers were kept awake all night by the German bombers. Seeking a way out, the War Cabinet decided to do what officialdom often does in crisis, it created a committee, in this case a Committee on Air Organization and Home Defense against Air Raids, to be chaired by Lieutenant-General Jan Smuts. On August 17, just as the bombing war was turning against Kagohl 3, General Smuts submitted a far-ranging report on "the air organization generally and the direction of aerial operations"; the report, adopted by the War Cabinet on August 24, would ultimately work profound changes in the British conception of air power.[44]

In the meantime the London press was in full hue and cry, armchair strategists found ready audiences, and in Parliament there were debates of unusual violence; after one particularly heated exchange in the House of Commons the Speaker ordered Noel Pemberton Billing removed from the Chamber. The people's tribunes were obviously in a state of agitation, but what of the people themselves? Some claimed that the population of London was living on the raw edge, that its morale was slumping. This very argument was being made in Germany by Captain Rudolf Kleine, who had taken over Kagohl 3, and was struggling to continue his mission: If the campaign against London were continued, and if possible intensified, the city would surely crack.[45]

Some in London were reminded of those tense days in 1915 when there were rumors of gigantic super-Zeppelins, and Scotland Yard was advising families how to cope with poison gas bombs. Then, too, there had been signs of incipient panic. John Slessor had a nightmarish experience straight from one of the apocalyptic novels of war in the air, one so vivid he included it in his memoirs. He was driving through London in an R. F. C. truck when the vehicle was suddenly surrounded by a swarm of agitated Londoners: "There were angry cries, and we were mobbed til we had to pull up and get a policeman to stand on the step on either side of the driver's seat of the tender to get through at all."[46]

But there is other testimony about the temper of London in those critical days and nights, a detached, indeed a clinical assessment, provided by the city's physicians and duly recorded in the pages of *The Lancet*. Its editor was interested to know how the bombings affected patients in hospitals, whom he described as "a particularly vulnerable section of the population." A physician attached to a military hospital filled with men from the front recorded the effect of the air raids on his patients: "Nearly frantic with terror, numbers of them writhing under their beds . . ., their eyes transfixed and their twitching faces wearing a look of abject horror." But these were "nerve-shattered men," victims of what the medical profession then called "shell shock," who suddenly found themselves back amidst the terrors of the battlefield and reacted accordingly.[47]

A survey of the civilian hospitals produced quite a different story. At Charing Cross Hospital "the calmness of the patients was wonderful"; at Middlesex Hospital they behaved "admirably"; the same was true of the Hospital for Sick Children, on Great Ormond Street, save for a few upset mothers who were "foreigners." At the London Fever Hospital the boys suffering from scarlet fever "took to active vocal verbalisms, derogatory to the 'fat-heads', 'square heads', and 'pigs' of Germans." The editor of *The Lancet* himself toured outpatient facilities in the raided district after the July 7 raid, and talked with physicians in the area, who reported few signs of apprehensiveness and sleeplessness after the raid. After the series of nighttime raids another *Lancet* survey produced equally reassuring findings: "The recurrence of the dangers has tended not to exaggerate those dangers, as the enemy hoped fondly would happen if attack followed often upon attack, but rather has made the circumstances more tolerable; and it is this growing bravery that has become a part of our psychology." That same "psychology" would manifest itself again in London in 1940 and 1941—and in Berlin in 1944 and 1945.[48]

=4=

The Development of Aerial Combat

Men are going to fight in the air for the same reason
that they fight on the ground and under the ground
and on the sea and under it—because a true soldier
attacks the enemy wherever he finds him. And since
it is certain and beyond a doubt that there will be combat
in the air, we must immediately forge the weapons
for this combat.

This call to arms was issued in December 1913 by two French officers named Sensever and Baillif; they were the authors of *Le combat aérien*, probably the first book-length treatise on aerial combat. When war came to Europe seven months later, their call had not been answered, for neither the French Air Service nor that of any other belligerent had on the line machines intended for aerial fighting, though there is some evidence that they were moving in that direction. Serious speculation about coming aerial battles actually went back to the dawn of the century, when the dirigible began to emerge as a viable weapon. R. P. Hearne, an early authority on airships, foresaw duels between them using such weapons as compressed air and spring guns, petroleum and liquid air bombs, aerial mines, fire-tipped arrows, javelins, detonating darts, and aerial torpedoes, the latter being a kind of guided missile, or as Hearne described it, "some form of miniature airship loaded with high explosives and perhaps in the perfected state steerable by wireless electric means from the airship itself."[1]

As the German dirigible fleet grew into a palpable menace, and as the airplane appeared as a possible antidote, in both Britain and France some thought was given to arming it as a Zeppelinkiller. The French Army's *Troisième Bureau* noted in its analysis of the 1912 maneuvers that the airplane "could have real offensive power against dirigibles," and by 1913 the French had acquired the Guerre "incendiary arrow," a large two-pound, benzine-filled dart equipped with hooks that would catch on the fabric of the dirigible's envelope. For its part the Royal Flying Corps was working on the "sweeping" concept in which an airplane would trail a bomb at the end of a wire and hopefully detonate it against an airship.[2]

Several French aviation pioneers wrote about combat between airplanes. Clément Ader saw the possibility in the 1890s, and Ferdinand Ferber dwelt on it at some length in 1908. He foresaw aerial battles in which the chief weapons would be hand grenades, revolvers, hooks, and harpoons, with the victory generally going to the protagonist who had the advantage of altitude. As experimentation with airplanes revealed their value for reconnaissance, the question of "command of the air" came to be linked to facilitating the work of one's own observation planes and barring the enemy's aerial observers from one's own airspace, and chiefly the latter. A British general had put the case quite clearly after the 1912 maneuvers: "Personally, I think there is no doubt that before land fighting takes place, we shall have to fight and destroy the enemy's aircraft. It seems to me impossible for troops to fight, while the hostile aircraft are able to keep up their observation. That is to say, warfare will be impossible until we have mastery of the air." Major Frederick Sykes, then commander of the Military Wing of the Royal Flying Corps, told the Royal Aeronautical Society in February, 1913 that it was necessary to gain command of the air "in order to obtain information ourselves and to prevent enemy air reconnaissance from doing so."[3]

Among those who speculated on the future of air power there was some difference about how hostile airplanes might be destroyed. A contributor to *Engineering* wrote in 1909: "Obviously the way to combat flying-machines will be to build opposing flying machines;" but he confessed it was impossible to know what "the future fighting machine of the air" would be like. Captain W. A. de C. King of the Royal Engineers believed that while some planes would be armed to take the offensive, ground fire would be more important, for "it does not seem reasonable to expect that hostile aircraft can be destroyed or driven away by armed aircraft only." Two German writers of 1912, Olszewski and von

Elgott, gave it as their considered opinion that "airplanes will not be able to harm each other without sacrificing themselves;" this was an allusion to deliberate ramming, a desperation tactic which was sometimes proposed against dirigibles. Official opinion on the possibility of combat between airplanes could perhaps be described as reserved and tentative. A staff report prepared for the French Minister of War in 1912 concluded that "combat between airplanes is not to be envisaged at the present time." According to Raleigh and Jones, the R.A.F.'s official historians, "this fighting had been foreseen, but only as a speculative possibility."[4]

Olszewski and von Elgott, cited earlier, argued that true aerial combat was not possible for lack of a suitable weapon; when they wrote, the machine gun had already been identified as the "suitable weapon" and in several countries work was underway to adapt the arm to use in the air—for, like engines and electrical equipment, the machine gun had to be lightened and reduced in size before it could find its place in an airplane. The first such weapons, the American Gatling gun and the French *mitrailleuse,* were mounted on horse-drawn carriages; the next generation of automatic weapons that began to equip European armies at the turn of the century were still cumbersome and heavy: on the German Maxim gun of 1908 the water-cooling system alone weighed over 40 pounds. Many of the guns had feed systems that permitted horizontal firing only, or threw expended cartridge cases about—and just one such cartridge case, thrown into an airplane's propeller arc, could shatter the wooden propeller, provoking a forced landing or worse.[5]

The first machine gun with the potential for use on an airplane was invented by an American Army officer named Isaac N. Lewis, and first demonstrated to American military authorities in 1911. In 1912 Lewis took sample weapons to Europe, where they favorably impressed airmen in several countries and produced some sales; in May of that year, American airmen at the Signal Corps Aviation School in Maryland gave the 25-pound weapon its first airborne firing tests, firing at ground targets from several hundred feet up; the tests were encouraging, even though the gun used had no sights. One year later, at the Salon d'Aéronautique of 1913, the Hotchkiss aerial machine gun made its début. It was light in weight (22 pounds), compact (less than a meter long), and could be fired in any direction, including straight up.[6]

The marriage of airplane and machine gun had at this point

become inevitable; in fact the first attempts to unite the two had been made somewhat earlier. In a Berlin exposition of 1911 there was an Euler airplane with a machine gun mounted in a fashion that was "more symbolic than practical." In Italy the authorities made extensive tests with aircraft carrying machine guns, testing their potential against other airplanes and dirigibles as well. In Britain, too, the idea had its partisans, and several embryonic fighter aircraft were devised. In 1912 there were experiments with a Maxim gun mounted on an F.E. 2 pusher, and early the following year an F.E. 2 was rebuilt as a two-seat gun carrier, the beginning of a "Fighter Experimental" type of pusher biplane designed at the Royal Aircraft Factory; at the same time the Vickers firm was developing an armed biplane for the Royal Navy. Peter Lewis, who has studied the evolution of the British fighter in all its details, has concluded that "by 1913 it was obvious that both the Army and Navy had reached a firm appreciation of the value of being able to mount guns, either large or small, on their aircraft for dealing with an enemy."[7]

The fact remains that during the first months of the war there were no fighter planes worthy of the name and very little by way of aerial fighting. Sir John French, in his despatch from France dated September 10, professed wonderment that his airmen had engaged in any such combat at all, for he reported that "by actually fighting in the air, they have succeeded in destroying five of the enemy's machines." A writer in *The Aeroplane* explained that there were no aircraft adequately armed for it, but also "aeroplanes avoid one another purposely." This was often the case. They usually flew on a mission—almost always reconnaissance—and the completion of that mission was paramount. The French captured a memo addressed to German airmen which acknowledged that French aviators sometimes "amused themselves" by firing at German planes; but there was "nothing to worry about" since the danger was nil, and German air crews were in no event to take up the gauntlet.[8]

What little fighting there was seemed to have been the result of individual initiative and improvisation. The aircraft designer Gabriel Voisin had acquired six Hotchkiss guns, and these he gave to the aviators of Escadrille V-24, who were flying his machines. There was talk of bizarre and desperate measures; pilots were said to fly with trailing grapnels in hope of snagging an enemy plane; it was rumored that French pilots charged with the defense of Paris had taken oaths to ram any Zeppelins that approached the city. A German pilot wrote home that when he and his comrades went up to meet intruding French aircraft, they went "armed to the teeth," carrying among other things small bombs. A British aviator recalled being told that "the correct procedure on meeting hostile aircraft was this:—if possible overtake him, then dive in front of him, and as you passed do a turn. The air pockets caused by this turn, I was assured, would be quite sufficient to send him crashing to the ground."[9]

But it would be wrong to draw too strong a contrast between the initiative of the airmen and a lack of that initiative of the "higher-ups," for the latter reacted rather quickly when the theoretical possibility of aerial combat became a daily reality, and this was notably the case with the French High Command. In late August 1914, when the city of Paris seemed in grave danger from the rapid German advance, the city was declared a special fortified area, the Camp Retranché de Paris. Among the forces mustered for its defense were eight hastily organized escadrilles, created from airplanes and pilots held in reserve at Saint-Cyr. Several of the planes were armed—some with 37mm cannons taken from the Eiffel Tower. They flew their first mission—probably the first genuine fighter mission of the war—on August 30, 1914. Soon the danger receded and most of the military build-up around the city was dispersed, but the idea of using the airplane as a destroyer of enemy airplanes was not forgotten. In a plan for expansion of the air service submitted to the minister of war at the beginning of October, 16 of 65 escadrilles projected would be specialized in reconnaissance and chasse—fighting or, more literally, hunting.[10]

General Joffre, who passes for one of the more conservative and less imaginative of the generals of 1914, was nonetheless an early advocate of the fighter: in a note on army aeronautics dated November 10, 1914, he stressed the offensive roles the airplanes could undertake, including that of "chasing and destroying enemy aircraft." He proposed that the planes for that purpose be both "armed and armored." To be sure, it is more than likely that the note he signed was drafted by the chief of his air service, Major Barès; nonetheless, when Joffre signed it he gave a solid endorsement. As the conception of the fighter plane sharpened in the official correspondence, so did notions about aerial fighting. A French note on the use of aviation, dated February 11, 1915, contains a reference to the *barrage,* a sort of aerial blockade which would "deny the enemy access to our lines by continual flying back and forth, and by this means mask movements behind our front." The first such barrage was probably set up for the French attack at Eparges in the second half of February. Within the first six months of the war, then, the French military had made considerable progress in identifying the fighter and defining its role, progress that appears to have put them in advance of the other belligerents; thus there is some justification for the argument recently made that the fighter arm was essentially the product of "French initiative."[11]

While the French High Command and the military leaders of the other belligerents were weighing the functions and future of air power, the air war was continuing apace, and in it the fighter was beginning to make its presence felt. The early aerial engagements—more often duels than battles—helped demonstrate what the fighter plane should be. The first attribute needed was speed, so that the predator could overtake its prey; as early as March, 1915, Joffre was complaining that aerial engagements were more often the result of accident than design, for lack of fast planes. The fastest aircraft in 1914 were the lighter, smaller machines which economized on weight by carrying only a pilot; on the Allied side the Morane-Saulnier monoplane best met these criteria. The quick and nimble Model N single-seater seemed particularly suited to this work, though it had originally been cast in the role of an unarmed "scout," a label that clung to early fighters. A different concept was applied with the Vickers F.B. 5, a pusher airplane carrying a pilot and a machine gunner, the latter enjoying a sort of balcony seat in the plane's nose. The F.B. 5, which made its appearance in the summer of 1915, was the outgrowth of a peacetime initiative taken by the Vickers firm.

Initially the Germans were hard pressed to match the Allies. With no suitable machine guns available, they issued pistols and automatic rifles to their aviators. A German airman told a *New York Times* reporter: "We find the best defense against their machine-gun fire is to get up close to the French aeroplane and then dodge and twist in sharp dips and curves, spoiling the aim of their mounted machine gun, and giving us an advantage with our revolvers." Despite such brave talk, German airmen felt keenly the disadvantage under which they fought; what is more, the German Air Service had no equivalent to the Morane. Spurred by losses of observation and reconnaissance aircraft, the Germans turned for help to the young Dutch designer Anthony Fokker, who produced for them the Fokker *Eindecker* (monoplane). The Eindecker may be called the first true fighter plane, built and armed expressly for aerial combat. The airplane itself offered no novelties in design, in fact it closely resembled the Morane single-seater; but in the Fokker Eindecker the marriage between the fighter plane and the machine gun was consummated. It had been argued, with some justice, that a pilot flying alone would have his hands full with maneuvering the aircraft, keeping his bearings, and scanning the skies, and would have no time to aim and operate a machine gun. Lieutenant Pichot-Duclos, writing in 1912, estimated that it would be a "heavy burden" that the distracted pilot would not be able to perform satisfactorily.[12]

It had been appreciated well before the war that the pilot's task would be much lightened if the machine gun could be made to fire along the plane's line of flight or "axis," so that the pilot could aim the gun by aiming the airplane—at the same time, the challenges of deflection shooting would be much reduced. For that purpose a way had to be found to fire through the propeller arc of the tractor machine, and work in this direction was under way before the war broke out, with patents for synchronizing systems taken out in France, Germany, Italy, and some other countries as well. At the beginning of the war a French aviator named Roland Garros had found a makeshift solution in fitting the propeller with steel deflector plates, so that bullets that encountered the propeller (about 1 in 10) would harmlessly bounce off. Fokker's solution was a device that ensured that a bullet was fired only when no propeller blade would encounter it. The Eindecker with its synchronized gun was demonstrated to German pilots in May 1915, and thereafter the machines began to flow to the front; the new fighter achieved its first aerial victory on July 1, inaugurating a new phase in aerial combat. "A technical marvel," one German pilot called the new plane, "with it a man can really hunt down the enemy."[13]

The impact of the new German fighter was not felt for some time, at least not at the front. During the entire month of August 1915, the R.F.C. recorded only 16 aerial combats. More noticeable was the effect of the enhanced fighter force on French bombing missions into Germany. These had been conducted at relatively little cost, but then in a raid against Saarburg on August 2, the

French lost nine planes. It was the beginning of a pattern of losses that would eventually bring an end to daylight bombing. In the meantime the Eindeckers arriving at the front saw only limited use, first of all because they were not to be taken across the lines where they might fall into enemy hands (the Allies only captured their first Eindecker in April 1916, some nine months after its introduction). Then, too, the Fokkers were sent to two-seater units as supplementary aircraft, to be flown when the occasion or opportunity presented itself. The same policy was being followed by the Allies with the new single-seaters they were introducing, the Nieuport XI "Baby" and the Bristol Scout. There was one exception: Escadrille N. 65, located at Malzéville, near Nancy. It was equipped with Nieuport XIs and given a dual assignment: to escort French bombers operating from Lorraine, and to defend the skies over Nancy. This escadrille, and the R.F.C.'s No. 11 Squadron, flying Vickers F.B. 5s, could well be considered the first fighter units.[14]

Aerial activity intensified that fall; if the Germans had felt the losses from fighter activity in the spring, now it was the turn of the Allies. Late in November the French Air Service called on the aircraft industry for a long-range fighter that could protect its bombers, for whom German airspace was becoming increasingly dangerous. Despite bouts of bad weather that curtailed operations, the R.F.C. recorded the loss of 20 aircraft between November 7 and January 12. These were manifestations of the "Fokker menace" which became the talk of Allied airmen, and ultimately of governments and the press as well. By the beginning of 1916, then, a new arm was clearly in evidence; but the full range of its capabilities had yet to be explored, and the tactics inherent in its use had not gotten beyond animated discussions in the squadron mess. But in the great struggles of 1916, at Verdun and along the Somme, the new arm came into its own.[15]

The Germans had made elaborate preparations for the attack at Verdun, which began on February 21, and had assembled a large number of airplanes for use in the battle. The bulk of these were committed to the *Luftsperre,* a German version of the barrage designed to form a screen impenetrable to Allied aircraft, or nearly so. The Fokkers were not used for this work, which was done by the more numerous two-seaters of the Fliegerabteilungen, which cruised up and down the German side of the front in great numbers. At first, the score of fighter planes, grouped into *Kom-*

mandos, were charged with the interception of French planes which made it through the Luftsperre. But as the offensive ground on, the number of fighters was increased by drawing them from other sectors, and they began to take up other tasks. It was not sufficient to bar the French from the German side of the front; German reconnaissance and artillery observation planes needed security as they "worked" the battle zone, and the German fighter force undertook to clear the air for them. Flying more offensively now, the German fighters began to appear over the front in formations of two or sometimes three. These changes are associated with an already-famous fighter pilot named Oswald Boelcke (he and his colleague Max Immelmann had earlier experimented with the two-man patrol). Within a matter of days the Germans had made a practical reality of the hitherto speculative term, "air supremacy."[16]

When the storm broke before Verdun the French were as ill-prepared in the air as they were on the ground. To combat the sizable concentration of German aircraft they had only two escadrilles, N. 23 and N. 67, and these were simply overwhelmed. To redress the situation General Joffre ordered Philippe Pétain to undertake the defense of Verdun, and to direct the struggle in the air Joffre called in Major Tricornot de Rose, of Escadrille M.S. 12, and gave him carte blanche. De Rose concentrated Moranes and Nieuport XIs in the Verdun–Bar-le-Duc area, skimmed the various escadrilles of their best pilots, and put together a fighter force of 15 escadrilles which he formed into a *groupe de chasse* under his command. (SPA 124, the celebrated Lafayette Escadrille, saw its first action over Verdun in May.) On February 29, 1916, General Pétain initialed the orders for the reconquest of the air over Verdun: "Offensive patrols will be carried out on a regular basis at times fixed by the commander of the *groupe.* By reconnaissance is meant patrols, flown by airplanes flying in a group. The mission of the escadrilles is to seek out the enemy, to fight him and to destroy him. They will patrol by escadrille or by demi-escadrille. They will adopt a formation that will place them in echelon in all three dimensions."[17]

What followed was an independent war of sorts fought between two fighter forces, the first such confrontation of the war. It was characterized by formation flying, with formations increasing from two or three planes to a half-dozen. To coordinate the fighter effort, the planes were placed in larger and larger units.

The Germans deployed their fighters in two groups, one on each side of the Meuse. As the year wore on the French grouped more and more escadrilles into *groupes de chasse,* and beginning in August the Germans began forming *Jagdstaffeln* (hunting squadrons) with a theoretical complement of 14 planes each. By then the contest for control of the skies over Verdun had been largely won—by the French. Much of the explanation lay simply in the larger number of fighters the French were able to commit. Though they also had some first-class fighter pilots there, in fact for both air services Verdun became, as someone said, "a rendezvous for virtuosos." By March the airspace over Verdun had become less dangerous for French "working" airplanes, and more so for German ones. By April, German plane incursions over the line were becoming rare; by May the German artillery was relying chiefly on observation balloons for ranging its cannon, and toward the end of the month French fighters, armed with air-to-air rockets, began a campaign of destruction against the balloons. And as the effectiveness of the German artillery declined and that of the French improved, the casualty rates in the trenches tilted against the Germans; then at the end of the year the fighting petered out. The French claimed the victory, such as it was, and the French air service could claim its full share of the laurels.[18]

For the French and the Germans, Verdun carried eloquent lessons. The notion of the barrage was demonstrated to be essentially unworkable; more than that, the battle demonstrated the immense range of advantages that accrued from air superiority and the critical role of the fighter plane in obtaining that superiority. The struggle on the Somme, which occupied the most attention during the second half of 1916, witnessed another lesson in the value of air power, which the Germans once again learned the hard way. In part it was once again a question of numbers—one authority has suggested the Allied superiority approached three to one—and in addition the Allies, too, now had fighters whose machine guns were synchronized to fire through the propeller arc. In addition to the other disadvantages brought by inferiority in the air, the German ground troops suffered something of a morale crisis, provoked by the frequent presence over the battlefield of Allied planes and the almost total absence of German ones. In August 1916, one frequently encountered in German trenches and command posts crudely lettered signs reading "*Gott strafe England und unsere Flieger*" ("May God punish England and our flyers"). The Somme offensive finally bogged down in the mud. As the front became quiescent, the German fighter pilots began to receive replacements for their Eindeckers, and the German Air Service was given a thorough organizational overhaul. When battle was joined again in the spring of 1917 the reinvigorated Jagdstaffeln made a very strong showing. Led by such men as Manfred von Richthofen and flying new fighters such as the Albatros, they gave the British in particular a mauling that goes down in R.F.C. annals as "Bloody April." But later in the year the Allies regained the ascendancy in the fighter war and held it until the end.[19]

The year 1916 was critical for the evolution of aerial combat. The French say that the fighter arm—as opposed to the fighter plane—was "born" at Verdun. Major Wilhelm Siegert, second in command of the German Air Service, said the Somme served as a "finishing school." In the years 1916 and 1917 the doctrinal guidelines and the tactical principles were worked out by the airmen themselves—men such as Tricornot de Rose, Boelcke, and the R.F.C.'s James McCudden—and then refined, codified, and disseminated through such vehicles as the R.F.C.'s *Notes on Aeroplane Fighting in Single-Seater Scouts* of November 1916, and its *Fighting in the Air*, which appeared in March 1917.[20]

The *Notes* of 1916 indicate clearly that a tactical revolution has taken place with the spread of formation flying. The paragraph on "Fighting Tactics of the Single-Seater" is explicit in this regard: "As a general principle a single-seater should never cruise alone, and an attack by an isolated single-seater should be the exception." The introduction of the two- and sometimes three-fighter patrol was in part inspired by the defensive pairing of observation craft which appeared in 1915; in the case of Feldfliegerabteilung (A) 263, for example, notes from its *Kriegstagebuch* (war diary) for that summer indicate that one two-seater would be sent across the lines to gather information, with a second two-seater assigned to accompany it in a protective role (though the unit had by then received at least one Fokker Eindecker, the fighter plane was always retained in German airspace). The French and British also experimented with various escort techniques, and the R.F.C. made the escort system virtually mandatory in January 1916. As the fighter's potential victims found advantages in flying in groups, so did the fighter. A British memorandum of December 1917, on the "Development of Aerial Fighting," clearly indicates that this was the experience of the Royal Flying Corps. Having described the emergence of the escort system for reconnaissance planes in the course of 1915, the memorandum noted that a little later "the fighting scout also found that more than one machine working together had a better chance of bringing a combat to a decisive end and they, in their turn, commenced working in pairs."[21]

Fighters flying together also derived some defensive advantages; among them, said *Fighting in the Air,* were "mutual cooperation and support." The single-seater was particularly vulnerable to an attack from the rear, and formation flying reduced this danger by making several pairs of eyes available for scanning the flanks and the rear of a formation; the leader of the formation, largely relieved of this concern, could concentrate on what lay ahead. But experimentation soon proved that the advantages of formation flying did not necessarily increase as the group grew larger. After trials with two- and three-plane formations, and then four—what the French called a *quadrille*—consensus by 1917 placed the optimum number at six; Massenet de Marancour, a French fighter ace who wrote a treatise on his specialty just after the war, said the ideal fighter patrol should be no less than five and no more than seven. Anything smaller was too weak, anything larger was too unwieldy.[22]

The classic formation was in a "V" pattern, the leader forming its leading "tip," with the other patrol members behind him and spaced left and right of him and flying higher in stepped formation—a formation the French described as in triple echelon. Since the members of the formation could communicate only in the most rudimentary fashion, they often got together before the mission to go over the details. Then the leader fixed the location and altitude for the rendezvous, the shape of the formation, and each man's place in it (the greenest pilots usually on the flanks immediately behind the leader; an old hand, often appointed sub-leader, flew in rear/most position or between the two arms of the "V." Very often a rallying site was stipulated in case the members became separated, and the leader explained any special signals he intended to use. The leader would convey such conventional commands as "stand by for a maneuver," "attack," etc., by firing his guns, or by maneuvering his plane in certain ways—such as wagging its wings slowly or quickly, making it "porpoise" etc. In some cases, flares of various colors also served as signals.

Many formation leaders flew at considerably less than top speed, so that a pilot in the rear who saw something important could fly to the head of the formation and "report" it by signals and gestures.[23]

Formation flying was a demanding activity. The leader rarely set a straight course. Over enemy territory, where there were strong antiaircraft batteries, frequent changes in direction had to be made. Then, too, it was hard for the lead pilot to keep a watch straight ahead, since his view was usually obscured by his engine cowling. To see what lay on his route, as well as to check the positions of those following him, he would fly something of a zigzag course. Those following had to give close attention to keeping position, which required "wangling the throttle and petrol supply continuously." Jean Puistienne stressed the difficulties of formation flying in such circumstances: "It's difficult to stay grouped in the air. To keep the right position vis-à-vis one's comrades in three dimensions while going 200 kilometers an hour is tricky business. . . . You've got to keep your eye on the leader, be ready for his every move and signal, and at the same time scan the space about you, watch the ground, listen to your motor, keep an eye on the manometer, thermometer, tachometer, and check your altimeter, your map and your compass. You have to fly, calculate, and reflect all at the same time; the man at the controls of a fighter is pilot, machine gunner, and observer all rolled into one. It's no picnic."[24]

For all the precautions its members took, a formation remained vulnerable to attack from one direction, and that was overhead. Staggering the aircraft in altitude gave some protection, but as operational ceilings went up to 16,000 feet and more, a better precaution was to place another patrol overhead; this additional element might itself need protection, so a third, higher formation might perform this function. For the system to be effective the patrols had to be separated by a vertical distance of no more than 4,000 feet or so; it was possible to have formations "stacked" as many as four high. And when opposing forces arranged in such layers engaged each other, the result was often a battle in multiple "tiers." In a big fight over the Ypres salient in July 1917 there were 37 planes fighting at 8,000 feet, 40 more at 12,000 feet, and another 17 at 17,000 feet—in all, nearly 100 single-seaters. It is difficult to say how frequently such large battles were fought, but they seem to have been exceptional.[25]

More common were squadron and *Staffel*-sized clashes; in some sectors those occurred with a regularity that almost suggested prearrangement. One British pilot recalled the battles in which his squadron was frequently involved, once again in the vicinity of the Ypres salient: "The fun used to begin about 7 P.M. as a rule, just east of Polygon Wood, and the death-flirting usually went on till dusk and sometimes even later." The two opposing groups would maneuver around each other, seeking advantage of altitude or perhaps a better position vis-à-vis the sun. Then the battle would be joined, and more often than not the formations would come to pieces in the swirl of combat. The result would be that wildly turning mêlée, the *Kurvenkampf* (swirling dogfight or "mix-up"). The aerial sparring near Polygon Wood often ended in this manner: "About thirty machines could be all mixed up together, and viewed from a distance it seemed as if a swarm of bees were all circling around a honey pot."[26]

Here is the classic image of aerial combat, the one that remains indelibly fixed in the popular mind more than seven decades after the Great War came to an end. But the fighter pilot and his machine were more often engaged in other duties that were unglamorous and unsung. There was the "line patrol," a sort of attenuated *barrage,* with the fighters serving as aerial sentinels. Then there was the work most fighter pilots regarded as tedious and unrewarding—the task of escorting reconnaissance or bombing airplanes. In the French Air Service the four-plane *section de protection* was usually staffed by the junior pilots. An American airman wrote that there were "two classes" of fighters: "The first does escort work about half the time, the second does nothing but parade up and down the lines hunting for trouble. The last are the elite among airmen." General Porro explained that such plodding work was "contrary to the character and the instinct of our fighter pilots." And the German fighter pilot Karl Degelow wrote that he and his comrades felt too "tied down" by an essentially defensive role. The fighter pilot preferred to make his escort role a loose one, enabling him to "hunt" the neighboring airspace, while the observation plane's crew liked him to stay close at hand. Massenet de Marancour wrote that when the escorting fighter was not within eyesight the observer lived "in a state of perpetual nervousness. He does not do his work well, and he's going to stay that way, even if he knows from the communiqué that two Albatrosses were shot down over Etain and three over Mont-faucon."[27]

The other extreme was what the French called *chasse libre* and the British a roving mission, a sortie in which one could roam freely, hunting enemy planes. Some of the more skilled and prestigious pilots flew alone on chasse libre missions right to the end of the war; these were the "lone wolves" and the "head-hunters," seeking to boost their scores. Probably more frequent were small patrols of two or three planes at the most—these missions usually involved stalking and surprising an enemy, and the larger the patrol, the fewer chances of achieving surprise. The more experienced pilot who led the patrol might let a colleague make the actual attack, while he stayed above to provide cover. Or more ungenerously, he might make all the kills himself. Karl Bäumer, who flew such missions with the German ace Werner Voss, recalled with some rancor that Voss did all the attacking and shooting down, "while I, miserable neophyte, covered him from behind and kept him from being surprised."[28]

Interestingly enough, about two out of three air battles, large and small, took place on the German side of the line, and this was by a mutual if tacit agreement. The British stressed carrying the air battle to the enemy, in a sense attacking him psychologically as well as physically. General Hugh Trenchard was an outspoken advocate of this policy which, for the British fighter arm, resulted in aggressive "distant offensive patrols" challenging the Germans to battle well behind their lines. The French favored the offensive as well, but their fighters were more generally kept at the army's beck and call for escort and protection of other aircraft. Only perhaps in the spring of 1917, when Major de Peuty directed the French air effort, was there a thoroughgoing commitment to deep offensive activities. The Germans, for their part, were generally willing to receive Allied air incursions, what was known in German fighter parlance as "letting the customer come into the store." This accorded well with the basic German decision early in the war to maintain a defensive posture, and also with the inferior numbers of planes the Germans had on the Western Front. Then, too, over their own airspace German fighter pilots would count on their efficient antiaircraft artillery and air-warning systems.[29]

The fighter might on occasion be mobilized for missions that were normally someone else's job. The fighter pilot could be sent on a reconnaissance mission, to make a quick confirmation of some activity in the enemy's rear, for example. Then, on days of a big push, fighters might be charged with direct support, machine-gunning the positions friendly troops were about to assault—the Italian ace Francesco Baracca lost his life in this hazardous low-level work. Occasionally, too, the fighter could become a makeshift bombing plane. Then there was another highly specialized fighter function that emerged in the course of the conflict, and this was night interception. The British and French got the earliest experience here in trying to protect London and Paris from nighttime attacks by dirigibles and bombing planes; the British went so far as to set up a night-fighter school early in 1917. There were also continuing attempts to utilize night fighters at the front. The French began experimenting in 1915; the German night fighters claimed their first two victims—French Caudron bombers flying out of Malzéville in Lorraine—in February 1917.[30]

What sort of pilot would be required to assume these demanding roles? We will have occasion later to examine in greater detail the men and the machines of the air war, but it might be well here to note the peculiar challenges which the fighter arm posed for airmen and aircraft. Some argued that for the fighter pilot, as for any aerial predator, keen eyesight was the most essential quality. "As with the bird," wrote Hans Buddecke, "so with the aviator. His life, his whole existence depend on the eyes, which he must use to the utmost." Curiously, Buddecke placed last in his list of qualities the airman's flying technique. Like the birds once again, this was something the good pilot did subconsciously. But other pilots felt the ability to maneuver was the essential part of aerial fighting, and the most demanding part. Still others, including crack fighter pilots such as René Fonck and Billy Bishop, insisted that it was shooting ability that separated the good fighter pilot from the bad one, and indeed the live from the dead. Finally, there was the pervasive argument, heard most often from the British, that the exceptional fighter pilot needed *all* of the above skills and something else as well, a certain quality of heart: "The chief characteristic . . . of a fighting pilot is a fixed determination to bring down the greatest possible number of adversaries." Such was the judgment of the R.F.C. in November 1916.[31]

There was also a bewildering variety of views on the qualities inherent in the fighter plane. As late as the spring of 1916 French aviation circles were agitated by the suggestion that the single-seater fighter plane might well be dispensed with as a distinctive type, since two-seaters used for reconnaissance and light bombing could, if their armament were enhanced, defend themselves without fighter escort, and even take an offensive role in aerial combat. (Beginning in 1915, pilots and observers changed places in new two-seater tractor designs, the observer moving to the rear seat where he had better play for his machine gun.) The German Air Service stressed an offensive air role by giving the two-seater bombing plane the designation *Kampfflugzeug,* or battle plane. A British flying officer argued at the end of the war that the two-seaters "made up in field of fire what they lost in maneuverability," since they carried two mobile machine guns in the hands of the observer as well as one fixed to fire forward. "It is still a debated point," he wrote, "as to whether a two-seater thus armed is more than a match for a scout machine or not." But Massenet de Marancour had no doubts—the single-fighter would win.[32]

Generally the single-seater was admitted as the most valid concept, provided the correct qualities were built into it. The British *Notes on Aeroplane Fighting* of November 1916 describe the ideal fighter as being "fast, very easily handled, a good climber, and capable, owing to its penetration through the air and the stoutness of its build, of diving with great speed on an adversary." Most fighter pilots would have no quarrel with this list of qualities, but an engineer might have great difficulty incorporating them all into the same airplane. What was the fighter plane's most essential characteristic, the one to which the others might be sacrificed? Albert Caquot, who had moved from balloon design to the development of the Spad XIII fighter, said that the most important attribute of the good fighter plane was its ability to gain the advantage of altitude, and a number of accomplished pilots agreed with him. But others insisted the key quality in an aerial fight was superior speed, for with it one could initiate the battle and break it off at will; still others insisted that maneuverability was most often the key to victory. Such considerations—often competing ones—figured prominently in the evolution of aircraft design, which must be considered later in detail.[33]

On one point there was broad concensus: the machine gun was the most efficient weapon at the fighter pilot's disposal. Air-to-air rockets, such as the French Le Prieur system, were only effective against large, slow-moving, or stationary targets such as dirigibles and tethered balloons. The aerial cannon, which seemed to offer great promise, proved incapable of much accuracy or rapid fire. If the machine gun held its place of prominence, it was in part because the weapon was improved steadily. The Hotchkiss was soon retired because its mechanism did not lend itself to synchronized fire, and because its magazine capacity of 25 rounds was insufficient. The Allies came to rely heavily on the Lewis gun and the Vickers, and by 1917 many fighter planes were carrying two Vickers guns fixed to fire on the axis. The Germans used the Parabellum and the Maxim or Spandau, and the Austrians their Schwarzlose. The use of tracer bullets helped in aiming, and incendiary bullets, which were in common use by 1917, were particularly useful against hydrogen-filled balloons and dirigibles.

The machine guns generally fired the standard service cartridge filled with smokeless powder and carrying a bullet of the 8mm/.30 caliber size. These projectiles, fired at the rate of about 10 per second, could cover 100 yards in a ninth of a second with a "drop" of only four inches. Even with such weapons the challenge was formidable. "Firing and hitting in the air," wrote a British officer, "is somewhat akin to shooting a high pheasant with a rifle, one that is doing 100 m.p.h. at that." Deflection shooting, incorporating the principle of correction or "leading," was taught in the gunnery schools, and a variety of gunsights were introduced to help the gunner in this regard. Yet few seem to have been very good with deflection shots. There was a tendency to underestimate the speed of the enemy plane and "undershoot"; at the same time airmen tended to underestimate distance. James McCudden recalled seeing a Camel pilot "firing at a Gotha at over half-a-mile range, and had that same pilot been asked the range at which he was firing after he landed, he would, no doubt, have said two or three hundred yards." A Frenchman named Frantz, who may have been the first aviator to shoot an enemy plane down with a machine gun in October 1914, was among the first to endorse the method of firing that became the fighter pilot's favorite—from the rear and "on the axis" of the enemy plane.[34]

Frantz acknowledged that "the difficulty was not in determining the way of proceeding, but in carrying it out." In the case of Frantz the difficulty lay in the fact that the Voisin he flew was three or four miles per hour slower than the German Aviatiks he was fighting. Gunnery and tactics were closely linked, and in the latter there were bewildering variables. R.F.C. authorities queried their airmen several times before they amassed sufficient hard data on tactics to publish their first tactical guidelines in November 1916. The complexities of aerial fighting are clearly visible there: the tactical "recipe" varied, depending upon whether the opponent was an enemy fighter craft or a machine of some other type. Two fighters operating together have two attack options against a single German airplane; against two German aircraft still another procedure is described. But this is not all. Edward Sims, who has written the most extensive work on the evolution of fighter tactics, isolated no fewer than 16 factors that affected the outcome of aerial battles in World War I. These included such things as speed, engine and gun reliability, and weather conditions. There are other considerations Sims failed to mention—for example, the amount of ammunition a pilot had left had tremendous influence on his comportment in a fight. Then there were the "wrinkles," the techniques and tricks that an accomplished pilot had in his repertory: the dive, pull up on one's back and then half-roll—the Immelmann—that put a pilot back on his target after an initial pass; the slip turn, done with the rudder only, that a pursuing enemy would detect too late; and the small details such as wearing clean goggles, which James McCudden believed made "all the difference between getting and not getting a Hun."[35]

If aerial combat was admittedly an affair of great complexity, still there were rules to the game, and if a pilot learned them and applied them, then he should have victory within his grasp— this was the reassuring message of the tactical manuals and the flight school lectures. Then came the reality of combat. One must wonder how well the precepts were applied in one air battle a German captain described after the war. It came toward the end and it was fought in appalling conditions. There were perhaps 100 planes contending in limited airspace, flying at less than 3,000 feet under a ceiling of thick cloud; antiaircraft fire, particularly threatening at that altitude, was constantly arching up from below. On the ground the German and British armies were locked in combat. The pilots caught occasional fleeting glimpses of the battlefield with its drifting clouds of gas and the bright streaks of light made by flamethrowers. Above, the airplanes twisted and climbed and plunged "like wild things." The captain continued: "In the rain and mist the danger of midair collision was added to all the other hazards. Other planes would suddenly appear like phantoms. An adversary would emerge as a shadow for a fraction of a second, then vanish into the black clouds. There was something uncanny, sinister, about this flying in rain and storm, cloud and mist." The pilots, German and British alike, were "half-dead, exhausted and worn to tatters by the inhuman strain and the nerve-shattering tumult." It was eery and unearthly, like some "frantic witch's sabbath in the air." Such was the recollection of Captain Hermann Goering.[36]

=5=

Harnessing Air Power

A Luftwaffe general once described the German air force as an "incomparable razor," a precision instrument with unique capacities and characteristics. The simile is a good one and it is equally applicable to the air services of the Great War. We have seen the major functions of air power as they developed during the war, but the bomber and the fighter plane were only the edge of the razor, and it would be well at this point to look at the entire instrument and its place in the considerable panoply of weapons the generals of the Great War had at their disposal.

If the air service were to be compared to the other constituent elements of the army, the infantry, the engineers, and the other arms and services, its most salient characteristic would be its remarkable smallness, for it was a lilliputian among giants. The 500 airmen that Germany mobilized in 1914 were no more than a microscopic part of her armed force of over 4 million; Richard Hallion, writing of those critical months of late 1916 and early 1917, noted that the R. F. C. then made up no more than 3 percent of the total British Expeditionary Force. And General Porro has written about the 2,000 airmen with which Italy ended the war—and the 3.5 million in the ground forces. A similar gulf separated air casualties from those on the ground. On the first day of the Somme, when the Royal Flying Corps lost five airmen, 57,000 British soldiers were killed or wounded on the battlefield below.[1]

A second characteristic of the air war was its heavily incremental nature. The number of men and planes grew constantly, and sometimes exponentially. By 1918 Germany had 5,000 airmen, 10 times the number with which she had started the war, while the total of Germans in uniform did not change appreciably from 1914 to 1918. But the growth could be seen in many other ways, in the consumption of gasoline, for example. In 1914 the German Air Service used about 600,000 kilograms per month. By 1915 the monthly consumption had climbed to 3 million, and by 1916 to 4.5 million. The average monthly consumption in 1917 was 5.5 million kilograms, and in 1918 7 million. As there was more flying and fighting, so there were more casualties. According to recently compiled figures the French air service suffered 75 percent of its casualties (killed, wounded, missing) in the last two years of the war. As for losses in 1918, if adjustments were made for September and the first 10 days of November, for which no casualties were given, the French suffered 48 percent of their losses in those final months of war. This is eloquent testimony to the growing intensity of the air war; it is a no less eloquent refutation of the arguments sometimes advanced, that in the last months of the struggle the French failed to carry their part of the burden in the air.[2]

The air services were not the only elements in the armies that underwent rapid expansion, for there was a rather more general shift, as the proportion of infantry in the various armies declined and the proportion of manpower allotted to the more technical arms and the logistical services increased. The French Army is a good case in point. In 1914 infantry made up 67 percent of the Army, a drop of perhaps 10 percent since the time of Napoleon. But by 1918 the proportion of infantry dropped to only 45 percent. The major beneficiaries were the *armes savantes,* as the French call them, the artillery and the engineers. Between 1914 and 1918 artillerymen increased from 16 percent of the Army to 26 percent, while engineers went from 3 percent to 7 percent. The *train,* or supply department, went from 4 percent to 7.5 percent. The air service, which in 1914 was a fraction so small that it was simply listed as "zero," made up 3.5 percent of the Army at the time of the Armistice.[3]

The air services were characterized by what is called today an unfavorable "teeth to tail ratio," that is to say that the proportion of men who flew and fought was very small, and the non-combatant "service" proportion was very high. In a British squadron there were perhaps 10 men who stayed on the ground for every man who flew; but behind the squadrons there were even larger numbers of men in purely support positions, in depots, repair facilities, fuel dumps, and the like. Richard Hallion has estimated that pilots made up no more than 2 percent of Royal Flying Corps personnel. Of the 90,000 men in the French Air Service at the time of the Armistice, only one-third were even at the front. And the Armistice found the U.S. Air Service with 116,000 of its 195,000 men in the United States. These heavy commitments of manpower, added to massive investments in rapidly consumed matériel, made an air service a relatively expensive way to project military power. As an Italian aviation historian put it, "an hour of flight by an airplane represented the expenditure of an enormous sum of energy, of matériel, and of personnel."[4]

As the war progressed the proportion of non-flying personnel in the air services tended to increase, in part because the complexities of high technology warfare required it, but also because at the outset the services lacked the command structures and the organizational linkages needed to use air power to its full potential. In the other arms, those structures and linkages had already been tested in war; those of the air services rested essentially on what a German officer called "speculative-academic" estimates, and the war quickly revealed their weaknesses.[5]

In most European air services the only field unit in 1914 was small and quite mobile, modeled on the French escadrille. It was built around six aircraft and their crews, a force that prewar maneuvers had seemed to indicate was adequate to supply the reconnaissance needs of an army corps composed of three or four divisions. (The British squadron of 1914 had 12 planes divided into three flights because "it was feared that there were too few experienced officers readily available to command a larger number of individual units.") The escadrille and the German Feldflieger Abteilung were under the operational command of the army or corps to which they had been assigned; in administrative and logistical matters, however, they were still subject to the authority of the Directorate of Aeronautics in the French system, and to the Inspectorate of Flying Troops in the German organization. Once the units were mobilized and went into the field, while the Directorate and the Inspectorate remained in Paris and Berlin respectively, distance and difficulties of communication made the units orphans of a sort. Nor was there any mechanism for them to have contact with one another, to share intelligence, or to transmit it to a common evaluation center. Moreover, they received their orders from corps commanders who often had little idea of the airplane's capabilities and limitations.[6]

One early development was the use of the liaison officer. A British officer who served as the link between the staff of an army corps and a reconnaissance squadron wrote that his job was "to find out what the staff wanted done in the way of reconnaissance, counter-battery shoots, photography of enemy lines, and contact patrol work; to transmit it to flyers before they took off; to collect and collate their reports as soon as they landed; and to pass it back by reports and the telephone-lines as soon as possible." Corps and army commanders had a much better idea of what the airplane could do for them if there was an air officer at hand for them to consult, so eventually these found their way on to army staffs.[7]

The Germans solved the problem of a senior air authority in the field by creating a *Feldflugchef* early in 1915, the post going to Colonel Hermann von Leith-Thomsen. The British elaborated their command structure by introducing the wing, which could contain up to four squadrons, and the brigade, composed of two wings of airplanes and a balloon wing. The brigade, commanded by a brigadier-general, supplied the air needs for an army. In the French system the escadrilles came to be collected into *groupes*, the bombers as early as 1914, the fighters two years later; several groupes could in turn be assembled to form an *escadre*, which might contain 100 planes or more.[8]

As the airplane assumed more roles and as specialization set in, air units came to be classified into two distinct groups, the "working" units and the combat units. The working units labored for the direct benefit of the ground forces to which they were attached; typically, they sighted in its artillery or flew observation and photo-reconnaissance missions for corps headquarters. In the British system such squadrons formed an army's "corps wing," while fighters and bombers made up its "army wing." A British airman recalled: "An Army squadron might be called upon to do work normally falling to the Corps squadrons, just as Corps squadrons frequently engaged in combat, but their essential or basic functions were distinct." In the German organization the "working" planes tended to get the *Fliegerabteilung* designation, while combat planes were grouped into *Staffeln* (squadrons) and *Geschwader* (wings).[9]

Further differentiation came about with the introduction of airplanes designed for a specific function and unsuitable for any other. Strategic reconnaissance aircraft such as the German Rumpler C. VII Rubild were built specifically for high-altitude, long-distance flying; they had little in common with the observation planes that worked the battle zone; as a consequence, strategic reconnaissance planes came to be grouped into units of their own. Similar was the case of the heavily armed and armored ground-attack aircraft that appeared toward the end of the war; they were eminently suitable for one task and poorly conceived for any other; the Germans, who pioneered in these aircraft, created whole squadrons of them.

The linkages between air and ground units developed through trial and error, and for the most part embodied the lessons learned in those first months of the war. It quickly became apparent that the tasks of aerial observation and artillery spotting were more effectively done when air units were paired with ground elements on a stable and reasonably permanent basis. An artillery battery and an aerial observation team worked more smoothly and harmoniously as they made acquaintance and developed mutual confidence. An observation unit working for one corps day after day also did a better job, but for a different reason: the observers developed an intimate knowledge of their sector, and if they were transferred it would take them some time to develop the same familiarity with the new sector.

On the other hand it made sense for strategic reconnaissance to be attached to an army, since it provided information of broad and general value; likewise it made sense to profit from the airplane's remarkable powers of mobility and concentration by placing bombers, and then fighters, within the broader purview of the army, which could direct them to one or another sector as needed. In the latter half of the war, air forces were formed into even larger masses and placed in the hands of the supreme command for intervention anywhere along a vast front. This was the case with the German Bogohl, or *Bombengeschwader der Obersten Heeresleitung,* a concentration of bombers at the disposal of the German High Command; the French *Division Aérienne* and the Italian *Massa di Caccia* were similar concentrations, held and committed by the highest military authorities.[10]

As the war continued, the air services developed close links with certain other services. The fighter arm learned to cooperate with the antiaircraft batteries. The Germans, whose antiaircraft defense was consistently superior, developed a procedure whereby the guns could signal by their fire the presence and location of Allied aircraft to German fighters cruising above. On the Allied side this same arrangement existed at least in fragmentary form, for it was used by the Lafayette Escadrille:

> If a German aircraft crossed over the lines in a certain sector while the Lafayette patrol was in another, French ground troops telephoned to the antiaircraft batteries in the sector where the Lafayette was operating. A French battery then sent up one, two, three, or four shells to indicate by the number of bursts the sector in which the Germans were then flying, setting the shells to burst above or below the assigned altitude of the SPA 124, thereby giving the approximate altitude of the intruders.

By the end of the war there was an elaborate aircraft warning system on each side of the line, covering not only the battle zone but also the interior. Spotters in the front lines relayed reports of enemy incursions, and these were passed by telephone to plotting centers and ultimately to fighter fields. So intimately did air defense seem linked to the air service that in a major reorganization in 1916 the German High Command confided all air defense— the antiaircraft batteries and the *Flugmeldedienst* or warning system—to the German Air Service, rechristened the *Luftstreitkräfte* (Air Force).[11]

Air operations were intimately bound up with the weather— indeed, some called the air service a "fair-weather weapon." Well before the war the authorities had realized the extreme value of weather forecasts for airship and airplane operations. In most countries what scientific observatories there were received military subventions, and in Germany they became linked with the *Heereswetterdienst* or army weather service. The number of weather stations expanded tremendously during the war, and the weather bulletin became a key element in air operations, and in any kind of operations for that matter. In France a bulletin destined especially for the air service was broadcast from the Eiffel Tower every morning and every evening. The German Air Service maintained a *Wetterdienst* that was in continuous contact with other meteorological agencies.[12]

An administrative history of the various air services would no doubt make tedious reading, but it would reveal an almost constant tinkering with forms and structures and frequent shifting of responsibilities and functions. This was no doubt necessary for a new service untried in war; at the same time the very newness of the service made changes easier to accept. Even so basic a matter as unit size was subject to frequent changes. Between 1914 and 1918 the French escadrille was variously composed of 4, 6, 10, 12, and 18 aircraft. In 1917 the German Air Force decided to change the numbering system of its Fliegerabteilungen, and some units were assigned new numbers—a measure that would have been impossible in an older arm such as the infantry (in fact some of the German air units felt very keenly the loss of their "old" number). In 1916 the French pulled their fighter units at Verdun into a groupe, then after a few weeks disbanded the groupe and parcelled the escadrilles back out along the line; after a few weeks more the groupe was once again constituted. Perhaps most remarkable of all, in that same year the French "redesignated" 10 reconnaissance escadrilles and converted them into fighter units.[13]

As the air services adapted themselves to the exigencies of positional warfare, the armies they served sought to fit them into the order of battle. By the spring of 1915 the airplane had made its presence sufficiently felt for generals to expect more of it than simply reconnaissances of the enemy's rear. When General Haig was preparing for the British offensive at Neuve Chapelle in March 1915, he had the foresight to ask his air commander, General Trenchard, "What will you be able to do?" By the time the British First Army assaulted Aubers Ridge in May a comprehensive air-support plan had been prepared, and the R.F.C. undertook not only reconnaissance but also artillery "shoots," contact patrol work, and some bombing on rail objectives. By the end of 1916 air support for an offensive was sufficiently important for the attack to be postponed if the planes could not fly.[14]

For the Germans the great assault on Verdun, beginning in February 1916, was the occasion for their "first attempt at a regular aerial deployment, a centrally directed tactical employment of the air weapon, and a systematic utilization of an arm of the service prepared to wage its own battle in the arena of the third dimension." Beginning in December 1915, they moved four aerial reconnaissance units into the area, and these systematically photographed every foot of the Verdun salient held by the French Army. Masses of other aircraft were moved into the area; these included Fokker fighters; the elite bombing units, Kampfgeschwader 1, 2, and 3; and a sizable number of other aircraft to man the *Luftsperre* and to supply air units to all infantry divisions participating in the assault. At the same time elaborate plans were laid to cripple the French in the air. Cannon were registered to fire simultaneously on the observation balloons and on the winches to which they were tethered. Long-range guns were sighted to bring the French fighter fields under fire. The British offensive at the Somme later in the same year amassed even greater resources—some 200 planes, to be used in an elaborate multi-stage air plan.[15]

Fitting air power into a battle plan was not accomplished easily or smoothly. The new arm was so different and its capacities and limitations so difficult for outsiders to grasp, that friction was inevitable. There was a sort of mutual incomprehension, and since the airmen tended to note down such things, it is easy in reading about the air war to conclude that all the fault lay on one side. Certainly there was abundant evidence of the failure of army authorities to understand the airman and his problems. One R.F.C. liaison officer recalled trying to explain that a long-distance reconnaissance the ground commander wanted would be impossible because on the return flight the pilot would have to fly against a 40-m.p.h. wind. A British general in the Intelligence Section exclaimed: "But the wind makes no difference to you!" The air officer, a lieutenant, probably did not try to argue with the general; but the story of their encounter was probably repeated in the squadron mess as another instance of incomprehension on the part of ground officers. Nor were British air officers the only ones who encountered such problems. General von Bülow has written that the German military leadership failed to take more seriously the clues indicating British preparations for an offensive in the Somme area, because those clues came mostly from air intelligence; moreover there was a disinclination to accept the arguments of air officers in staff discussions because the aviators were considered merely technical specialists rather than tactical advisors.[16]

The men who flew often had serious doubts about the missions they were ordered to undertake. Perhaps the most serious charge of misuse of air resources made after the war was that levelled at the German High Command for tying up much of its air strength at Verdun in the vast and futile Luftsperre scheme. Many of the planes assigned that thankless and largely useless effort were bombing machines. Had they been able to attack the perilously slender French supply system, which relied on a single vital road, the French might well have lost the battle from lack of supplies and replacements.[17]

Among all belligerents there was a tendency for the high command to regard airplanes as multipurpose weapons, a view that increasingly lost its validity as specialization proceeded. Particularly at moments of crisis, generals had a tendency to throw every available airplane into the breech, much as cooks and drivers and military policemen were sent forward as makeshift infantry. At a critical juncture of the Verdun fighting French fighter planes were ordered to attack enemy depots, though the bombs they carried were miniscule and the planes were not equipped with bombsights. In the last year of the war the Germans committed their large strategic bombers to support of the Army; in the crisis after their rout at Caporetto the Italians used everything they had to stem the enemy's advance, including airships and flying boats. Right to the end of the war General Foch used the same recipe, *tout le monde à la bataille.* To many of the airmen who flew such missions they seemed fruitless and a perversion of their role, the sort of thing that happened when generals wielded air power without understanding it.[18]

It was not just in the realm of operations that the air service encountered difficulty in fitting in, for there were frequent *querelles de compétence* regarding staff, administrative, and logistical matters. In these domains the air services felt their special needs were often ignored. There was a strong argument that airmen needed special medical treatment by a physician versed in the demands of flying—in a word, the flight surgeon. But the army's medical corps fought with almost universal success against a separate service. The German Air Service fought a strenuous battle with the Gewehrprüfungs-kommission in order to have its own armament service for the development of air weapons. This battle it won, but shortly afterwards it lost another when its wireless operators and equipment, both on the ground and in the air, were placed under the *Nachrichtentruppe,* the German equivalent of the Signal Corps.[19]

These collisions led inevitably to a desire for greater autonomy. The most immediate goal was recognition of the air service as what the French called "the fifth arm," with status equal to the cavalry, infantry, and other combat arms. The French and British Air Services had this status at the beginning of the war, Italian airmen achieved it in 1915, and the Germans in 1916. There had been efforts in the U.S. Congress as early as 1913 to separate Army aeronautics from the Signal Corps, and the issue flared up again in 1916, with young airmen the most outspoken partisans of the change. There were outspoken young men in the German Air Service as well, and they applauded the emergence of the autonomous Luftstreitkräfte.[20]

But autonomy seemed to many only a waystation on the road to independence and equal status with the army and navy. In 1916 Colonel Leith-Thomsen put forward a proposal for the creation of the Kaiserlich Deutsche Luftstreitkräfte, the Imperial German Air Force. It was to incorporate all air elements of both land and sea service and take its place beside the two older services. The proposal came to naught, being bitterly opposed by the German Navy and by the Bavarian government, which wanted to preserve the status of its own air service. Where German airmen failed, the British ultimately succeeded with the creation of the Royal Air Force in April 1918. Much of the wartime discussion was discreet and muted, except in Great Britain. One often gains the impression that independence for the air force became an issue only in the interwar period, but such was not the case. To many men in the escadrilles and the staffeln at the close of the war, the emergence of independent air power was only a matter of time.[21]

=6=

The Machines

On June 5, 1917, members of the Aeronautical Society of Great Britain assembled to hear a lecture by Captain B. C. Hucks, of the Royal Flying Corps. Captain Hucks was an old hand at military aviation who had already addressed the society back in 1914, so he entitled this second lecture "A Further Three Years' Flying Experience." He told his listeners that he had recently flown a Blériot airplane powered by a 50-horsepower motor, a plane that had been a "premiere machine" in 1914. Captain Hucks had not been up in a Blériot for a considerable time. At first he thought there was something wrong with the plane, that it was "a very bad specimen of the breed"; but as he flew on he came to realize that *all* Blériots had flown that poorly, and that it simply took time "to again get used to such inefficiency."[1]

The French pilot Roland Garros had a similarly revealing experience, though he found himself suddenly stepping forward in aviation history rather than backward. After three years as a prisoner of war in Germany, Garros managed to escape in 1918 and make his way back to France, where his first thought was to get back into a fighter plane. But the planes had changed—so much so that Garros, still famous for his air victories of 1915, had to go back to school before he could join a fighter squadron.[2]

By 1918 the tremendous strides in aircraft performance were obvious to all. It was often said that the speed of aircraft had doubled and so had their ceiling, while horsepower available to them had quadrupled and their load bearing capacity had increased many times over; as Major Siegert put it, the airplane

93

of 1914 viewed from 1918 was as ancient and as extinct as an archeopteryx. And the changes in aircraft capabilities were the key changes underlying the evolution of aerial warfare; much as one might talk about the "human factor," and the importance of valor, spirit, and pluck, at bottom everything rested on what the airplane could do. John Slessor acknowledged as much: "The best pilots, the best armament and ancillary equipment in the world are no good in a really inferior airplane." It was the determination not to have the inferior airplane that spurred the phenomenal wartime progress; and at the same time it was important not to be inferior to the enemy in the number of airplanes one had, a consideration that placed heavy burdens on wartime economies.[3]

The demand for more and better aircraft went spiraling up, first of all because they were being consumed at a rapid rate. An informed estimate of 1918 put the service life of a British warplane at "barely six months." Production figures for several of the major belligerents suggest a high turnover: at the end of the war the French, British, and Germans had a front line aircraft strength of 3,700, 2,600, and 2,500 respectively, though over the preceding four years they had a combined production of about 150,000 planes (the French and British slightly over 50,000 each, the Germans slightly under that figure). To be sure, aircraft were often withdrawn simply to be replaced by improved designs. The Germans used over 200 different types, and the French about the same number; the Italians produced 84 of their own models, manufactured 27 foreign models under license, and imported foreign planes of 8 more varieties. Then, too, planes removed from the Western Front might continue to fly in schools or on other fronts. Still, what the R.F.C. called "wastage" must have been quite high. Between July 1 and November 17, 1916—the period of the struggle on the Somme—British squadrons "struck off" 782 aircraft; the average rate of replacement was 10 planes per squadron per month.[4]

There were prodigies of achievement. A new airplane that existed only in the designer's mind in January could be in prototype in March; the first production planes might reach the squadrons by the end of the year. The first prototype of the Spad VII flew in April 1916, and the first two production models were delivered in September. Probably the best known success story in American aviation annals was the development of the Liberty engine. It was designed in Suite 201 of the Willard Hotel in Washington during six frantic days and nights beginning on May 29, 1917. The first motor was assembled in the laboratory of the Packard Motor Company and shipped to Washington on July 3. The first Liberty-powered airplane flew on August 29. Liberty engines were still powering American warplanes two decades later.[5]

This sort of progress had a high price, one that would not have been paid in peacetime. Resources—money, matériel, and sometimes lives—were committed lavishly and indeed recklessly. There was a strong impulsion to save time and cut corners. New designs were not thoroughly tested for the stresses they would have to undergo. T. O. M. Sopwith, designer of a series of successful aircraft, recalled that no stressing at all was done for a good part of the war. "It was a constant gamble, in a way," Sopwith continued, "some of us were lucky and some of us were not." Then, too, the evaluation of prototypes was often such a hurried affair that serious defects were not discovered until production models became operational and complaints began to come from front-line units. Germany's L.F.G. "Walfisch" was found to have a dangerously restricted view forward. Early models of the British S.E. 5 had a poorly mounted radiator that ruptured in rough landings. In some cases the errors could be corrected—a strut was added here, a new rudder fitted there. Motor designs often suffered from "short cuts" that led to expensive, wasted efforts. The British government once placed an order for 3,000 Sunbeam motors of a new type that had not been thoroughly tested; the entire lot had to be scrapped.[6]

One is sometimes tempted to think that poorly designed aircraft were after all the understandable mistakes of designers and builders who were essentially amateurs rather than professionals, obliged to proceed by intuition and experience for want of scientific principles. In point of fact, an imposing number of the designers of the World War I era had formal training in scientific and technical fields; many of them—men like Geoffrey de Havilland, Anthony Fokker, and Louis Bechereau, the creator of the Spad fighters—were engineers well-grounded in aeronautics. General Christienne is quite explicit in the case of French builders: "Contrary to legend, the industry's leaders were in the great majority certified engineers." And Howard Wolko, who has traced the evolution of aviation technology, says that by the First World War the formative period of aerodynamics was over, so that the builders of that era could rely upon its principles and seek answers to their problems by mathematical analysis, rather than by intuition and trial-and-error procedures. Wolko found this trend less well-established among British designers than among their European colleagues. The British builder A. V. Roe, though an engineer, confessed that he designed many of his creations "by eye and by his own innate sense of what was fitting in a flying machine." In this same vein a British aviation writer argued that "the ultimately perfect mechanism is always extremely eyeable."[7]

The engineer's grasp of such aerodynamic forces as lift and drag was solid but not complete. Here and there were other largely unexplored phenomena. The shear center for a wing, for example, was not identified until the 1920s, and failure to identify it on the Blériot XI made that plane prone to shedding its wings in flight. By the same token, the phenomenon of wing flutter was baffling—and for pilots who flew Nieuport and Albatros fighters it was sometimes fatal. On the other hand, designers and builders knew how to build this or that desired quality into an airplane, and they knew that as they enhanced one quality they might diminish another. For example the ability of a plane to bank or roll quickly—desirable for a fighter—could be increased if its wings were reduced in size. But there would be other consequences, as a German engineer pointed out: "In order to generate the same lift as before, there must be an increase in speed, and the airplane's ability to reach altitude will decline." The engineer went on to give figures: If the wing loading (expressed in the number of pounds per square foot, i.e. the plane's weight divided by its wing area) were increased by 10 percent, the speed would have to be increased by 5 percent and the plane's ceiling would drop by 1,000 feet.[8]

It is often assumed that what airplanes the armies acquired before the war were simply civilian craft adapted willy-nilly to military use, and that what one could call properly military planes were a product of the war itself. The story is a little more complex than that. From about 1910–11 the military gave thought to what it wanted in an airplane and invited aircraft firms to submit models for trials and possible purchase. For example, when the U.S. Army's Signal Corps decided to acquire a "speed scout" type in 1911, it made public the specifications of the airplane it was seeking; there were no fewer than 12 specifications, including a speed of at least 65 miles an hour, the ability to climb 1,500 feet in three minutes, and to carry enough fuel for three hours' flying.

The Austrians laid down similar specifications in 1912, but added precise requirements on how pilot and observer would be housed, with "a perfect view for the observer, and for the pilot one as little restricted as possible to the front, to the side, and even to the rear."[9]

In several countries competitions were held and contracts let on armored planes, and on planes that could be quickly disassembled for transportation by truck. Almost invariably military models were required to have strong undercarriages that would withstand rough use in the field. Several air services questioned the use of monoplanes on the grounds that they were unsafe, and their suspicions tended to bring the type into general disfavor. On the other hand the German military were instrumental in keeping in production the obsolescent Taube monoplane. In countries such as Germany, where the civilian market was still small and the Army's orders sizable, the military largely dictated the type of planes that would be built. John Morrow's researches on the German aviation industry in 1914 have shown that the army had succeeded in imposing essentially military models on the industry, notably "a rugged, dependable two-seat reconnaissance craft with a reliable water-cooled, in-line engine."[10]

For the balance of the war the design and building of military aircraft mainly followed the practices of the prewar era. A technical organ of the air service would formulate needs and solicit designs from private industry, then monitor the production process. Development was often carried out with the assistance of public or private laboratories and testing centers. The French, for example, used the laboratory and wind tunnel of Gustave Eiffel, designer of the Eiffel Tower and early contributor to aerodynamics. In the German service the agency which oversaw aircraft procurement was Idflieg, or Inspektion der Fliegertruppen; the Italian equivalent was the Direzione Tecnica dell' Aviazione Militare. The French had a Service des Fabrications de l'Aviation, with Captain Albert Etévé in charge of new airplanes; Etévé recalled that his service encouraged manufacturers to produce advanced designs which were at the same time relatively easy to build.[11]

The British system was somewhat different in that an official agency, the R.F.C.'s Royal Aircraft Factory at Farnborough, held a near-monopoly on design and development, at least in the first part of the war. British airplane builders were very few when the factory was founded in 1911, and there was a feeling that those companies "could not be depended upon." Thus the factory designed the plane and then parcelled out orders for it. There was some advantage in manufacturing and maintaining a "standard" model as against having the dozen different types with which the French began the war. But the factory's designs had their flaws: they were solid and workmanlike but uninspired, and all too quickly obsolescent. A British airman recalled that "the factory machines were beautiful aeroplanes, but bad war craft, owing to their inherent stability, which detracted from their maneuverability." The B.E. 2c was such an airplane. The mainstay of the R.F.C. in 1915 and 1916 and still seen at the front in 1917, it was a derivative of a prewar design badly outclassed by the middle of the war. Noel Pemberton Billing and C. G. Grey, the editor of *The Aeroplane,* were severe critics of the Factory's designs, and more recently the whole design policy has been called "short sighted."[12]

During the war the impetus for new designs came from a number of sources, and quite often it came from the frontline units, particularly when airmen became convinced that the enemy's planes were superior to their own. Sometimes the enemy supplied impulsion by introducing a new design that had to be "matched." Generally each side acquired examples of the other's newest models rather quickly, most often through motor failure on the wrong side of the lines, or pilot error. The British were particularly unlucky in this regard. The FE 2d was a case in point: "The very first one with a Rolls Royce engine, complete with a high-ranking staff officer, was handed over intact to the Germans by its pilot who had lost his way and landed at Lille by mistake for St. Omer." A similar error delivered a new Handley-Page bomber into German hands.[13]

Veteran pilots often tried out newly captured enemy planes. After flying the British Sopwith triplane, Manfred von Richthofen pronounced it the best airplane the Allies had, and his pronouncement helped decide the German authorities to rush into production a triplane of their own. The aces could foster the development of new models in other ways; Georges Guynemer was intrigued by the idea of mounting a cannon on the Spad fighter so that it could be fired through the propeller hub. He took a hand in the experiments which led to the Spad XII.[14]

Because of the lag time between the conception and the production of aircraft, air service leadership tried to anticipate future needs. Thus Lord Weir, a member of the British Air Board, argued in 1917 that the Allies would shortly have such command of the air that specialized aircraft designed for ground attack could work the battlefield without fear of attack from the air, hence a heavily armed and armored plane should be built in anticipation of this opportunity. The eventual result was the Sopwith Salamander, which made its appearance at the end of the war. Also in 1917 the British decided they would need a heavy bomber that could reach Berlin; the outcome was the Handley Page V 1500. The first of these were assembled on Martlesham Heath and ready for a raid on Berlin when the Armistice came. At the same time the Allies were trying to foresee their fighter needs. At one point when formation flying was being widely adopted there were arguments that the new tactic and the limits on maneuvering which it imposed would reduce the value of the single-seater and put a premium on superior two-seaters. This prediction proved wrong. And then there was the problem of determining the future power plant, accurately traced by the historian of the Liberty engine: "It was thought in May, 1917 that a 250 hp eight-cylinder would be the engine for the spring of 1918. Two months later a 300–350 hp twelve was required, and by September 1917 the horsepower race required 400–450."[15]

The time factor was only one of many constraints that affected wartime design and development. There were first of all the shortages of critical materials. Early in the war magnetos were in short supply in England, for the Germans had dominated the market, notably the Bosch firm. The unprecedented demand for certain types of wood for airframes and propellers could not always be met; there was a world-wide shortage of spruce, for example. The demand for linen also exceeded supply, so cotton often had to be employed for covering airframes. In the end the shortages of critical materials were most keenly felt by Germany and her allies. German builders had to substitute steel springs for rubber in shock absorbers; because there was not enough copper they were forced to use radiators made of iron; these were less efficient and rusted out quickly. A dearth of castor oil, the only effective lubricant for rotary engines, limited the use the Germans could make of this type of powerplant.

Then there were the shortcomings in the various elements that went into a warplane; they were often unreliable, with their lack of dependability increased by hasty wartime manufacture.

The machine guns had always to be mounted so that the men who fired them could get at them to change magazines or clear jams in their mechanisms (not until the mid-thirties were machine guns sufficiently reliable to be mounted in the wings of fighter planes). Motors had to be easily accessible and capable of rapid removal and replacement, for some required overhaul after as little as 20 hours of running. The specifications for the German R-planes called for the engines to be accessible for repair *in flight*. The motor most widely used by the Germans was of the six-cylinder, in-line type. It was fairly reliable but had a distinctively high profile. If German engineers had found a way to invert it, designers could have created airplanes with better visibility, better weight distribution, and a shorter and less bulky landing gear. Theoretically such an inversion was possible, and after the war it was accomplished; but in the press of wartime it could not be done.[16]

If there was a single, overriding consideration in aircraft construction during the war, it was the quest for greater performance: for planes that could lift greater payloads, that would fly higher, faster, and farther. There were basically three ways in which this could be done: by giving the aircraft a form with greater dynamic efficiency, by lightening it, and by increasing engine power. In the end the third of these options was the one most used, largely because the other two had severe practical limitations. With the then existing "state of the art," it was not possible to go very far in the direction of aerodynamically "cleaner" or streamlined craft. To the end of the war the dominant form of airplane was the braced-frame biplane with its "cluttered" construction, wind-catching struts and wires, etc.; that drag-inducing appendage, the fixed landing gear, remained a fixture on aircraft until the 1930s.

It was very difficult to lighten the airframe of 1914 without compromising its strength. This had been the basic weakness of the monoplanes of 1914: in order to build a plane light enough to fly with the lift of a single wing and the weak motors of the era, the machine's weight was pared down to the point that it simply became too fragile. The trend during the war was in fact toward heavier aircraft. As horsepower increased, giving builders some "margin" to work with, the payload was increased, but also the planes were built more solidly. To give a case in point, the Morane type N of 1914, the first French fighter, had an empty weight of 635 lb. and a loaded weight of 981 lb.; the Spad XIII, the fighter with which the French Air Service ended the war, had an empty weight of 1,255 lb. and a loaded weight of 1,808 lb. The Spad was a far more robust machine, capable of standing the stresses of high-speed maneuvers.[17]

There was a great deal of experimentation in aircraft construction techniques both before and during the war. There was for example monocoque construction, in which the fuselage was a strong, hollow shell, much like the boat hull which inspired it; it was generally too expensive for use in mass-produced military craft. There was increasing use of plywood as the war progressed, and before the conflict ended the first all-metal planes had appeared; yet the airplanes most widely used consisted of a braced wooden framework covered with fabric. Making airframes was not so much an industry as a craft, with a great deal of hand working, particularly in the shaping, fitting, and assembling of wooden parts. John Slessor wrote "it is hardly an exaggeration to say that any reasonably competent perambulator manufacturer could turn his hand to building airframes." France, then a nation of cabinet makers and other artisans, was particularly well-equipped for this type of construction. In other countries a wide range of light industries converted to airframe manufacture with relative ease. The Grand Rapids Airplane Company was a consortium of American furniture makers; the makers of the Bristol Scout had earlier been the Bristol Tramways Company, and Igor Sikorsky constructed his giant bombers in the shops of a Russian railway car manufacturer. Once the plane was assembled and covered (the fabric often being sewn on by hand—10 stitches to the inch for R.F.C. planes), it was "doped," with several coatings, usually laid on with the brush. The completed airframe for a typical plane of 1918 made up only a third of the weight of a fully loaded machine; the motor might weigh another third, and crew, armament, and fuel would comprise the rest. A completed two-seater contained perhaps 50,000 parts and was the fruit of some 4,000 hours of human labor.[18]

The very lightness of the wood-and-fabric construction sometimes saved an airman's life in an accident that would have been fatal in a modern plane. One day a French Nieuport collided with a Voisin at a height of 3,000 feet. The two planes, locked together, pinwheeled down, dropping into a grove of trees where they both lodged. The airmen climbed down, emotionally shaken but without a scratch. And Sholto Douglas recalled that he was once flying very low in a Martynside Scout, looking for a student who had landed somewhere in the area. Too late Douglas looked ahead and saw he was headed into 20 or 30 telegraph wires strung along some railroad tracks; it was too late to go over or under the wires, and the Martynside flew straight into them: "They acted as a net which caught the aircraft, pulled it up all standing, and dropped it down on its back on the railway lines."[19]

But there was another side to the coin. Such planes tended to deteriorate rapidly unless they were kept under shelter. When left outside they were supposed to be pegged down and placed facing the wind so that sudden gusts would not blow their control surfaces about and damage them (the British had 30 aircraft destroyed by high winds in a single night). The airframes easily caught fire, producing perhaps the worst catastrophe an airman could encounter at altitude; intensive research into fire retardant paints and self-sealing gas tanks did little to reduce the danger. It was said that a heavy-handed pilot could "break" any machine through violent maneuvers, but those were just the types of maneuvers necessary in combat flying. Builders usually tried to test the solidity of their creations and their ability to withstand various stresses by means of static tests; for example the test planes would be turned upside down and sandbags stacked on the undersides of their wings until they collapsed. But the only dynamic test was to put the plane through its paces, at the hazard of someone's life. This was the function of pilots like those of the R.F.C.'s Testing Squadron.

But other things could happen. It was said that if a single bullet struck the main spar of a German L.V.G. two-seater, it would collapse like a house of cards. If the gun-synchronizing system malfunctioned, as it sometimes did, one could shoot off one's own propeller. The calamity was greater if only one blade were shot off, for the unbalanced propeller would continue to turn, even if the motor were shut down, and the vibrations it built up could tear the motor from its mounts or simply shake the plane to pieces; it is thought that this sort of accident cost Max Immelmann his life. Then there were the baffling cases in which an airplane flying peacefully along simply disintegrated in the air—just such an accident took the life of the well-known French aviator Marcel Brindejonc des Moulinais. The Experimental Flight attached to the R.F.C.'s Central Flying School investigated such mishaps and could sometimes determine the cause.

When a DH 2 came apart in midair it was determined than an external valve rod on the rotary engine had broken off "and had torn away the tail-boom's cross bracing wires, causing the whole rear structure to fail."[20]

The motor was frequently and aptly described as the heart of the airplane. It's pulsations brought the machine to life and gave it movement. When it stopped beating the consequences could be fatal. It is often said that the airplane inherited the automobile engine, but the needs of the two machines were not identical, and the aviation engine very quickly evolved as a specialized type. The car motor had to be inexpensive to manufacture and run quietly, weight was not a major consideration, and the engine ran a full regime only part of the time. In the aero-engine weight was critical, and so was the ability to operate reliably at full throttle for extended periods of time. Cost was certainly not a major consideration; some of the complex engines of 1918, the Rolls Royce Eagle and the Liberty, for example, cost about $7,000 to manufacture at a time when Henry Ford was selling his Model T touring car for $400.[21]

The aircraft motors used in the Great War were of two basic types: the rotary—an engine that itself turned while its crankshaft remained stationary—and the fixed or stationary type. The latter were usually built in one of three forms determined by the arrangement of their cylinders. There was the radial, in which the cylinders were grouped around the crankshaft in star formation; the in-line, such as the six-cylinder Mercedes-Benz, the workhorse of the German air service; and the "V" configuration, of which perhaps the best known models were the Hispano-Suiza and the Liberty. The motors were also classified by their cooling systems; the rotary was an air-cooled engine, the radial might be cooled by air or liquid, and the in-line and "V" motors were liquid-cooled. During the war, motors were turned out in very large numbers. The French, who led in wartime production, built over 90,000. Not surprisingly, carmakers switched heavily to aero-engine production; by war's end there were planes whose motors bore such prestigious names as Rolls-Royce, Duesenberg, and Isotta-Fraschini.[22]

At the beginning of the war the most popular aircraft engine was the rotary, of which the French Gnome, later the Gnome-Rhône, was the best known design. It has been estimated that in 1914 nearly 80 percent of the power plants in all airplanes were

Gnomes. The rotary had the great advantage of lightness, its horsepower/weight ratio being unexcelled in 1914. The seven-cylinder 50 horsepower Gnome Oméga, introduced in 1908, weighed only 167 pounds; a strong man could pull it from its mounts and carry it across the shop to his work bench. The spinning engine cooled itself very effectively, thus saving perhaps 20 percent in weight that a cumbersome and vulnerable water-cooling system would require. The rotary had the additional advantage of running with very little vibration—the whirling motor had the damping effect of a flywheel. It also had disadvantages: the spinning mass of the motor produced a torque effect, tending to make the airplane turn in the opposite direction; this phenomenon could be quite pronounced on small aircraft of limited wing surface, and sometimes made handling somewhat tricky. Then too, the rotary was a very thirsty engine, consuming 7 gallons of fuel where a fixed engine of the same capacity might use 5. Lubrication was also a problem, for only castor oil would retain its lubricating qualities when associated with gasoline. At the end of the war the French alone were using 170,000 kilograms of castor oil each month.[23]

What ultimately dethroned the rotary engine and ushered in the era of the fixed type was the unending quest for greater power. Very large rotary engines were not feasible for several reasons, and increasing power by raising revolutions per minute was not feasible either. Increasing the r.p.m. made the engine use more of its energy—20 percent and more—just in overcoming increased air resistance; then, too, it increased the destructive effects of centrifugal force for an engine which even at moderate speeds was known for its habit of throwing off valve rods, rocker arms, and even whole cylinders. For a variety of reasons, then, the rotary could not be counted on to produce much more than 200 horsepower. From that point on the fixed engine took over.

The fixed motors were made to yield more horsepower by several means, of which the most obvious was to increase displacement. But better than making a bigger engine was making one of modest size and weight turn out more horsepower. One technique was to increase the compression ratio, which was commonly around four-to-one in 1914, and had edged up higher than six-to-one by the Armistice; the limiting factor here was the poor quality of gasoline (45 to 70 octane), for which no chemical additives were available. Engineers were also successful in getting the engines to turn faster; and a redesign of cylinders and pistons, an improvement of carburetion, and other changes added further to the engine's efficiency. The addition of a supercharger enhanced performance at high altitudes. These gains brought their own problems. As engine rotation moved above 1,500 r.p.m., it exceeded the most efficient speed for the propellers of the day; the propeller could no longer be attached directly to the crankshaft, but had to be coupled to it by means of a reduction gear. When horsepower moved much above 100, manual starting—having someone simply pull the propeller around—became difficult, and ultimately the sweating mechanic had to be replaced by a mechanical starter.[24]

If there was a single motor that stood out at the end of the war, it was probably the remarkable Hispano-Suiza. It was the brainchild of Marc Birkigt, a Swiss engineer then living in Spain (hence Hispano-Suiza). Birkigt was already an accomplished motor designer when the war broke out and he decided to "make himself useful" by designing an aircraft engine which he submitted to the French government. It was so revolutionary in design and construction that governmental authorities gave it unusually rigorous testing; it was stipulated that the engine would have to run continuously at full throttle for 50 hours, which it did without mishap. The Hispano-Suiza was a V-8 consisting of a crank case and two rows or banks of cylinders, each row being incorporated into a single block, what came to be known as the monobloc system; equally innovative was the use of aluminum alloy for the engine body. The designer Louis Bechereau built a series of highly successful Spad fighters around the new motor. In 1916 the Spad VII broke all existing speed records; the "Hisso-"powered Spad XIII was the most widely manufactured fighter of the war, with over 8,000 built.[25]

Engines such as the Hispano-Suiza V-8 and the American Liberty were "modern" in configuration, but not in performance; much improvement was needed in that regard. Consider that the Liberty Engine of 1918 and the Rolls Royce Merlin of World War II were powerplants of about the same displacement, 1,650 cubic inches; and yet the Liberty developed 400 horsepower while the Merlin produced 2,000 hp (perhaps 40 percent of this enormous increase in power output was due to higher-quality fuel). The engines of the Great War also left a great deal to be desired in reliability. Sophisticated high-strength alloys lay in the future;

metal-working tolerances were broad, with much hand fitting; day-and-night production and hastily trained workers made things worse. In some engines there were clearly design flaws that were detected and corrected only after a considerable time lapse. The lack of reliability was proverbial even before the war, and was the basis for arguing that the cavalryman could be counted on for reconnaissance while the airman could not: "Save in very rare cases, the cavalryman can always count on his horse. But the airman has in his motor an instrument that is still delicate, despite progress made to date; its failings can leave him immobilized at any time."[26]

During the war pilots were trained to make "dead-stick" landings on the assumption that they would not fly long before they had to cope with engine failure. The good pilot kept an ear out for any change in the rhythm of his motor, and he was particularly attentive over enemy territory. A French fighter pilot said that "the great preoccupation of a pilot across the lines is the regularity of the pulsations in that mechanical heart." And an American echoed the concern about flying over "*Bochie*, where motor-trouble means a soup diet until the end of the war." Some engines had notorious reputations. The Gnome 100 h.p. Monosoupape was one of these. An officer attached to R.F.C. headquarters in 1915 related the case in which the pilot of a Monosoupape-powered Vickers machine had 22 forced landings in 30 flights. Although the motor was gradually improved, another British airman recalled that "the Mono never, throughout its career, succeeded in living down its reputation for insincerity." The D IVa engines of the Gotha bombers gave so much trouble that they were eventually replaced by other powerplants; even those replacements were far from satisfactory, so that 12 percent of all Gothas headed for England had to abort because of mechanical problems.[27]

All of the engines of the Great War required much more maintenance than powerplants of today. A piston engine on a modern airplane might be a candidate for an overhaul after 2,000 or 3,000 hours of flight; an in-line engine of 1916 would need the overhaul before it had flown 300 hours. The rotary required even more frequent attention: after only 20 or 30 hours it would need to be disassembled for what the French called *révision générale*. In between it was wise to check spark plugs for fouling and do other maintenance. A German complained that "the motor of an airplane is as sensitive as a young girl; it reacts spitefully to the slightest neglect."[28]

Much the same thing could be said of the rest of the airplane, for scrupulous and frequent inspection and maintenance were the keys to a safe and efficient machine. These were the functions of the ground crews; in the British service, the fitters took care of the motors and the riggers concerned themselves with the airframe. If a propeller developed a scarcely noticeable warp, it could still affect the performance of the plane significantly. If an enemy bullet had gone through a spar, the wing might fail unless the damage was detected and repaired. Then, too, the airframe (like the engine) had to be kept "in tune." It was essentially a braced structure, its parts held in correct alignment by struts and wires. Periodically, with plumb bob and spirit level the riggers had to align or "true" the machine, chiefly by tightening and slackening the bracing wires. To help prevent fuel line blockages, a mechanic would often strain gasoline through a piece of chamois before putting it into "his" pilot's plane, or he would sit and patiently fit rounds into the breech of a plane's machine gun to make sure there were no irregularly shaped cartridges that could jam the gun. "How much depends on them!" So one German pilot wrote of his *Monteure:* "It's not simply a question of the correct performance of their duties; no, our very lives are always in their hands. The slightest negligence, forgetting to put in a screw or tightening a cable the wrong way can cause a fatal crash, especially here at the front, where so often we strain airplanes to the limit." The airman insisted that he would rather fly a mediocre airplane that was well maintained than the best machine serviced by a careless *Monteur.*[29]

Even with the best of maintenance, if six planes of an *escadrille* were ordered into the air, chances are one would not start and another would return to the field with a rough engine, leaving four planes to do the work of six. The increase in the size of air units during the war was in part to compensate for this lack of dependability. (Nor was it a phenomenon only encountered at the front: at the British flight school at Upavon, one fourth of the planes were out of commission at any given time.) And even when all six planes of an escadrille did fly, their performance was not the same. There were airplanes that seemed inherently better or worse than others of the very same breed, and no one knew quite why. Two Sopwith Camels, apparently identical, would not have identical flight characteristics; one could go higher than the other; and, if they both flew with throttles wide open, one would edge ahead of the other. In 1917 the British Air Board received many complaints from pilots at the front that they had received "bad" Camels that could not reach altitude. Many airmen felt the best guarantee of a "good" plane was to have one with airframe and motor built by the parent firms, those that had designed them; thus the most desirable Camel was one built by the Sopwith firm, and with a Clerget motor manufactured in the Clerget shops.[30]

Then of course some models of aircraft simply flew better than others; at first glance this is so evident as to seem a commonplace. Yet what one might call the qualities of an airplane, its speed, rate of climb, ceiling, etc.—things that could be expressed in cold, precise figures—were not necessarily the same as its perceived qualities or more simply its "reputation." This distinction is important because sometimes the reputation of a particular type of aircraft could be at considerable variance with its actual capabilities; even where there was a weakness or a strength, it would be magnified by a sort of psychological "multiplier." This is traceable to the enormous importance of the planes to those who flew them or met them in battle.

U.S. Army psychologists who were with American forces in the North African campaign of 1942–43 were among the first to probe the role the airplane held in the thinking of the airmen, a role that had no parallel among ground troops. The airplane and preoccupation with it was found to be "the central unifying force" in the Air Corps. More specifically, the psychologists found that airmen reacted to the various types of aircraft "as they would to individuals they meet, forming loves, hatreds, and jealousies out of all proportion to the realities of the situation." No one can read far in the aeronautical literature of the Great War without encountering the airplane in this guise. The appearance of a new type of plane generated immense interest. "The really important news," one British pilot wrote in 1917, "is that the Camels are coming." Rumor and speculation abounded, and then one day the new models arrived. "Days of high spirits," one French pilot noted, "we have received Spads! Now we're finally going to show the Fritzes about speed and maneuverability." A German pilot recalled vividly the first day he saw the "trim, powerful machine," that would be "his" A.E.G./G IV. It was the beginning of a long relationship, or indeed friendship: "My A.E.G. and I— we remained loyal to each other, day and night, in storm and sunshine, through fog and snow, until the day came when together we laid down our arms."[31]

The machine, then, sustained the man. Yet that was not always the case; when the aviator decided that he flew a plane that was unsafe or dangerously inferior to the one the enemy had, morale would suffer, and sometimes military operations as well. In the R.F.C. this problem developed in connection with the B.E. 2c, the standard corps machine of 1916, and also one of its successors, the R.E. 8. At first the airmen's criticism took the form of humor; B.E. was said to signify Beast Extraordinary, and the plane was lambasted in an ironic version of the Twenty-Third Psalm ("Thou preparest a crash for me in the presence of mine enemies," etc.). Ultimately the morale problem became serious; a government spokesman acknowledged in Parliament that six flying officers had refused to go up in the R. E. 8, and Pemberton Billing denounced the plane as a "murder machine." Most modern authorities agree that both planes were inferior, and that the R.E. 8 was a very demanding and unforgiving craft.[32]

But other planes were stigmatized in the squadrons with far less cause; such was the case with the De Haviland DH 2 and the Sopwith Tabloid, which carried sinister reputations "like an invisible label." The Sopwith triplane was said to have a weakness which made its wings "fold up" in a dive; yet research has turned up no instance in which this occurred, leading a historian to conclude recently that "it was all nonsense about a supposed weakness in the Sopwith triplane." Even the celebrated Camel had to overcome an early reputation as a mankiller: students in British flight schools were told that more people were killed learning to fly the planes than ever flew them overseas. British authorities seem to have accepted this state of affairs philosophically: "Trenchard himself was quite clear at this time that to study the tastes and preferences of the pilot, even when those tastes were prejudices, was the only way to efficiency. So if it was rumored that such and such an aircraft had bad habits, above all if it was said to be prone to spinning, its prospects were damned."[33]

There was another dimension to this image of the machine, and that was the tendency to overrate the aircraft of the enemy. Any innovation on the other side was of consuming interest to the airmen at the front, and they were inclined to attribute their reverses to it. Thus in early 1915, when the Germans learned some French pilots had mounted machine guns on their airplanes, they reported encounters with such planes everywhere, though in fact the French only had a few of them; every reverse came to be laid at the door of the new enemy weapon, and in the front-line units there was a rising clamor for similar arms.

If the technological surprise were a new enemy plane, it would know a fabulous phantom existence in the squadron messes opposite. Whatever qualities it had would be enhanced, and in addition it would often acquire totally mythical attributes. The most spectacular example of this phenomenon was the "Fokker Scare," which reached its height at the beginning of 1916. In January of that year "the deadly Fokker" was the subject of debates in the British Parliament and in the French Chamber of Deputies; *The New York Times* dedicated a front-page story on the *Eindecker*, while London's *Daily Mail* warned the plane would be accompanying German dirigibles on their next raid. The public was told that this remarkable aircraft "stands on its head and dives straight for its victim, loosing off a stream of bullets. . . . By making the descent ever so slightly spiral, the straight stream of bullets becomes a cone of fire, with its apex at the gun, and with the victim inside, so that whichever way the lower machine tries to escape, it must pass through the cone."[34]

The editors of the more responsible aeronautical journals, who had a more informed idea of what the Fokker Eindecker could and could not do, denounced the "fatuous sensationalism . . . which appears to have got such a firm grip upon most of the editorial departments of the ha'penny papers." The whole affair was a journalistic fabrication that made "fit company for the air raid scare." There is no doubt that the British and French press contributed to the panic, as did any number of ill-informed politicians. But there is also no doubt that the whole myth of the deadly Fokker came from the front, and from the men who had to face it in battle. The Eindecker pilot had, as we know, a superior ability to fire his gun on the axis, but beyond that the plane was not extraordinary, being neither particularly powerful nor fast. A number of Allied types had nothing to fear from it; the French Nieuport IX fighter, for example, was decidedly faster. Nor were the Fokkers very numerous at the front. John Morrow has estimated that there were never more than 50 Eindeckers operating at the same time, and this along a front nearly 300 miles long. In January 1916, when the clamor was very loud indeed, British air losses on the Western Front were only 10 planes.[35]

But the Eindecker was a new and unknown presence, and therefore a menacing one; it was distinctive in appearance—"an evil-looking monoplane"—and it had some successes. The "multiplier" went to work and made the Eindecker deadly, at least in the eyes of Allied airmen. Albert Ball said the Fokker was "twice as fast" as the plane he flew. Cecil Lewis recalled that in his squadron "rumor credited it with the most fantastic performance! It could outclimb, outpace, and out-maneuver anything in the R. F. C. You were as good as dead if you as much as saw one. . . ." Morale sank. In April General Trenchard reported he had reduced operations "enormously." The crisis soon blew over with the appearance of new Allied fighters and the increased use of formation flying and fighter escorts. When the Allies finally laid their hands on an Eindecker they found it to be a very ordinary machine. Mock combats with Allied fighters showed the Fokker at a disadvantage. Cecil Lewis was there for one of the demonstrations when the French Morane outflew the Eindecker: "A cheer went up from the ground. The bogey was laid."[36]

But there would be other bogeys, and eventually those who directed the various air services could all acknowledge the truth of an observation by a member of the British Air Board: Once captured and submitted to a cold, clinical testing, the enemy's airplanes "were constantly found to have an inferior performance to that reported from the front." It must have seemed a baffling phenomenon; the explanation lay partly in the rapidly evolving realm of technology, but perhaps more in the world of the men who flew, and it is that world that we must now examine.[37]

=7=

The Men: Selection and Training

"Military aviation is apparently the most dangerous sport man has discovered since the contests of the gladiators." This judgment made by a French aviator of 1914 expresses very well an attitude that was extremely widespread during the Great War. The danger associated with flying—an often exaggerated danger—colored the public's perception about flying and had no small effect on the flyers themselves.[1]

Fatal flying accidents were newsworthy because they involved airplanes, and also because they were often spectacular—as when one of the airplanes in the Paris-Madrid race of 1912 plowed into a crowd of spectators, killing the French minister of war and badly injuring the prime minister. The tabloids marked each airman's fall, and the deaths increased in number. In Germany, for example, there were 4 deaths from flying accidents in 1910, 13 in 1911, 29 in 1912, and 43 in 1913; a similar trend appeared in other countries. The figures were probably not that grim, considering the rapid growth in the number of airplanes—Frederick Janes placed the number at 2,000 in 1912—and in the growing numbers of pilots "taking their tickets" each year. But flying kept its reputation as a perilous activity and any number of people gave it up. Winston Churchill did so at the urging of his wife. Ernst Heinkel, who survived a bad crash in 1911, never again flew in any of the planes he made if he could possibly avoid it.[2]

There was special concern in military aviation circles. If the death toll from the simple act of flying had to be added to the casualties that would result from wartime operations, then the attrition rates for airmen might be very high indeed. When the Royal Flying Corps was created in 1912, it was estimated that in event of war the entire flying personnel would have to be renewed every six months (R.F.C. authorities were very relieved early in 1915 when they found that after five months of war they had lost less than 3 percent of their airmen). Peacetime losses in themselves were problem enough: early in 1914 the U.S. Congress became involved when it learned that 8 of the 14 qualified aviators in the Signal Corps had lost their lives. The French Senate also began an inquiry into aviators' deaths, and there were questions in the British Parliament. A number of changes were introduced in the various air services, with the French generally leading the way. In 1911 they prescribed a special military pilots' license with more rigorous requirements than the civilian license; the German authorities made the same change and so eventually did most European armies. From 1912 on, the seat belt was mandatory on French military aircraft, and the cork and leather crash helmet became a feature of the aviator's dress. As an acknowledgement of the special risks of the air service, it was everywhere recruited on a voluntary basis, most often from the ground arms. As an inducement to their aviators, in 1912 the French introduced flight pay, a measure quickly copied in other countries.[3]

In most European air services only single men were accepted for flying, another recognition of its dangers. Congress decreed in 1914 that U.S. Army aviators had to be unmarried lieutenants of the line under the age of 30. Curiously, the U.S. Navy had no such restrictions, but it could be understanding in this regard. In 1913 it transferred a Marine pilot to other duty when he complained that "my fiancee will not consent to marry me unless I give up flying." There was also a certain "turnover" in flying personnel as some who had volunteered—perhaps the more prudent—decided that flying was not for them and asked to be transferred to other duties (Lieutenant Henry H. Arnold, who had several friends involved in serious crashes, returned briefly to the infantry). Of the 52 French military pilots who learned to fly in 1910, two years later 3 had been killed, 3 had been invalided out of the service after serious injury, and another 14 had left the air service and returned to their original arm or service. It is probable that well before 1914 this sort of winnowing-out, added to the special requirements for airmen, had already produced a body of specialists who were quite distinct from the rest of the military establishment. They were young (as a rule 30 was the age limit for pilot trainees, with observers taken somewhat older); they were unattached; they were not repelled by the risks involved, and most of all they were captivated by the idea of flying. Well before 1914 the rest of the army regarded the airmen as a reckless, rambunctious breed. In the Italian Army they had become the *scavezzacolli*, the daredevils.[4]

After the war began, the question of motivation became more complicated. Some were attracted by the higher pay. Some volunteered though they had no particular interest in flying. One young man confessed he had done so "because he was always asked why he was not in the army." Many who were already in uniform volunteered in hopes of escaping the hell of the trenches. Usually the soldier's commanding officer had to give his consent to the transfer, and that consent was more easily obtained by a malingerer or a troublemaker than by a dutiful soldier. There is no doubt that the lure of flying continued to attract men all during the war. When a number of British flyers were asked toward the end of the war what characteristics the good pilot should have, they frequently listed "keenness for flying."[5]

Well before the war the air services had decided that the military pilot needed more than "the flying hunger" and a reputation for daring. The services began to lay down special requirements for flying personnel. In September 1912, a French ministerial circular called for the pilot to have excellent eyesight, a sound heart, and good hearing; that same year the U.S. Navy required its pilots to be free from color-blindness (colored flares were then much used in signaling) and other serious visual defects, have "normal" hearing, and a "healthy" nervous system. In Germany and in some other countries the military themselves, notably the medical corps, successfully opposed special physical requirements for airmen, so that little was done until after 1914. Rational standards for personnel selection, and the special field of aviation medicine upon which they were based, were in large part products of the war.[6]

Fixing physical criteria for aviators was difficult since most of the earlier experience and observation dealt with balloonists, whose role during their ascensions was essentially passive. But the pilot, the observer, and the bombardier or machine gunner had to work, to function during flight. Then too, in that early stage of aviation medicine, myth was still mixed with fact. Some physicians believed that the aviator would have to contend with caisson disease, or "the bends;" others thought blood vessels would dilate at altitude. Even as late as 1919 an American scientist acknowledged that "the idea is still prevalent that hemorrhages occur under low barometric pressures." Then there was the mysterious disease known as *mal des aviateurs* which could work subtle and fatal changes on the airman's body. The story that flying would enlarge the heart was so prevalent among German airmen that in 1918 the German Air Service distributed a "fact sheet" in the flying units. There were articles in medical journals on "aviator's heart."[7]

Then there were those who believed that the essence of good flying lay not in physical qualities or even in training but in the "flyer's temperament," which would manifest itself by a sort of natural selection. This notion was especially popular in Great Britain. And there were those who believed that the ideal airman was a distinct and recognizable physical type. Martin Flack, who played a significant role in the personnel selection program of the Royal Flying Corps and later the Royal Air Force, suggested that studying photographs of good and bad pilots might be useful. He felt that what he called "the bird-like type" made the best aviators: "not like a parrot, which might be compared to the man who flew badly and landed badly—but alert men rather like a sparrow; the quick, keen and alert type."[8]

Finally there were those who believed that the best pilot was a recycled cavalryman. This notion was strong in the French service, where the airmen sometimes referred to their planes as "mounts." Among British pilots a highly desired quality was "hands," a deftness and dexterity in hand movements common to the good horseman and the good pilot. Into the 1930s British airmen were encouraged to ride horseback as a way of improving their flying. In Germany the same notions obtained, and the Von Richthofen brothers, both former cavalrymen, were held up as proof of the close relationship between horseback riding and flying. In reality there seems to have been very little connection. Of the 65 most distinguished German airmen of the Great War,—those who received the coveted *Pour le mérite* or "Blue Max"—only a minority came from the cavalry. The same was true of

The aerial weapon goes back two centuries. Sole survivor of the world's first military air fleet, this French observation balloon was captured by the Austrians in 1796. *Heeresgeschichtliches Museum, Vienna.*

Two pioneers: Captain Ferdinand Ferber (top, left) was an early partisan of aeronautics in the French Army, and in 1909 he became the second Frenchman to die in an airplane accident; Giovanni Caproni of Italy (top, right) designed a multi-engined airplane for use as a bomber before the outbreak of the war. *Service Historique de l'Armée de l'Air; Museo Aeronautico Caproni.*

Lieutenant Thomas Selfridge, U.S. Army, lies dying after an airplane crash at Fort Myer, Va., on September 17, 1908. His death, the first from a crash of a powered airplane, began a series of fatalities that made prewar flying seem a particularly hazardous activity. *National Air and Space Museum, Smithsonian Institution.*

The dirigible *La France* (top), designed by two French Army officers, Charles Renard and Arthur Krebs, made a highly successful flight in 1884; it was handicapped by its battery-powered electric motor. Count von Zeppelin's newest airship (bottom) created an international incident in April 1913 when it accidentally crossed the French frontier and landed at Lunéville. *Service Historique de l'Armée de l'Air; Karl Schneide Collection.*

"Panic in Trafalgar Square." Such was the title of this cartoon which appeared in the German humorous weekly *Lustige Blätter* in 1914 a few weeks after the war broke out. A number of German political and military leaders shared the cartoonist's view that the appearance of German dirigibles over England would create popular unrest. *Lustige Blätter.*

A. 1725. Dans la Marne.
Capitaine observateur
dans la nacelle d'une saucisse.
10.5.17.

A French officer checks out his telephone before the ascension of his observation balloon. His parachute is in the container attached to the right side of the basket. *Karl Schneide Collection.*

The top photograph shows a German Drachen; the figure of the soldier beside it gives some idea of its size. The bottom photograph caught the fiery end of an observation balloon, whose observer has successfully parachuted. *Peter M. Grosz Collection; National Air and Space Museum, Smithsonian Institution.*

The Caudron G. 3 (top) was used extensively by the French for observation and artillery spotting in the first part of the war. The bottom photo is an airman's view of the Western Front and shows a gas attack launched by the French. *Service Historique de l'Armée de l'Air; National Air and Space Museum, Smithsonian Institution.*

Two innovations in the air war: the Le Prieur air-to-air rockets, shown here on a Nieuport 16 fighter, were the invention of a French naval officer and were used with some success against observation balloons; the glider shown in the bottom photo was designed to be released from a German dirigible, and was only one of several attempts to develop radio-controlled aircraft during the war. *Musée de l'Air; Peter M. Grosz Collection.*

the 200-odd French pilots who each downed five enemy planes; more of them came from the infantry than from anywhere else.[9]

Even if some rules for selection had been in existence in the early years of the war, it is doubtful they could have been applied; the French in effect set aside selection guidelines for a number of months after October 1914, when they were pushing the expansion of their air service; men who had been declared unfit for service in the infantry because of wounds were accepted as aerial observers. Any number of other young men with infirmities talked their way into the various air services, including John Slessor, who had been lamed by infantile paralysis. The British took to recruiting their observers among those who had washed out of pilot training, and the Americans imitated them. Beyond the almost universal eye test, many of the early screening procedures seem haphazard and naïve. The applicant for flight school might be asked to stand on one leg for a length of time, to walk along a chalked line, or to hold his breath for at least 45 seconds. The French came to put considerable emphasis on good hearing, in the belief that the pilot should be able to detect the slightest change in the rhythm of his airplane motor; the Americans, on the other hand, seem to have seriously entertained the idea of letting deaf men become pilots, on the grounds that no pilot could hear anything over the roar of the engine anyway.[10]

Screening techniques were continually refined and more rational guidelines evolved as the air war itself evolved. The Germans found, for example, that as airplanes became more powerful and their lifting capacity increased, the weight restrictions on flying personnel could be dropped; also, the airmen of 1918 were piloting larger and heavier planes, and manipulating heavy cameras or training their machine guns against a stronger slipstream generated by greater speeds; thus the airmen needed to be stronger. In Italy and particularly in France, where the greatest strides were being made in aviation medicine, scientists recruited from the universities were devising more sophisticated testing procedures. They tested the airman's reflex reaction time by having him press a button as soon as he saw a light flash or heard a bell ring. They sought to test the "solidity" of a candidate's nerves by applying pneumographs and vasomotor recorders to his body, and then suddenly slapping him on the nape of the neck with a wet sponge or firing off a revolver behind his back. The British were far less enthusiastic about such tests, though one medical officer devised an apparatus for evaluating "hands." Procedures for discovering "temperament" were deemed more important in the R.A.F. Medical Service, including a proposed test for emotional self-control and "pugnacity." The officer who proposed the test felt it was not necessary to measure self-control among British candidates, since the quality was inherent in them; on the other hand it could be quite useful for evaluating "the more emotional latin type." Pugnacity—a quality especially desired in fighter pilots—could be tested by making "disparaging remarks" to the candidate, and a "a prompt response would be considered satisfactory."[11]

By the end of the war selection techniques had changed radically, like virtually every other aspect of aviation. Some of the more naïve ideas of 1914 had fallen by the wayside, and the various tests and examinations devised during the war were probably helpful in culling at the outset those candidates who would never have made it through flight school; at the very least this represented a considerable saving in time and in money, for the British estimated that every pilot who washed out was a lost investment of £2,000. But the tests and the screening could not predict who would be the superlative pilot, nor did they always identify those whose flying would be marginal at best. General Sefton Branker, who in 1917 was the Royal Flying Corps' Director of Organization, and therefore thoroughly conversant with its selection and training programs, acknowledged in a meeting of the Royal Aeronautical Society that "the most unexpected people make good pilots and very often the most promising ones never attain more than mediocrity in the air."

The shortcomings in the selection system were well known to the airmen themselves, who took a wry pleasure in pointing them out. Edward Parsons, who flew with the Lafayette Escadrille, recounted in his memoirs that he and a number of other pilots from the escadrille were called before an examining board of the U.S. Air Service and subjected to what Parsons called "a long series of rather ridiculous physical demonstrations." After careful deliberation, the board gave the pilots the results of its findings: "Not one of us, despite hundreds of hours in the air, most of us aces, all thoroughly trained war pilots with many victories to our credit, could ever be an aviator."[12]

Whatever the impact of the selection process, it seems to

have placed little emphasis on a candidate's cultural background
or social standing. This is perhaps understandable in a new branch
of the service lacking in tradition and unencumbered by association
with any particular class. One has only to read the capsule biographies of the more successful pilots to appreciate the enormous
variety in their backgrounds. The extensive mixing of various
classes in the Royal Flying Corps, and later in the Royal Air Force,
was apparent to contemporaries themselves. Two R.A.F. officers
writing at the end of the war in *The Lancet* stressed this very
point: "Flying is not now confined to the public school boy, the
cavalry officer, or the athlete. We take many of our pilots at present
from the lower middle classes and the artisan class." To prove
their point, they listed the "occupation in civil life" of 61 R.A.F.
pilots who had filled out their questionnaires; these ranged from
student to barrister, to farmer, to "window designer and dresser."
The varied—and often modest—social origins of the German *Pour
le mérite* recipients were also remarked on; before the war, 3 of
the 65 had practiced the trade of roofer.[13]

Still, there is evidence that the upper and middle classes
were somewhat overrepresented. The public school boy, the "gen-
tleman-pilot," was particularly drawn to the British fighter arm,
where he seems to have set the tone. General Charles Christienne
has written that in the French Air Service men from the lower
classes were present in limited numbers only. It is also clear—at
least on the Allied side—that the airmen came above all from
the cities. The backgrounds of Canadian airmen have been carefully analyzed, and the results indicate that the rate of enlistment
among city dwellers was over three times that of young men from
the countryside. "It was, apparently, the urban dweller, presumably somewhat familiar with engines and things mechanical, or
having the benefits of a better education, or perhaps more easily
reached by the recruiting advertising, who was more likely to
join one of the flying services than was the 'wild colonial boy'
sometimes popularly thought to make up the bulk of Canadians
in the flying services." By the same token few Frenchmen of the
peasant class preferred the air service to the trenches. As General
Christienne put it: "The mud was already part of their lives; the
air was the unknown."[14]

The exigencies of coalition warfare and the constantly increasing demand for airmen had the effect of drawing men from ever
more varied backgrounds into the training programs. The British

were soon calling on the manpower of the Empire, and by the end of 1917 there were 15 training squadrons in Canada and another 5 in Egypt. The German, Austro-Hungarian, and Russian Air Services all sought flying cadets among the various ethnic groups within their empires. The German government undertook to supply training and technical assistance to the Turkish and Bulgarian air services. From 1916 on, British and French schools received both flying cadets and mechanic trainees sent by the Russian government. After the United States entered the war, the British, French, and Italian Air Services all opened their training facilities to American students. The French flight schools often contained a bewildering range of nationalities: Serbs, Japanese, Belgians, Greeks, Russians, and even students from neutral countries who had enlisted in the Foreign Legion and then transferred to the air service.

Oddly, the outbreak of the war had the effect of bringing training to a halt everywhere, as pilots and planes headed for the front. The French schools at Avord and Pau simply closed, not to open again until the end of the year. The R.F.C.'s Central Flying School at Upavon, though nominally open, had been depleted of everything but clerks and filing cabinets. The German training facility at Döberitz lost all its planes in the mobilization and could get no replacements. The commander bought or borrowed any airplane he could. The result was "a museum" of outmodeled and discarded machines.[15]

With the decision to expand the air services after the first few weeks of war, the schools reopened in a rush; the scope and pace of training began to change drastically. Upavon, with its 40-student capacity, became inadequate overnight, as did the prewar training program of the French Air Service with its leisurely, year-long progress to the military pilot's license. Rapid, even dizzying growth set in; for some of the air services enough figures survive to indicate its magnitude. The expansion of the training program in France can be seen in the wartime production of military pilots:

1914—134

1915—1,484

1916—2,698

1917—5,608

1918—8,000

In all, the French turned out 18,000 pilots; British records indicate a total of 21,957 pilots "trained and graduated" during the conflict. The German Air Service began the war with 500 airmen and ended it with 5,000; in the last year of the war it was replacing pilots, observers, and machine gunners at the rate of 750 per month.[16]

As the functions of airmen expanded and diversified, so did the training programs. While many early bombing units were put to work with little or no instruction, most specialties required formal training. The aerial machine gunner, who had not existed in 1914, was one of the easier specialists to train. The gunners who manned French Breguet bombers towards the end of the war got a brief gunnery course at Cazaux (Americans who trained there called it "Kazoo"). If weather conditions were favorable the course could be completed in less than a month. The gunnery students began by firing shotguns at clay pigeons and red balloons, then graduated to the rifle and machine gun. Much of their firing was at targets towed by speedboats across the lake at Cazaux; this enabled the students to see where their shots were striking and to correct their aim accordingly.[17]

Formal training courses for observers had been devised before the war, and could take two months and more. There were lectures in which the candidates learned that enemy soldiers in the streets of a town were probably infantry, while concentrations of them in courtyards meant they were cavalry. There were practice reconnaissances and exercises in which the observer learned to estimate numbers of troops. A French observer learned that a German infantry battalion in order of march was 400 meters long. A British airman recalled practicing artillery observation "in a hangar where a model village had been built, enabling the would-be observer, mounted on the roof, to spot and locate the flashes of tiny bulbs concealed variously on the ground. Locations and corrections were signalled down by the observer by means of a Morse buzzer."[18]

There was talk of continuing the observer's instruction by training him as a pilot as well. General Douhet had urged such a measure as early as 1912, on the grounds that in an emergency the observer could fill the pilot's functions. And when the war came, and any number of observers were carried helplessly to their doom with a dead or badly wounded pilot at the controls, in many units the pilots took it upon themselves to instruct their observers in the rudiments of flying, and there were cases in which the observer, leaving his cockpit and crouching alongside that of his disabled pilot, successfully landed the aircraft. After the war several air services adopted the principle that the observer should also be trained as a pilot.[19]

But for the period of the war itself there was no question of admitting observers to the flight schools. These were already operating at capacity, and at accelerated pace. As a rule, more subjects of study were packed into a shorter training period. In 1916 a German pilot named Franz Schlenstedt was appalled by what he found when he left a combat unit to take an assignment as flight instructor. Schlenstedt, who had learned to fly before the war, had difficulty adjusting to the pace and the frantic activity: "We were manufacturing pilots on an assembly line." There were also frequent complaints from the front that the pilots coming from the schools were hastily and incompletely trained; and a common feature of front-line airfields was the new pilot turning about the field to learn the ways of his "mount." But when combat units ran short of pilots, that consideration overrode all others, and right to the end of the war there were instances of airmen rushed to the front before their training was completed.[20]

On balance, however, instruction was more effective as the war progressed. The simple flying school gave way to a series or progression of installations where specialties were taught and skills honed in preparation for combat. Hands-on training improved measurably. In 1914 British pilots were being dispatched to service at the front as "qualified" with as little as four or five hours of solo flying. By the end of the war the Royal Air Force boasted a minimum of 35 hours, including 5 in the type of airplane the pilot would be flying at the front; in fact, few pilots were going across the Channel with less than 50 hours of solo time behind them.[21]

The training techniques varied from one country to another, and indeed from one school or training squadron to the next. In their haste to expand training facilities the authorities often took over or contracted with private flying schools, which had their own ways of doing things; the German government gave a premium to private instructors who trained pilots quickly, and this no doubt influenced their training methods. According to Sefton Branker, the British avoided developing precise guidelines for training for fear it would stifle initiative. The individual instructor needed a free hand, along with the qualities of "a man whose business it is to break young horses." Flight instruction could also differ fundamentally from one French school to the next. Dual-control aircraft were used at Buc; at Pau, they were not.[22]

The first stage of training was usually conducted exclusively on the ground, and was heavily military in content, as if to remind the students that they were soldiers first, and then airmen. The French gave men and non-commissioned officers what was essentially a course in infantry training, with a good bit of close-order drill to combat "the individualistic tendencies to which the aviator can fall prey." The British Cadet's School dispensed two months of "military subjects, pure and simple." For volunteers fresh from the civilian world, the military life offered some rude challenges. In their letters and their diaries the men voiced the usual complaints about early hours and bad food, and there were the denunciations civilians newly in uniform always make of military discipline and conformity.[23]

Early in the training program there was usually a considerable amount of classroom instruction on various aspects of flight. The future pilots made some acquaintance with the science of navigation, though they rarely perfected or even used that knowledge thereafter. They flew by reference to the landscape, rather than to a compass, and followed roads or railways rather than a charted course. (Naval pilots, who had no such landmarks available, were more diligent students in this regard.) It was felt that a pilot should know his airplane, so the students were introduced to the world of spars, turnbuckles, and obturator rings. These lessons, too, seem not to have had great impact on the pilot's subsequent career. While in their diaries and letters airmen wrote constantly of flying, what they wrote was rarely very technical. Here and there a pilot with the aptitude and training might take a hand in the rebuilding of his engine, and a few aces like Georges Guynemer could do so. But most pilots left such matters to their mechanics. Two British authorities on airmen and their ways believed the average pilot knew little about his airplane from the technical point of view, though his *amour propre* usually prevented him from saying so. They reasoned it was just as well for the fighter pilot, especially, to remain in ignorance: "From the very nature of his work he must be prepared to throw the machine about, and at times to subject it so such strain that did he realize how near he was to the breaking-point, his nerve would go very quickly." And a veteran pilot who had flown 14 different types of airplanes put it simply: "If you have not got an extensive knowledge of engines and you have a dud engine you go on and don't worry."[24]

But the goal of flight school was learning to fly, and here there were two basic approaches. In the first, which was pioneered by the French and widely used by them, the student was placed— by himself—in a succession of airplanes and given increasingly complex maneuvers to do with them until eventually he was flying. The other system used the dual control airplane, a type that had been pioneered by the Wrights. The dual control system was embraced by the British and widely used elsewhere since it offered the possibility of training pilots quickly; indeed, by the end of the war a number of French schools had switched to *la méthode anglaise.*

Still, an enormous number of World War I pilots learned to fly without ever having anyone else in the airplane with them. At the end of the war this system was still in use in the French flight school at Avord, probably the largest such school in the world, with its 1,000 students and 1,300 aircraft. An American volunteer named Reginald Sinclaire learned to fly at Avord in 1917. A half-century later, aided by his log book, he was able to relate his experiences to a U.S. Air Force oral history committee in fascinating detail.

Sinclaire climbed into his first airplane on June 20. It was a Blériot with a 25-horsepower engine and cropped wings, both of which guaranteed it would not leave the ground. Such a plane was known, aptly enough, as a penguin. Sinclaire and the dozen other students in his class had to guide their planes at full throttle across a mile-long field; there waiting ground crewmen picked up the penguins' tails and turned them around for the return trip: "The idea was that you should hold it in the position, and learn the position, where you were in what the French termed *ligne de vol* or line of flight, which would be the position of the airplane when it was in flight, with the tail up in a horizontal position. I didn't have any difficulty with the class, and I enjoyed it very much—it was fun. But I did find that you had to be real quick with your feet."[25]

On July 17 Sinclaire moved up to the *rouleur* class. Here the planes had larger engines and full wings. Though the *rouleur* plane could leave the ground, the goal was to cross the field without flying: "when it would try to leave the ground, you'd just back off a little bit on the throttle." Five days later Sinclaire was promoted to the *décolle* or take-off class; using the same planes as previously, the students ran their machines across a field a mile and a half in length. There was a depression in the middle of it so that when the airplane passed over it for a few seconds it became airborne. On July 26 Sinclaire moved to the *piqué* class, in which the student allowed the airplane to rise to 100 feet or so, and then brought it back down, still flying only in a straight line. Next came *tour de piste*, a flight half around the field, then "spirals," cross-country flights, and finally the military *brevet* or license on October 1, after 47 hours of flying. Thereafter Sinclaire reported to the fighter school at Pau, where he flew Nieuports and Spads and learned aerobatics (17 hours); he moved on to the front in December.[26]

Sinclaire's progress took some six months, and this was considered about average for pilot training. When there were variations, they were usually caused by bad weather. In Germany the rule was that winter training always took longer. An exceptionally long period of bad weather at the beginning of 1916 set the Italian pilot training program back by two months. The ideal weather for flying school was a dead calm or nearly so. Since the heat of the sun stirred up troublesome convectional air currents during the day—what the British called "sun bumps"—beginners usually did their flying very early in the morning or in the evening (in some French schools the students could make their morning flights in pajamas).[27]

The instructor was a central element in the student's life and the subject of frequent comments in letters and diaries; there was the instructor who stuttered uncontrollably, an affliction the students felt was "attributable to an earlier crash while flying," and there was the instructor who stretched out in a chaise longue to follow his students' evolutions as they flew over the field. If the students are to be believed, the advice they were given was sometimes bizarre at the very least. An instructor in a French school told his class that if the motor suddenly stopped—every pilot's nightmare—while flying over a wooded area, it was best to land in an apple tree; and an Italian instructor told his students that if the plane caught fire—an even worse nightmare—his recommendation was: "Shut off the gas and commend your soul to God."[28]

The instructors were the subject of considerable complaint

in official circles as well. Sefton Branker acknowledged they were frequently inadequate, while French instructors were accused of imposing a sort of stultifying formalism, punishing students who showed initiative. Much of the problem was traceable to the fact that the instructors were often combat pilots who were *abgekämpft*, as the Germans said—fought out, or suffering from combat fatigue. Such men could be short-tempered and irritable. Because some instructors were "recuperating their nerves," as one contemporary put it, "their method of telling the student is somewhat forcible." In truth, the instructor did not always have an easy time of it, and flying with an edgy novice at the controls did nothing for "recuperating" the nerves. "All instructors carried their lives in their hands—and feet," wrote one airman. "No one could foresee when a normally cold-blooded pupil might suddenly go bonkers and, freezing on to the controls, send himself and his tutor plummeting earthward."[29]

For those who learned to fly on dual-control airplanes, there came the momentous day of the solo. A German pilot named Eddebüttel recalled that at his training field a special yellow flag was run up when there was to be a solo, and the air was cleared of all other planes: "After the flight the inevitable cigarette was lit up and the Kodak was brought out and a picture made in full flying costume so that 'she' and a faraway 'Mama' could admire the 'hero of the air.'" And an Italian pilot had vivid memories of his first flight: "I landed in triumph, happy, envied, surrounded by comrades not as far along in their lessons, and welcomed now by the group that had preceded me."[30]

Some did not make it to the solo. Ten days after an accident in which he suffered minor injury, A. J. Insall took off with his instructor and flew without difficulty until it was time to land: "As soon as I had throttled down and we were approaching the ground, I began to feel physically sick, and had to shake my head vigorously and relinquish control to Darley." Three days later the same thing happened again; Insall abandoned his hopes of being a pilot and became an observer. For some, the solo flight was just too daunting. They too were culled, with the notation "could not face the responsibility of flying alone," or "when ready for solo refused on account of fear." An 18-year-old R.F.C. trainee who had crashed on his first and second attempts to solo was withdrawn from the program as "temperamentally unfit" when he confessed he had "a sense of impending disaster." And there were men who cleared all the hurdles training presented, yet showed no progress thereafter. They remained awkward and uncomfortable when they were in the air. One British medical officer coined the term "aerosthenia" for their condition, which he believed was permanent. As he put it, "it is not given to all men to fly."[31]

And there were those who did not get their wings because they lost their lives in the attempt. A fatal crash at a training field had a profound effect on all who witnessed it. The sound itself was unforgettable. One airman spoke of "the ghastly crunch that an aeroplane can make once, and once only, in the course of its lifetime"; another said "I know of no sound more horrible than that made by an aeroplane crashing to earth." When such a thing happened it was often the custom to cancel all flying for the rest of the day, ostensibly out of respect for the deceased, but also because the students had been badly shaken. The students in Jean Puistienne's flying class witnessed a terrible crash at 7:30 one morning, and Puistienne noted in his diary "we don't dare fly any more"; but by four that afternoon they were venturing back into the air.[32]

Throughout the war, stories circulated of the high fatalities in the flying schools. Historians of the French training programs said there were persistent rumors of "veritable hecatombs," particularly at Avord and at the fighter school at Pau. Among the airmen themselves there was also talk of 30 or 40 or 50 percent of the class killed, with the figures of course hushed up by the government. Early in 1917 there were particularly heated exchanges in the British Parliament. Noel Pemberton Billing, who was something of a gadfly on the issue, charged that "hardly a day goes by but two or three pilots are killed in this country." The stories persisted long after the war, and the high loss rates in the flight schools have found their way into the history books.[33]

Accidents of the minor sort seem to have been epidemic in most schools; particularly in those where dozens of "penguins" were released at once, collisions were the order of the day. Landing was regarded as the most difficult operation for a neophyte, and many of these too ended in some damage to the airplane, but with relatively little harm to the airmen, who seem to have accepted a mishap as part of the learning process. To wreck a plane in German airman's argot was *Kleinholz machen;* and the French called it *casser du bois,* both of which mean to split wood; both terms were in constant, almost casual use. (Among Americans trained at Avord the story was that after he damaged three airplanes a student was assigned to night bombing; if he damaged five he went to the infantry.)

On the other hand the sort of accident that led to total destruction of the airplane *and* serious injury or death to its occupants seems to have been less frequent than is often supposed. For the French, some global figures have survived: in the flying schools the number of fatal accidents per 1,000 hours of flying were 0.37 in 1916, 0.35 in 1917, and 0.25 in 1918. In the *écoles de perfectionnement* that "converted" the new pilot to the latest combat models—schools which had a particularly bad reputation —the deaths per 1,000 flying hours were 0.85 in 1917 and 0.75 in 1918. Perhaps more significant is the figure supplied by General Christienne, which puts the number of student pilots killed in French flight schools at 300. Since the schools produced 18,000 pilots, there would be one student killed for each 60 who got their wings. The death rate based on these figures would be 1.6 percent, but in fact it would be even lower, since there was another group in the flight schools—at least 10 percent of those enrolled—who ultimately dropped out for a variety of reasons.[34]

In the case of the British, the testimony is often contradictory, and so are the figures on training casualties. A Royal Navy surgeon named H. Graeme Anderson wrote early in 1918 that in six months at one R.N.A.S. training installation he had been present for some 9,000 training flights—about 4,000 hours of flying—and had witnessed only 58 serious crashes, of the kind that destroyed the airplane or very nearly so; those 58 crashes had produced injuries for 16 airmen—and death for none; in two years of such work Anderson had seen only four deaths. His conclusion: "School flying is fairly safe and compares favorably with other high velocity forms of transit." And in March 1917, under the Parliamentary assaults of Pemberton Billing, a spokesman for the British government consented to give some details. As for Pemberton Billing's query about "30 or 40 percent," the spokesman said the percentage of R.F.C. flight trainees lost was "nothing like that." As for the deaths of "two or three" airmen per day, that Pemberton Billing had spoken of, the truth was that for the months of December 1916, and January and February 1917, the number of airmen killed in the United Kingdom was 58.[35]

Records for January–October 1918 indicate that in R.F.C./ R.A.F. training establishments there was one death for every 790 hours of flying, suggesting a loss rate that is hardly a hecatomb. Yet there are references to earlier loss figures which do seem appallingly high: one death per 90 hours of flying, for example. The R.A.F.'s official history touches on this subject but lightly, though it does dwell on reforms introduced into the training program in 1917 by Major R. R. Smith-Barry; these were aimed at giving the new pilot a better understanding of his machine and a longer period of tutelage under his instructor. There is ample evidence that reforms were needed. In that same year of 1917 the R.F.C. at various times calculated the "wastage" in its flight-training institutions at 17 percent, 20 percent, and 28 percent. Wastage referred to the percentage of a class that failed to finish the program for any reason, usually including about 10 percent who were culled as lacking aptitude or the "flyer's temperament." Even with the Smith-Barry reforms, flight training in the United Kingdom was apparently more costly in lives than elsewhere. The rate for 1918 of 1.34 deaths per 1,000 hours of flying is significantly higher than that in French schools, while the rate obtaining in Canadian flight schools for 1917–18 was only one death for each 1,902 hours of flying. German figures indicate only that their air service suffered 28 percent of its flying fatalities in *Heimatdienst*, that is during flying inside Germany, much but not all of it in flight schools. For other belligerents no such figures are available, but in general it seems likely that the flight schools were not the slaughterhouses depicted in more than a few books on early aviation.[36]

The risks of flying—real or imagined—do not seem to have preoccupied the students overmuch, perhaps because at the age of 20 one's own mortality is not that easy to grasp, but also because the very idea of flying excited them far more than it frightened them. Most, in fact, were probably drawn into the training schools by the basic lure of flight. For Mario Fucini it was the central motivation: "The shock of discipline, the privations, the heat and the cold, all these things I put up with without difficulty. The lack of privacy in our quarters, the grime, the sometimes vulgar company, all, all of that seemed as nothing compared with my desire to fly." And a Canadian who learned to fly in 1917 recalled: "We lived for flying and were in despair when shortages of machines, sickness, orderly duty, etc. grounded us."[37]

In many flight schools it was the custom to whet this desire by taking new students up for a demonstration flight. It almost always had the desired effect. The students were often profoundly moved by the experience, as their letters and diaries show. Robert Kröger wrote his mother that there was something "unendingly beautiful" about flying; there he found himself "in a wonderful detachment, far from the cares and bustle of our little world." Jean Puistienne, who had dreamed of flying—literally—as he lay on the operating table while surgeons worked to repair the wounds he suffered as an infantryman, found that the reality of flight was even more exhilarating than the dream: "We're flying—I'm flying—and I'm stupefied. . . . Everything is limpid, everything is light; a sort of primitive, animal joy washes over me. . . . Here I am in this machine, setting off to explore space; giddy from the sensation of it, I start up the great staircase that has no steps." Even when that first flight ended badly, the exhilaration was no less there. A German student was taken for his first ride by a fledgling pilot who crashed on landing. The student was pulled from the wreckage, unhurt but shaken; he took several puffs on the cigarette they lit for him and then said in a timid voice "it was beautiful!"[38]

Once they had gained confidence and had advanced sufficiently to fly without close supervision, many were prone to undertake all sorts of aerial stunts and pranks, occasionally with disastrous results. In the summer of 1917 there was a clamor over French pilots losing their lives while "showing off" or "playing the clown." In June 1918 the British Air Ministry called attention to accidents resulting from "stunting at low altitudes, especially by pupils not sufficiently experienced to do so." All air acrobatics were to be conducted above 1,000 feet; pilots were to cease low flying over grazing animals and roads with horse traffic. Appended to the Ministry's order was a list of airplanes, including the gentle old Maurice Farman and the Sopwith Baby seaplane, which were not to be "looped or spun." Still the antics went on. Pilots training at Camp Borden in Canada liked to overtake the Toronto Express, flying the length of the train at minimal altitude and dropping down from time to time to bump their wheels on the roofs of the cars. German pilots liked unorthodox takeoffs like the *Affenfahrt* or Monkey Ride, and the *kühne Sprung* or Daring Leap; in the latter the pilot continued to fly just above the ground until he had built up enough air speed to zoom skyward at a sharp angle.

This was forbidden, but, as a pilot confessed, "that specially tingly feeling it gave you was too hard to resist."[39]

By the time the new pilots had finished their training, flying had become the central element in their young lives. "We talked aviation all the time, of course—day and night"; what was true of Reginald Sinclaire's class at Avord was also true of Döberitz and Upavon and Mirafiori. They were the initiates into a new craft, and they had learned its first secrets. And they now spoke a new language, peppering their speech with words they had not known six months before. Fifty years after their training in France, American airmen of the Great War could talk volubly of *vrilles* and *piqués* and *renversements*, to the bafflement of their oral history interviewers. But it was not just their enthusiasm nor their newfound jargon that marked them apart. When they took to the air they crossed some shadowy frontier, so that thereafter they were never quite the same as other, earthbound men. They had acquired what the R.A.F.'s first historian called "the temper of the air."[40]

=8=

The Men:
En Escadrille

Hubert Freeling Griffith was a British infantry officer assigned to liaison work with the R.F.C. He found himself more and more involved with aviation and ultimately arranged a transfer to No. 15 Squadron, where he flew as an observer. Griffith was also an excellent observer of the milieu in which he lived; as a consequence his reminiscences give us a privileged glimpse into that collective existence all airmen knew, "squadron life," or, as the French called it, *la vie en escadrille.*

Like most soldiers who transferred into aviation, Griffith was struck by the difference between the life he had known in the infantry and the ambience in the squadron: "My feeling was that I was being invited to a party after quitting the gates of a penitentiary. . . . And if the atmosphere, in contrast with the staidness of an ordinary infantry battalion, had on first impact something of the craziness of a Wild Western movie—it was a change that I was personally very glad to welcome." Young pilots coming from the rigors of training made essentially the same discovery. A newly minted Italian pilot was profoundly impressed by his first meal with the officers of Squadriglia 25: "Was this really a military mess? It seemed to me more like a banquet of libertines. The only thing missing was the pretty girls! It was impossible to remain downcast or dejected in that general hubbub." And chaplains with the American Expeditionary Force, who were particularly well placed to detect nuances, reported: "The average American aviator at the front regards life in a lighter vein than any other man in the service of Uncle Sam." Allied airmen who talked to German aviators taken prisoner found them kindred spirits in this regard; something of the same atmosphere prevailed in the Fliegerabteilungen and the Staffeln, which had less of the Prussian rigor so evident elsewhere in the Army.[1]

Writers who visited the airmen at the front rarely failed to evoke the same sort of images. The public was told that the aviators had a set of attitudes quite distinctive from the ground forces, and attributable to their being in the air a lot. As the author of *The Way of the Air* explained it, "The air does affect a man to a degree and endows him with the strange malady, flying temperament, that makes him reckless, and to a certain degree headstrong; [leading him] occasionally to get out of hand and to find rules and discipline chafing and irksome."[2]

Flying did make the airmen at the front distinctive in the same way that it had marked the students in the training schools— the infatuation with flight bound them together in a common enthusiasm. "The flying officer must be an enthusiast," wrote the authorities in *The Lancet*, and generally the enthusiasm seems to have been there. "We love it, this job of ours," said one French pilot, "after three years of war we are perhaps the only arm of the service that still does its work with enthusiasm." And another recalled: "Above all, our work didn't bore us, and it was even fun. It was a sport, and a captivating one, and now that we knew the rules, we were anxious to play." This fundamental satisfaction—probably unique among the combatants of the Great War— may go far in explaining the superior morale that was generally reported in the flying units.[3]

Then, too, military aviation was an institution without a past, so the airmen were not hemmed in by custom or burdened with tradition; there was little of the staidness that characterized the older arms. Early in the war the most prestigious figures in the air services were those who already had a reputation as peacetime aviators—*Friedensflieger,* the Germans called them. They seem to have brought into military aviation the same easygoing camaraderie that had prevailed among airmen in the prewar meets and rallies. In the French Air Service, for example, a mechanic might well *tutoyer* (speak familiarly to) the lieutenant whose plane he maintained, a practice that would have been unthinkable in a cavalry regiment; the officers and noncoms of an *escadrille* often shared the same mess.

The individual squadrons and Fliegerabteilungen had no past either, no battle honors and no traditions. At airfields all over France the first traditions were in fact taking root, but they were being nurtured by 20-year-olds. The squadron was a society of the very young, rarely leavened by the presence of older men. "They were boys in everything but achievement," Alan Bott wrote of his squadron-mates. "As a patriarch of twenty-four I had two more years to my discredit than the next oldest among the twelve members of our flight-mess. The youngest was seventeen and a half. Our Squadron Commander, one of the finest men I have met in or out of the army, became a lieutenant-colonel at twenty-five." It is not surprising, therefore, that many of the squadron's rituals and taboos smack of the fraternity house. There was the Lafayette Escadrille's "bottle of death," from which a man might drink only when he had shot down an enemy. There was Escadrille Spa 3, whose members made it a point always to mispronounce the word *escadrille,* a practice that was still current in 1940, as was their special way of drinking a toast, with the arm "at the horizontal." There was the "champagne fund" of the American Aero Squadron 95, maintained through a system of fines: "If anyone brought down a German he was fined five bottles; if he himself was brought down it cost him three, providing of course he was not killed. Should one of us crack up on the field the penalty was ten." When the fund reached a certain point, it was expended in a general bacchanalia. While the escadrille had no battle flag, it had its symbol, usually adopted after long and impassioned discussion, though the resulting emblem was often whimsical enough: the crews of Escadrille MF 1, whose planes were notoriously slow Maurice Farmans, chose as their emblem a winged snail. The airmen of Escadrille F 25, who did much night flying, chose the owl as their symbol; in their bar was a mural showing a conclave of owls, each with the face of an escadrille member.[4]

What came to be called "squadron life" was a rich distillate that varied slightly from one unit to the next with the cultural blend from which it was extracted. There were a few units of essentially homogeneous makeup. The Lafayette Escadrille was one; its historian found that "almost all of them were well educated, from fine families, had some money and position." Then there was Escadrille N 77, *"les sportifs,"* filled with French sports figures.

But these were exceptions; most of the frontline units were as much melting pots as the training schools which supplied them with aviators. Compared to the British Army regiment, whose officers were from the same region, and quite often from the same schools, R.F.C. squadrons had an "infinite individuality and variety." Squadron No. 15 contained within its small flying complement a mix of "public school boys with Canadians, Australians, a cross-country Jockey, a man who had had half an ear shot off in some American brawl, and a New Zealander who read Homer in the original Greek." The squadron members affected a Canadian-American dialect.[5]

The squadron could develop a collective personna of sorts, that development being fostered by the isolation in which most air units lived and fought. At the same time it was that isolation, rather than any "flying temperament," that lay at the root of many of the airman's attitudes. The same lack of formality, the same disregard for "spit and polish," could also be found in the land and sea services among coast artillery batteries or on patrol vessels—wherever small groups of fighting men lived a relatively isolated existence. German pilots who made the acquaintance of U-boat officers found they had the same way of looking at things: what mattered to both were the comrades who peopled their small world—and the machines that carried them into battle.[6]

The airman's home was the airfield, which often took its name from a nearby village. The field was usually 15 or 20 miles behind the front lines, sufficiently far back to rule out much contact with the men in the trenches. The essential element was the field itself, and the field was just that—even so important an airfield as Le Bourget had no paved runways until World War II. The settings tended to be bucolic and somewhat removed, with at best a village nearby and a town accessible by car. A British aviator recalled that "the aerodrome just by the village of Béthouart was occupied by a herd of cows, and that no-one took the least notice of them, each pilot taking off or landing in whatever direction seemed to be most suitable to avoid the animals." It was uncommon for a field to have more than one squadron or escadrille. Hubert Griffith remembered that in the summer of 1918 his squadron had shared Vert-Galant airfield with Squadron 59, whose huts were on the other side of the road—yet there was never a thought of inviting them over. "There was no question of unfriendliness between us. It was simply that we had got accustomed to living and enjoying our squadron lives, and they to living theirs."[7]

In addition to being rustic and remote, the airfield was a surprisingly permanent home. Since the armies did not "move" to any degree until the spring of 1918, neither did the air units attached to them. Fliegerabteilung (A) 263, for example, spent an entire year at a field near Cambrai, and 16 months at another called Boucheneil. For most combat units a move to another airfield seemed a considerable adventure, if for no other reason than because it gave them a new landscape to fly over. But in the normal order of things, "at the end of the mission each escadrille returned to its nest, a nest it had been able to fashion to its own taste, or at least endow with comfort and a certain charm." If there were a farm or village nearby, most of the personnel would be lodged there, and failing that in huts or tents or barracks specially constructed; on the Allied side they were often the bleakly utilitarian Adrian barracks, lined with camp cots and furniture made from packing crates. The airplanes were kept under canvas, with the French Bessoneau hangar much used. Shop and repair facilities often found a home in more permanent structures.[8]

For the 10 to 20 men who actually flew—rarely much more than a tenth of the unit's complement—home was their sleeping quarters and their mess (the French called the latter the *popote*) and their bar-*cum*-day room; the German term for these common facilities was the *Kasino*. These quarters were often decorated with trophies—including a rotary engine converted into a chandelier— and sometimes pictures of women torn from the pages of *La Vie Parisienne*. The places where the airmen spent their time had not only a distinctive appearance, but also a distinctive odor, that of burnt castor oil, which the rotary engines used—and threw about—in great quantities. It clung to the men themselves, to their clothing and their quarters, and could even be detected in the bars of London or Rome or Berlin frequented by the flying fraternity. "That smell," wrote one aviation pioneer, "was all early aviation in one."[9]

That tempo of the flyer's life was such that he often spent a great deal of leisure time with his fellows, and the chief reason for this was, oddly enough, meteorological: "When an aviator wakes up, his first thought is for the weather." More airmen than a few recalled listening for the sound of rain, which meant they could stay in bed. There were often days at a time—sometimes weeks—when there was little or no flying. The British had the conviction that they did more bad weather flying than their allies the French, and certainly more than the Germans opposite them: "We used often to wonder what on earth their pilots found to do to while away the time," recalled one British airman. But French pilots also complained that they were the only ones to venture up in marginal weather, and German pilots had that same conviction (perhaps in the poor visibility they simply failed to see one another). No aviator liked to admit there were times he would prefer not to fly—some insisted they had never known of a pilot seeking to avoid a mission—but the days of forced leisure spent in the mess or the *Kasino* were not always unwelcome. Alan Bott admitted as much: "I cannot deny that on occasions a sea of low clouds, making impossible the next job, is a pleasant surprise." The Germans used the expression *Flugwetter*, flying weather, for when one could take the air, and *Fliegerwetter*, flyers' weather, for when one could not. And there is something of the same refrain in a piece of R.F.C. doggerel called "The Pessimist and the Optimist":

> *P.* I think we'll have a beautiful day.
> *O.* I hope it's going to rain.
> *P.* Only a shower that will pass away.
> *O.* And then come on again.[10]

Hubert Griffith described this sort of existence as "half hectic and half pastoral," and another British airman put it this way: "If one believes his account of his own doings, he divides his time fairly equally between lounging idly in his billet, playing frivolous or deleterious games of chance, and amusing himself vainly in the nearest big town. Occasionally he spends a while in being horribly frightened over the enemy's lines." In all the air services, then, much of an airman's life was spent in the clublike atmosphere of the *Kasino;* with smoking, which medical authorities noted had become "almost universal" among those in uniform, and also with drinking, which the same authorities insisted "should never be used for the purpose of stimulation, either before or after a flight." There was usually a record player, but its music served only as backdrop to talk, card games, and coltish pranks and scuffles. Alan Bott tried to recapture the din that reigned among airmen at their leisure:

From the babel of yarning emerges the voice of our licensed liar:

"So I told the general he was the sort of bloke who ate tripe and gargled with his beer."

"Flush," calls a poker player.

"Give us a kiss, give us a kiss, by wireless," pleads the gramophone.

"Good-night, chaps," this from a departing guest.

"Chorus—"Good night, old bean."

There was endless conversation, often about men who were or who had been in the unit; about Lieutenant Lentz, who always came out of air battles unscathed, and whom everyone referred to as "the virgin"; or about the curious end of Maréchal des logis Moissinac, killed in an air battle along the Aisne: his Spad made a perfect landing and brought its dead pilot up to the gates of a little country cemetery; there his comrades buried him. When the weather was not too bad there were sports—venerable ones like tennis and soccer, but also improvised ones like rat-hunting with sticks. Not surprisingly, airplanes often figured in the diversions. André Duvau recalled sitting in the escadrille bar one winter afternoon and watching planes land on their snow-covered field— a risky enterprise, since the pilots could not judge how close they were to the ground. The men in the bar passed the afternoon placing bets on whether a plane would crash or not.[11]

The unit often had one or more non-human members who were also the object of much interest and concern. The R.A.F. authorized the periodic issue of a bar of soap for washing a squadron's "war dog." But the squadrons and escadrilles had as mascots an amazing variety of fauna: foxes, boars, goats, squirrels, geese, and even lions. When an American journalist visited a German Fliegerabteilung that had made a home for itself in a Polish vodka distillery, he was urged to interview "Icarus," the most distinguished flyer in the unit. Icarus proved to be a plump, much-pampered dachshund who had in fact logged considerable air time on bombing missions. In addition to Icarus, the airmen kept a *Lieblingsapparat,* a "pet" airplane; having survived many missions, it had been restored and put on semi-retired status.[12]

Visitors seldom failed to notice and comment on the casual nature and endless variety of the airmen's dress. This idiosyncracy of the flying fraternity was well known to army authorities and the subject of stern memoranda—yet aviators continued to fly,

and occasionally be shot down and taken prisoner, wearing pajamas or tennis flannels. American pilots with the A.E.F. lost no
time adopting the dress habits of their British and French com-
rades-in-arms; among the American military the two groups which
presented the worst appearance were "the airmen—and the chaplains." The aviators were in a sense justified in improvising, since
their uniforms were usually ill suited for flying—the high "choke"
collar of the American tunic would soon rub a fighter pilot's neck
raw, as he constantly turned his head to look in one direction,
then another. Then, too, operational altitudes moved up towards
20,000 feet, but heated flying suits did not appear until near
the end of the war. Other habits among the airmen were less
easy to defend: there was the *Kampfeinsitzer-Frisur,* wearing one's
hair "fighter pilot style." This involved greasing the hair and
combing it straight back, giving the appearance of a man perpetually facing into a strong gale. French airmen were much taken
with the Sam Browne belt (Guynemer was once photographed
wearing the belt backwards). The British Air Ministry's weekly
orders toward the end of the war reminded flying officers that
they were not authorized to wear the Italian Fatiche di Guerra
medal nor the American Military Society badge known as "the
Order of the Dragon"; the airmen were also told not to salute
with the wrist bent, or in a "perfunctory or cursory" manner.[13]

The visitor was almost always struck by the informality, the
casual, egalitarian atmosphere that reigned among airmen at their
leisure. In French escadrilles the *tutoiement* (informal manner of
address) was almost universal. When the aviator introduced himself he rarely bothered to mention his rank, and more often than
not his attire gave no clue in this regard. Yet the airmen lived
in a hierarchical order, each holding a rank for which there was
no badge. The unit's flying personnel were its aristocracy; at the
outset the elite among them were those who had the most experience flying, the *Friedensflieger;* thereafter one's status was based
more upon the amount of combat flying he had seen. In German
units the more experienced and successful aviators were called
Kanonen, and exaggerated stress was placed on their age and length
of time in the unit; the Germans used the term *uralt,* ancient, to
describe a veteran flyer, who might be in his late twenties. In
fighter squadrons it was much simpler to establish the hierarchy
because it rested largely on the number of victories, with the
aces, the *grosse Kanonen,* at the top. At the other end of the hierar-

chy was the newcomer to the front. Among Italian airmen he
was called a *pivello*, a young innocent; in German he was a *Häschen*,
a little rabbit. In the Royal Flying Corps the fledgling pilot was
called a quirk, or, curiously, a Hun.[14]

A new arrival underwent a time of testing, and usually accep-
tance was gradual. A French fighter pilot complained: "Everything
would be fine if we could get stable and homogeneous patrol
groups, made up of pilots who are used to one another and always
work together. But as soon as a plane is missing there has to be
a replacement. No matter how good he is, the new man destroys
the harmony and the perfect understanding of the team." The
new man often inherited the least desirable lodgings, the most
obnoxious roommate, and the oldest airplane on the unit's inven-
tory. If he were a new observer or machine gunner, there was a
good chance he would be paired with the most inept pilot. If he
were himself the pilot, he would probably make his first flight
under close scrutiny, carrying ballast rather than a passenger,
which for the official record would be entered as "Lieutenant
Sandbags." It was often noted that the highest casualties came
among the novices in a squadron, and one's chances improved
thereafter. It is usually assumed that this was a consequence of
increased flying and fighting skills, but it may be that in some
subtle way one's chances also increased because he had been accepted and incorporated into the group—and knew it.[15]

Hardly had the most recent arrival ceased to be called "the
new man" than still another replacement appeared, for the turnover in the personnel of frontline units was usually steady and
sizable. Escadrille Spa 3, "the Storks," had a complement of 6
pilots in 1914, increased to 18 by the end of the war; it carried
on its wartime roster the names of no fewer than 123 pilots.
The bulk of the replacements were not for pilots killed in action—
the escadrille had less than a score of those—but for men who
transferred to other escadrilles, or to ground service, or who went
to the rear for medical treatment and subsequent reassignment;
and during the war the Storks had no fewer than 8 commanders.
Thus it was possible for two former Storks to meet after the war
and discover they had no common acquaintances in the
escadrille.[16]

Despite the turnover in personnel, what could be called
"squadron feeling" was generally strong. "The men in it change
frequently," a pilot recorded, "but the community lives on as a

cut-off little world." "It is touching," wrote another, "to see the haste with which a pilot who lost his way gets word to his escadrille that he is all right." When Hubert Griffith was hospitalized after a crash, the separation from his comrades was very painful: "I missed every hour that I spent away from the squadron. I wanted to hear its latest news and its gossip, and be a normal part of its life again." And perhaps the most eloquent testimony to the solidarity that bound the airmen together was the collective refusal of the pilots of Escadrille Spa 48 to accept transfers to other escadrilles, even though they were promised promotions for doing so; what is more, they threatened to "turn in their stripes" if the authorities persisted in dissolving the escadrille.

Much has been made of the flyer's individualism, which could manifest itself freely in the tolerant atmosphere of the squadron; the quirks and idiosyncrasies of some of the more celebrated airmen are well known to students of World War I aviation. Even officialdom made concessions to the airmen's whims, concessions that had no parallel in the ground services. In most air services the "personalizing" of aircraft had official sanction. In French escadrilles and Italian squadriglie the pilot or crew of each plane chose a personal symbol in addition to the unit's emblem; Francesco Baracca, for example, chose a black horse rampant. The choice was sometimes humorous, sometimes macabre, occasionally downright bizarre. Lieutenant Léon Bourgade, who had interrupted his seminary studies to become a French fighter ace with 28 victories, named his Spad "Saint Theresa" and decorated it with the Sacred Heart. Some German fighter pilots chose distinctive paint schemes for their planes, with the scarlet fighter of Manfred von Richthofen being perhaps the most famous.[18]

But individualism had its limits. In the British service, for example, it did not take on such flamboyant forms as customized paint schemes. Billy Bishop recalled: "We wanted to paint our machines, too, but our budding notions were frowned upon by the higher officers of the Corps." But other British pilots felt the German custom of putting their planes "in gaudy dress" was in poor taste: "It is like going out to shoot birds of paradise," said one R.F.C. pilot; another complained "they spoil the sky." At bottom such manifestations worked against the collective identity, the "squadron feeling." The British were the most anxious not to let the individual diminish the image of the group to which he belonged, but the danger was recognized in the other air services as well when individual aces became popular cult figures. And within the squadrons, with their intense collective life, the extreme individualist—the loner—usually did not linger for long. As a rule, one joined the group or one was frozen out and moved on.[19]

The "squadron feeling" was not always one of harmony. Frequently there was a certain tension in the mess or the *Kasino;* jealousies and animosities were easily perpetuated in its hot-house atmosphere. Some of the more celebrated pilots were not easy to get along with: Billy Bishop often had strained relations with other squadron members, and Jean Navarre, the *enfant terrible* of the French fighter arm, possessed a "difficult" personality. Frank Luke, the "Arizona balloon-buster" and second-ranking American ace, has been described as "moody, withdrawn, at odds with his squadron mates." In the Lafayette Escadrille, Weston Bert Hall was a constant source of irritation. According to the unit's most recent historian "his basic problem was an abrasive, almost repulsive personality that made him something of a misfit among his more cultured colleagues." He was finally "asked to leave" the escadrille.[20]

Sometimes a unit contained a pariah, ostracized because his comrades suspected him of cowardice. There were stories of pilots whose planes frequently suffered a mysterious engine malfunction which obliged them to turn back just before crossing the enemy lines—and there were vague rumors of such men being shot out of the sky by their own exasperated comrades. Sergeant Lefoy was one such—a perpetually fearful man, one of two that Jean Puistienne encountered in the service. The sergeant never climbed into a plane without a crash helmet, which made him an object of ridicule. "But," wrote Puistienne, "Lefoy's prudence is not so funny for those who fly patrol with him. They start out three and before they reach the enemy lines they are two. Lefoy had his motor pack up or it started misfiring in an alarming way, and he 'thought he ought to turn back.'" The escadrille finally got rid of him; when his colleagues took to sending his name in as a volunteer for every dangerous mission, he asked for a transfer.[21]

Inevitably there were antagonisms between the leader and those he led, and these too tended to be exacerbated by daily contact in the closed world of the escadrille. Jean Puistienne found the chief of his escadrille somehow deficient in character: "He lacks that essence which characterizes 'leaders of men.' It is a rare and indefinable essence, a mixture of authority, of decisiveness and of optimism which gives an escadrille a kind of faith and confidence that reinforces the individual fortitude of the pilots." André Duvau's complaints about the leader of his bombing escadrille were more precise: "In the air he was not a good group leader. He made us climb to altitude too close to the lines, thus advertising our presence; he wasted too much time over the objective. In a word, he maneuvered stupidly and dangerously and to no purpose. One day after we had dropped our bombs he made a turn that was far too wide to suit us. The rest of us banked short and left him trailing behind. When we got back he was extremely angry and threatened us with punishment if it happened again; but he understood the lesson." And the leaders also had their resentments. Early in 1918 the German ace Rudolf Berthold confided to his diary the problems he was having with his Geschwader: "Instead of cooperation I encounter nothing but difficulties. It's odious and its wearing me down. The *Staffelführer* [squadron leaders] have organized some sort of plot to bring me down."[22]

Of all the relationships among airmen, the most critical were those between the two men who flew a two-seater airplane. In the French and British services, in which the observer or machine gunner was the junior member of the duo, his situation could be very unenviable, and he was ill-placed to change it. Hubert Griffith, for example, spoke of the "very real agonies of an experienced observer allotted to a dud pilot to contend with." A British medical study noted that many observers decided to become pilots in order to get away from an inept flying partner, and in doing so "have probably been saved from a nervous breakdown." André Duvau apparently had a string of bad pilots—his war record consisted of 47 bombing missions made with 10 different pilots. Each time the change was a delicate affair, requiring the support of the chief of his escadre.[23]

In the German system, in which the observer was the senior officer, there were also problems; for example, Franz Schlenstedt served grudgingly as the pilot for an enthusiastic Staffelführer who so overloaded their plane with bombs that each takeoff was traumatic. Occasionally there was a violent rupture: In May 1917, in a duel between French and German two-seater planes that took place on the Allied side of the line, the German plane took hits that disabled its motor. The Frenchmen followed the German plane as it spiraled down, and were astonished to see one of the occupants come flying out at a height of 200 meters. The German pilot, who remained on board, brought the plane down without serious mishap. Under interrogation he said that the officer-observer, who had been wounded in the air battle, ordered him to bring the plane down immediately so he could have medical attention. The pilot had refused, believing he could glide back to the German lines. With the motor off the two men became engaged in a violent argument. Then the officer leaned forward and began to strangle the pilot, who was forced to abandon the controls, turn around in his cockpit, and grapple with his attacker, finally throwing him from the plane.[24]

In general, however, the pilot-observer relationship was one unmarred by such antipathies. By one means or another the air crews sorted themselves out; compatible partners came together and stayed together. A German airman said the relationship was a "telepathic friendship;" for in the air, when conversation was impossible, one partner seemed to know what the other was thinking. Hubert Griffith spoke of the relationship as "peculiar, subtle, and binding." In some cases pilot and observer opened each other's mail, in others they arranged to take their leaves together. So strong was the bond that the Germans referred to it as a *Fliegerehe*, a flyer's marriage. And there were more than a few cases where this friendship stood even the test of death. The German ace Hans Buddecke remembered vividly the fate of a British two-seater and its crew: "Lawrence used the last ebbing strength in his body to bring his observer safely to earth, but the observer was already dead."[25]

Walter Kröger and his observer had a partnership like that; they were a skilled and highly efficient team, and in the spring of 1918 they succeeded in taking their high-flying Rumpler reconnaissance plane across Paris in a daring daylight flight. They had carefully devised a scenario to save them from the French Spads that frequently tried to intercept them. Kröger would *spiralisieren*, take evasive maneuvers sufficient to throw off the aim of the French fighter pilots, but not so violent that his observer could not bring his machine gun to bear with some effect. Then, one day in September 1918, when they found a half dozen Spads blocking their route, Kröger flew the Rumpler straight into the waiting swarm. Within a matter of seconds the Rumpler was a burning wreck, its crew saved by their recently issued parachutes.

Kröger was dumbfounded when his opened, for he had not re-membered he had one when he jumped from the plane; nor could he remember much that happened before that.[26]

Kröger was *abgekämpft*, the victim of a subtle, erosive force at work in every flying unit at the front, one that led a man to neglect his duty, jeopardize the lives of his friends, and ultimately lose his own. The phenomenon was not yet known as combat fatigue and its cause was much debated (the British, who called it "staleness," thought it might be brought on by oxygen starvation associated with high altitude flying). Kröger had what would today be considered classic symptoms: at the end of 1917 his hands began to tremble, so badly that he had to use two hands to bring a cup to his mouth; he found it impossible to get to sleep without taking a drink, and by the summer of 1918 he could sleep for no more than two or three hours at a time. He had carried out his last flight as if in a trance; when he saw the Spads ahead of him, the danger just didn't register. One did not have to look far in any air service to find such worn-out aviators. A medical examination of 92 men flying for the French Second Army in 1918 led to 15 of their number being declared unfit for further combat service. The numbers of airmen withdrawn from the front for this reason must have been considerable, but statistics for this category of casualty are lacking.[27]

The sheer physical fatigue that came from flying could quickly wear a man down, something not easy to understand for those of us who fly cosseted in the passenger cabin of a jet liner. First of all there was the thunderous, deafening noise of a motor three or four feet away, running at full regime with no trace of a muffler. Then there was the gale-force wind in one's face, laced with engine fumes if the motor were in front, and with a spray of castor oil if it were a rotary; at altitude the stream of air was glacial, and the open, unheated cockpit offered little protection. The aviator's seat was a primitive wicker affair, and it was not adjustable. Con-trols were temperamental and sometimes required brutish strength. There were no trim tabs to "set" the plane for steady flight; if it had a rotary engine, the pilot would have to compensate continually for the torque effect. After two or three hours of such flying, even on uneventful missions, it would sometimes be all a man could do to climb out of the cockpit. Then there was the stress that came from frequent brushes with violent death. In the summer of 1918 Kröger's unit suffered a series of calamities:

first their airfield was shot up by British fighters who suddenly appeared out of nowhere; then a pilot was killed within sight of the field when a brand new plane inexplicably broke up in the air; then two airmen were forced to bail out of their plane, once more within sight of the field—one was saved by his parachute, the other plummeted to his death when his failed to open. Kröger and his comrades had to search for the body, which took several days; then they attended their third funeral in a matter of days. When it was over the morale of Fliegerabteilung (A) 263 was so shattered that the whole unit was briefly withdrawn from operations.[28]

Death was a frequent visitor to the squadrons, where his passage left its mark. The sudden removal of one man from an intimate group of a dozen was often traumatic for the survivors. Sometimes they knew his fate—someone had seen his fall—but often he just failed to come back, and his comrades waited for a telephone call saying he had been obliged to land elsewhere, then for word from army headquarters that he and his plane had been found—then finally for word from the enemy, who was generally scrupulous about such things. And sometimes they never heard, neither plane nor pilot ever being found. For an appreciable time the missing man's things might be left for his return, and no one would sit in "his" chair. Then one day his replacement would arrive. Jean Puistienne noted in his diary for September 12, 1918, "Three new comrades have arrived to replace—the others. Now that I'm an 'old pilot,' I understand what it was in those looks that troubled me when I was 'the pilot who just arrived.' " To be sure, it wasn't always like that. If a unit were heavily engaged, with one mission after another, one had little time to grieve over a succession of casualties, though later, in time of leisure, the losses might be keenly felt. Historian Philip Flammer cited the case of a pilot named Edward Hinkle, who was once missing from Escadrille N. 124 for 24 hours: "When he returned to the N. 124 he found his possessions already divided up among his comrades. The man inheriting his best uniform had already lengthened the sleeves."[29]

Inevitably, the death of a comrade was a sober reminder of one's own likely fate. Harold Rosher, an R.N.A.S. pilot who normally sent humorous letters to his mother, wrote in another vein after hearing of the deaths of several friends: "If one goes on flying long enough, one is bound to get huffed in the end." His letter was dated February 9, 1916; he met his death 18 days later. And when in combat an enemy spun down out of control, that too compelled a man to reflect. Italian pilots, seeing an enemy falling to his doom, sometimes saluted him with the phrase: *"oggi a te, domani a me"*—"You today, me tomorrow."[30]

There were those who felt survival was a process of living by short stages: "if you can make it one week, you can make it two; if you can make it two, you can make it a month." Others found relief in banning such speculation from their minds; when veteran British airmen were asked what qualities an aviator needed, they often listed "lack of imagination," and by that they may have meant a merciful absence of the speculative faculty, and a habit of living only with the here and the now. "We lived supremely in the moment," Cecil Lewis recalled. "Our preoccupation was the next patrol, our horizon the next leave. Sometimes, jokingly, as one discusses winning the Derby Sweep, we would plan our lives 'after the war.' But it had no substantial significance. It was a dream, conjecturable as heaven, resembling no life we knew."[31]

There were others who placed their hopes in cheating death or charming it away. Aviators who were about to go on leave were regarded as prime candidates for fatal calamities, as if death found some grim humor in taking them just as respite was at hand. The solution was to excuse a man from flying just before he was to leave, and this custom became general. There were airmen who felt they were protected by charms or talismans or rituals. There were also believers in such things in the trenches— the taboo against lighting three cigarettes from one match was born there—but the airmen seem to have been particularly suscep- tible. "In no other arm of the service is there so much superstition as among the flyers," acknowledged one German pilot. Another confessed his life was governed by talismans and taboos, especially the latter: "I never allowed myself to be photographed before I took off—I never looked at a machine which had been shot down in flames—I did not wish a comrade "Good Luck" before he took off, but *"Hals und Beinbruch"* [Break your neck and legs]—I swore by my lucky numbers, 7, 3, 5, and 13."[32]

In Walter Kröger's unit every man carried some object that protected his life. Bülow never flew without a medallion given to him by his mother; Baron von Seydlitz always carried a silver cigarette case bearing his family's coat of arms; "other men had horseshoes, cloth dolls, little teddy bears, and some carried things

that they kept secret, for according to them, if they were shown
or talked about, that would be a sort of profanation." Kröger
continued: "One may think what he will about such strange habits,
but they undoubtedly had a positive effect. They raised self-confidence, they strengthened the spirit, they helped us get through
times of fear; they supported us and spurred us on to greater
achievements and even to prodigies of daring!"[33]

Kröger himself offered an example of the sort of blind trust
one could place in a good-luck piece. One day, just as he was
heading across the lines on a mission, his motor began to cough
and miss. He turned around and barely made it back to the field,
where mechanics swarmed over his plane. Suddenly Kröger recalled that he had left behind his lucky five-mark piece. He ran
to his quarters for the coin, then back to his plane, where the
mechanics told him they had not been able to find the trouble.
He waved them out of the way and took off again, his engine
running flawlessly now, as it continued to do the entire mission.
Such a story would not have raised eyebrows in the squadron
mess, it simply confirmed what was generally known and accepted
by everyone in aviation—including officialdom. Hubert Griffith
recalled that once "in some mess skirmish or other" he had broken
a silver ring he always wore: "I had come, rightly or wrongly, to
regard it as an omen of luck. I had gone straight to the Squadron-
Commander, and had said that I didn't want to be on the flying-
programme next day till after the ring had been mended in the
squadron workshops. He agreed in full seriousness to this gro-
tesque proposition."[34]

But there were also malignant signs and omens of disaster.
In the Lafayette Escadrille they repeated the story of a crippled
puppy named Archie who put a curse on anyone who adopted
him, and thus caused the deaths of three pilots. Some men knew
or thought they knew when their luck had changed for the worse,
and they prepared for it. A man of disorderly habits would be
shot down, and his comrades would discover that he had put all
his affairs in order. Captain René Doumer decided that his time
was coming and took measures accordingly. His comrades in Escadrille N.76 noticed that he began to fly missions in his dress
uniform, wearing all his decorations. He did not fly like that for
long; on April 27, 1917 he met death at the hands of Oberleutnant
Hahn of Jagdstaffel 19.[35]

But in most cases a man held on to hope. He flew on, sustained by the silver five-mark piece in his pocket or buoyed by the knowledge that it was Friday, a day which had always been lucky for him. Then one day he was gone, without fanfare and without farewell. Georges Guynemer confessed that just before he took off he always made a little sign with his hand to the ground crew standing by his plane. They took it as a casual "see you later," but he also meant it as a discreet "goodbye." And occasionally a man would leave a note behind, a few unpretentious lines, all the more moving for their simplicity. A French lieutenant named Penigaud prepared such a note before he took off for the last time on July 28, 1918:

> Dear Friends:
>
> Since you are reading this, you know that I've cashed in my chips. My turn was a long time coming. In the end it was bound to come. Well, too bad.
>
> Don't feel sorry for me, there's no need. Just remember that I tried to do my job as best I could, and that I did it in the best of company, among comrades who set me a good example. These few lines are just to thank you and to say goodbye. . . .[36]

=9=

A New Breed of
Heroes

"South of Dixude, aviator Lieutenant Garros brought down an Aviatik with shots from a machine gun." This brief notice in the French Army's morning communiqué for April 2, 1915, picked up and amplified by the Paris press, had considerable repercussions on French aeronautical circles and among the public as well. Roland Garros was a well-known aviator before the war and the first to fly across the Mediterranean in 1913. Now, having mounted a machine gun on his Morane monoplane, Garros was one of the pioneers in the art of aerial combat. His name came to public attention again and again as he shot down a second and a third German plane, and then was himself forced down and taken prisoner—all in the month of April, 1915.

Roland Garros was one of an initial group of aerial "heroes" produced in the first months of the war. Most of them, like Garros, had names already familiar to the public because of their prewar exploits. There was Garros' fellow-countryman Adolphe Pégoud, who had been the first man to loop the loop and the first to parachute from an airplane, and who became newsworthy again when he too began destroying German planes in the air. Then,

151

late in August, 1914, newspapers all over Europe noted the death of the well-known Russian aviator P. N. Nesterov. On August 26, near the Polish town of Lvov, Nesterov brought about his own death and that of an Austrian pilot named Baron Rosenthal when he deliberately rammed the Austrian's plane. Shortly thereafter the German public learned that Lieutenant von Hiddessen, a well-known *Friedensflieger* and the first German pilot to transport air mail, had again distinguished himself with a daring flight across Paris.[1]

Despite these highly publicized accomplishments, there was much complaint in the early months of the war over the dearth of information on aerial activity, and particularly on the achievements of individual aviators. Much of the complaining was from the editors of aeronautical journals, but the press generally sought more news as well, claiming the public wanted it. In September the editor of *The Aeroplane* protested: "We have been told absolutely nothing about the doings of the Royal Flying Corps, or of the Royal Naval Air Service." In France, too, there were complaints, for the journal *Flight* noted in November: "A considerable amount of criticism having been levelled at the lack of news from the aviation branch of the French Army, an official note was issued in Paris on November 8th." And in Russia an aviation enthusiast named P. Kritskii lamented the fact that "little is said and little is heard about military aviators." To remedy this lack of information, Kritskii published brief sketches of Nesterov and other Russian airmen of note.[2]

What angered the partisans of aeronautics, and eventually the press and public as well, was the policy followed by most belligerents of not identifying individual combatants by anything more than their last initial—consequently, combat accounts were filled with references to "Lieutenant M." and "Corporal E." There were two major exceptions to this rule: the first, that the cloak of anonymity would be removed if a man had done something sufficiently distinguished to be "mentioned in despatches," to use the British term. The German Army occasionally published names in its daily *Heeresbericht,* as did the French High Command in its communiqué on operations issued twice a day; but giving a man's name and his achievement—as the French did in the case of Roland Garros—was exceptional, and indeed being mentioned in despatches was a distinction akin to receiving a decoration. The other exception was when a man was in fact decorated. Then his name and achievements were made known to the public; the distinction was greater, but it was usually slower in coming, for there was considerable paper work, and the periodic honors lists tended to appear long after the event.

From the very beginning of the conflict, prominent figures called for special rewards and distinctions for airmen, among them H. G. Wells: "Every aviator who goes up to fight, I don't mean to reconnoitre but to fight, will fight all the more gladly with two kindred alternatives in his mind, a knighthood or the prompt payment of a generous life assurance policy to his people. Every man who goes up and destroys either an aeroplane or a Zeppelin in the air should, I hold, have a knighthood if he gets down alive." André Michelin had a different approach. In August, 1914 he announced that he was setting up a fund of a million francs from which to reward aviators who distinguished themselves. Pirelli, the Italian tiremaker, created a similar system of prizes. In both France and England cash awards were offered to the first airmen who would bring down a German dirigible. A wealthy American offered—and the French government accepted—10,000 francs "to be given in gifts of 1,000 francs to the first 10 aviators to bring down enemy planes beginning on June 2, 1916."

There was considerable discussion about the wisdom of offering such awards. Some argued that they were scarcely different from the peacetime prizes which had done so much to encourage aeronautical achievement, and some claimed that the awards could be compared with "prize" money given to sailors for capturing enemy ships. But others, especially prominent military figures, were indignant at the idea of offering men in uniform special rewards for doing what was after all their duty. When a wealthy citizen of Birmingham offered to pay £500 to any British airman who brought a Zeppelin down within five miles of the city, the editor of *Aeronautics* wrote: "Never was a more dire insult offered to a brave body of men." But prizes continued to be offered—and paid—until the British government prohibited the practice late in 1916; the French followed suit at the end of 1917.[3]

The airmen continued to receive gifts, often as a result of campaigns on their behalf. In 1916 it was fashionable for well-to-do Frenchwomen to offer their furs, which were then made into flight apparel; in Russia the Tsarina led a drive to provide aviators with warm clothing. Communities and professional and civic organizations found their own ways to pay tribute to the airmen. The British fighter pilot Albert Ball was given the freedom of Nottingham; inhabitants of a small village in Essex took up a subscription and presented three British aviators with silver cups, "suitably inscribed," for having destroyed German dirigibles. German industrialists presented a silver *Ehrenbecher* or trophy cup to each German aviator who downed an enemy. The Aero Club of France, which had presented gold medals for achievements in aeronautics before the war, now began to present them to pilots in the French air service; the Aero Club of America commissioned a medal for presentation to the most notable Allied aviators. The new decoration portrayed "the tenth muse—that of the air."[4]

By 1916 the names of the most accomplished airmen were becoming public property in most countries, thanks to a more liberal policy of reporting their successes. On September 26, 1915, the *Heeresbericht* contained a notice that "south of Metz Lieutenant Boelcke, who had gone up for a test flight, brought down a Voisin airplane." At the beginning of October the bulletin contained for the first time a report on the previous month's air activity, indicating Allied air losses far greater than the German ones. Then on October 11 the *Heeresbericht* carried for the first time the name of Max Immelmann, and the information that "this officer has brought down four enemy planes." Thus a tradition was established: when a man gained his fourth aerial victory he shed his anonymity.[5]

The Germans probably took a leading role in bringing the airman to popular attention, with the Kaiser himself playing no small part; the decorations, the personal letters, and the autographed portraits of himself he addressed to young flying officers holding the rank of lieutenant or captain were given the widest press coverage. By early 1916 the British were complaining that in trumpeting the successes of their airmen the Germans were violating the tenets of military decorum. An indignant writer in *Aeronautics* charged that "alone among the combatants the Germans have throughout failed to comply with this tacit rule of aerial etiquette, so that from time to time we find main headquarters pompously announcing that Lieutenant So-and-so on the previous day shot down his seventh aeroplane." But the French soon followed the German lead; airmen began to appear in the communiqué regularly in the summer of 1916, and not long afterward the French began to issue highly favorable reports of aerial activity.[6]

British authorities steadfastly resisted this tendency to personalize and popularize the air war. The issue boiled up in Parliament several times. In debates in the House of Commons in July 1916, an M.P. named Sir A. Markham demanded to know "why the name of the young aviator who shot down Immelmann, the Fokker champion, had been suppressed by the Press Bureau, and why the names of airmen who had distinguished themselves were not allowed to appear in the press." A government spokesman insisted British aviators themselves had approved the government's policy, and that they did not want their names put in the newspapers. Some observers, however, felt the flyers were all too hungry for acclaim. An anonymous writer signing himself "Berkeley" felt obliged to lecture the airmen on the necessity of contributing to the distinction of the corps, rather than seeking honors for one's self—an obligation that might not be well understood in "the newer units in the service." Others complained, especially in the aeronautical journals, that among the aviators of all the belligerents the British airman alone had his deeds unnoticed and unsung: "According to our present method of procedure," lamented a correspondent of *Aeronautics*, "it will be left to some bespectacled German professor a hundred years hence, to bring to the light the story of our aerial prowess." In fact that was not to be the case; by one means or another, through disclosures in parliamentary debates or in leaks and indiscretions of both press and officialdom, the names of the most successful British airmen became known to the British people; during the Battle of the Somme, for example, they learned the names and exploits of Albert Ball and James McCudden.[7]

Journalists played an important role in throwing the airman and the air war into high relief. From the first they tended to treat aerial activity as though it were a separate conflict; many newspapers used a special rubric dedicated to the "air war." More liberal press policies enabled them to humanize the struggle in the air, giving the aviator a name and a face. Then, too, as the tempo of the air war increased, there was a steady stream of reportage, and a succession of names and faces. The *New York World* sent the eminent journalist Herbert Bayard Swope to interview Captain Oswald Boelcke; the French daily *Le Figaro* gave its enthralled readers a close look at Georges Guynemer: "The young hero cannot stay still. He sits down, he gets up, he walks about, he sits down again, all the time telling about his exploits in pieces and snatches, as if he were talking about a football game or a hunting episode."[8]

Journalistic portraits of the airmen were often somewhat colored. There was the cool nonchalance of their bravery: "They mount their saddles in the morning, after a cigarette or two, as though they were just taking a taxi-cab to Picadilly Circus instead of mounting on frail wings into a wind-driven sky. . . ." Quite early journalists hit upon the difference between the airman's war and the contest on the ground. The air war was somehow "cleaner"; the airmen fought as individuals, in a realm where each could see and take the measure of his opponent. The aerial protagonists were more sporting, more knightly—for the chivalric theme was already in full flower in 1916. At the same time the unusual risks and perils of war in the air required a special courage of those who fought there and rendered them worthy of a special admiration. "If such fighters cry out," intoned a *New York Times* journalist, "their shrieks are only a whisper in that limitless space, until now a solitude. If those who come back alive from such experiences feel henceforth that they are a little apart and resplendent, touched with the radiance of that thinner upper air, who will care to deny them?" Thanks to such flattering portraits, aviators began to find themselves and their activities of consuming interest to the public. "Get on a train or a subway car," wrote Jacques Mortane, "and you will see that a pilot who has been decorated draws more attention than a man from any of the other services who wears the same decorations." Nor was that all. A French aviator confided to a friend in the infantry: "Ah, the girls, old man, once you've got those wings on your sleeve you can have as many as you want."[9]

Yet, some aviators were troubled by the distorted images that were being projected, and by the exaggerated notions widely current about their lives and their work. Hans Buddecke insisted that "only in books will you find that aviators begin the most demanding mission with a flippant remark. We know better than that." Alan Bott was troubled by what he called "the exaggerative ecstasies indulged in by many civilians when discussing the air services." He was also disturbed by excessively laudatory speeches in Parliament in which the airmen were hailed as "the superheroes of the war." Bott regarded journalists as major purveyors of the "exaggerative ecstasies." He explained in a letter to a friend that the term "intrepid birdmen" was simply "war correspondentese" for flying officers. Yet few airmen took up the pen in order to correct the picture, and some of those who wrote accounts of the air war contributed to the accumulating mythology; to be sure, those who wrote during the war itself did so under the restraints of censorship, while memoirs written after the war were often tinted with nostalgia. As a rule, the most successful books were those that catered to the reader's tastes, rather than trying to reeducate him.[10]

In official circles there was some concern that all the favorable publicity received by the air service would produce resentment and demoralization in the ground forces. In point of fact it probably exacerbated resentments already present; in the trenches there was an image of the airman from the outset, and it was not necessarily a flattering one. Eric J. Leed has demonstrated that the soldier in the lines found the situation of the aviator flying above him infinitely superior to his own: the airmen can fly over all obstacles, they "can see their work with their own eyes. They need not shoot into uncertainty and lie in wait month after month for an invisible opponent." Less abstract were the observations of a French soldier: " 'Oh, those aviators, they have it all!' That's what the anonymous, mud-covered and miserable *poilu* says down in the bottom of his trench when he finds in his newspaper a whole column dedicated to the latest exploit of one of our aces. And it's not just personal glory that the aviators enjoy. The way they live, why, between fights they can have hours of real rest, of complete relaxation, which is so exceptional for a man in the lines. They have comfortable billets near towns, where there is wine, civilians . . . and civilian women."[11]

The men in the trenches nursed their own myths about the airmen. First of all there was the *vie de château*, the comfortable existence the aviators lived, quartered in some sumptuous chateau, with clean sheets, haute cuisine, and the *châtelaine* herself looking to their every need. It was widely believed in the trenches that the airmen were constantly mentioned in despatches and that they had an easier path to promotion and took the lion's share of the decorations. Such complaints were not entirely without foundation: the flying personnel of the German Army reached a maximum strength of 5,000 in 1918, just over one-tenth of one percent of the Army's 4.5 million officers and men—yet, the airmen claimed 12 percent of the 687 Pour le mérite awards made during the war. Such resentments, which built up during the war were added to another, older one dating from peacetime, and that concerned the airman's special flight pay. Small wonder that Jacques Boulenger, who went from the trenches to the French Air Service, confessed in his memoirs: "When I was a footsoldier I couldn't stand aviators either."[12]

But in truth the ground soldier's view of the airman was a complex thing, involving more than simple envy. The infantry often accused the airmen of not being around when needed and more explicitly of avoiding a fight. In a tight spot one could always get a laugh from the British Tommy by shouting "Has anyone seen an airman?" Among Italian soldiers there was a widely repeated jingle:

> The flyer is a man
> who dashes through the skies.
> But once the enemy shows,
> He's gone within a trice.

But then it was a habit of mind in the infantry to feel neglected or abandoned by all the other arms and services, including the artillery and the supply corps. And there is the reverse side of the coin: when friendly planes were present and visibly so over ground troops—and especially toward the end of the war, when air-ground cooperation became more critical—their presence was clearly appreciated. General Keller recalled that when Kampfgeschwader 1 passed over the German front line positions, flying in close formation some 30 or 40 strong, "many a gray-clad soldier signalled to us from his dugout." And one day in 1916 the airmen of Escadrille C. 51 received a curious letter from a group of *poilus* in the front lines: "We infantrymen here in our holes watch you all the time. We see everything you do. You are our gods, our protectors. When a day passes and we don't see you, we are like children whose mama hasn't given them any dessert."[13]

The public, too, needed its gods, its heroes, but at first was hard put to find them. For the generation of 1914, which had on its parlor walls engravings of "The Last Cartridge" and "The Thin Red Line Tipped with Steel," the word "war" conjured up stirring images of martial prowess and *panache*. The war they came to know must have seemed a monstrous aberration, with the individual disappearing into the mass, and the masses trading ponderous and indiscriminate blows; death was anonymous and the sacrifices were made collectively. Such battles were not made for individual feats of heroism that could fire the public's imagination. It was fitting that in the end the highest honor was paid to a faceless symbol, the unknown soldier.

But that was the land war. In the sea war the Germans could fashion heroes from their U-boat captains. They had faces and names and discernible, measurable accomplishments in tonnages sunk; here were possibilities that government propagandists were quick to exploit. But paradoxically it was left to the newest arm to supply a hero from the classic mold in the person of the fighter pilot.

The destruction of an enemy plane in an aerial engagement was in itself a small thing, but it was a victory with an identifiable victor, a flesh-and-blood 20-year-old who was the sole author of his triumph. An aerial victory was gratifying, then, because it was a resounding affirmation of the individual; yet at the same time it could be an affirmation of the courage and the fighting skills of the nation's youth. In General Porro's words, the air heroes served "to exalt the heroic virtue of the race," and it was to that end that the French Chamber of Deputies voted to have Guynemer's name placed in the Pantheon. Significantly, air victories were attributable to men, not to the machines they flew, as if to underline the contrast with the ground war, where deadly machines dominated; in the popular mind the ace was equated with that warrior of the pre-machine age, the knight. Then, too, there was something refreshing about having heroes who were not military professionals of high rank; it has been said, for example, that Billy Bishop was Canada's first military hero who was not a general. It seemed somehow fitting in a war of peoples to honor young men new to war; at the same time their youth and modest rank protected them from the charges of wholesale and ineffectual butchery that stained the reputations of the "higher-ups."[14]

There were other ways in which the air battles offered a refreshing contrast to the struggle on the ground. Intellectuals in the trenches who analyzed the "aberrant" nature of their war were struck by the fact that in contrast to previous conflicts, the soldiers wore inconspicuous clothing and concealed themselves in holes in the ground, seeking self-effacement, invisibility. Wilhelm von Schramm believed that this "ideal of invisibility" completed "the decay of military style and virtues begun during the

French Revolution." But 5,000 feet above the trenches there was another battlefield where the protagonists sought each other out before the eyes of countless thousands; there at least the old virtues must survive.[15]

Here the fighter pilot was destined to play a role that no other airman could, for no other aspect of aerial operations had the same drama, the same competitive edge. Thus, from at least 1916 on, air-to-air combat—"the fighter's game"—began to monopolize public attention, while a small handful of the most successful fighter pilots did in fact become the superheroes of the war. In the popular mind they *were* the air war, and still are, for that matter. An American airman explained why: "The mere conception of two opposing flyers, each controlling, through the medium of a viciously high-speed engine, a little, flimsy spiderwork of wood and linen, and fighting with machine guns two or three miles above the earth, is enough to flog the laziest imagination." As for the other branches of the air services, they remained in the shadows. The more ambitious in the bomber and observation units sought transfers to the fighter arm, and some who made the change fought their way to renown. Most stayed where they were and did what men in uniform almost invariably do—their duty, grumbling all the while. In the "caste" system, as he called it, André Duvau considered that his job as machine-gunner on a bombing plane made him "the lowest of the low." But his view would have been challenged by a British observer, who called himself an "R.F.C. doormat." In 1918 American aviation leaders became so worried about "the lack of public regard for aerial observation" that an officer was detailed to organize a publicity campaign on its behalf.[16]

There were sporadic attempts to give greater recognition to other aspects of aviation, but for the most part they had little effect. Jacques Mortane proposed according the title of "ace" to an airman who had completed 300 bombing missions; the idea was never implemented, though the Aero Club of France did present medals to veterans in bombardment units. In Germany there is some evidence of an effort to redress the balance in the matter of decorations. Late in the war the Kaiser conferred the Pour le mérite on a handful of officers from bombing and observation units and on one lone balloon observer. Even so, at war's end fighter pilots had received 59 of the 68 decorations given to members of the German Army's Air Service. There was a similar imbalance in the distribution of the French Legion of Honor. In the summer of 1917 Jacques Mortane lamented: "People are surprised if an ace doesn't have the Legion of Honor after his seventh or eighth victory, but they find it perfectly natural for a bomber pilot not to have it when he has flown eighty night missions, and for an artillery observer not to have the Médaille Militaire after eighteen months of good work day after day."[17]

Thus, honors and acclaim flowed to the fighter arm, and the public heaped adulation on those individual fighter pilots whose names and deeds were revealed to it by the press and the communiqués. If this trend had unfortunate consequences for the rest of the air service, it could also have unfortunate effects on the young airmen in the spotlight of attention. Sometimes their egos seemed to grow apace with their reputations. The term "dandy" has been applied to Francesco Baracca, and could be used to describe other aces. Manfred von Richthofen's memoirs are the work of a young man eminently satisfied with himself; the reader is impressed to learn that von Richthofen once rode horseback a distance of some 60 kilometers while suffering from a broken collar bone—but would have been more impressed had the author not told the story himself. Sholto Douglas, who read the books of both Boelcke and von Richthofen, detected in them a certain arrogance, and many other readers have put them down with a similar impression. Douglas, who was himself a fighter pilot of some accomplishment, admits that he too sometimes traded on the "young hero" image his breed enjoyed: "Some of my friends in the R.F.C. undoubtedly were heroes, and I was proud to be associated with them. I knew that we were thought of as dashing, devil-may-care types, and I must confess that we often took the bit in our teeth." Even the American Charles Nordhoff, freshly arrived as a replacement in a French fighter escadrille, resolved to change the way he dressed and acted: "Though only a beginner, a *bleu*, I am Somebody, through the mere fact of being a pilot, and most of all a *pilote de chasse*—a most chic thing to be."[18]

The military and political leaders determined that with all the problems they caused, the new air heroes had their value, and even in Great Britain the no-publicity policy seems to have been relaxed somewhat. But it was necessary to "regulate" the production of heroes; the French seem to have taken the lead with what could be called the "ace system," with rules and procedures that were copied by others, notably the Americans, the

Italians, and the Austrians. An aviator's name was published in
the communiqué when he had downed his fifth adversary; his
name and often his picture were reproduced in newspapers and
the aeronautical press, with greater details about him and his
feat. The status of "ace" which came with the fifth victory was
never an official designation, but a title accorded by press and
public. The term is often said to have originated with journalists,
but there is evidence that it was in use in the escadrilles before
it was picked up by the newspapers late in 1916. The Paris papers
used the word in quotation marks into 1917, and the British for
a time translated it as "trump." It did not come into current usage
in Great Britain during the war, and of course the British never
adopted the "system." An American fighter pilot with the R.F.C.
wrote his sister: "Quit telling me to be an "ace" because we don't
have those things in the British Army, except four in each pack
of cards."[19]

The French ace followed a sort of *cursus honorum* that brought
him the Médaille Militaire, the Croix de Guerre, and finally the
"red ribbon," the Legion of Honor. Once he had these, subsequent
victories usually brought him palms for his Croix de Guerre, and
there were fighter pilots who earned a dozen or more. But the
ace's standing and his prestige rested essentially on the number
of his aerial victories and how they compared with those of other
aces—for each victory after the fifth was publicized, and newspapers and magazines published "scorecards" with names and rank-
ings. Almost all of the names on the listings belonged to fighter
pilots, but a few French airmen got their five victories the hard
way, in bombardment or reconnaissance units. A sergeant-machine
gunner named Du Bois d'Aische accounted for six German planes,
downing one of them with a rifle, and then applied for training
as a fighter pilot. His application was approved despite the fact
that he was 45 years old.[20]

As the war intensified and as fighter units increased in number, so did the toll of aerial combat. It became easier to reach
the fabled number of four or five victories and the number of
aces grew—but the distinction and the exclusiveness of that status
declined accordingly. To combat this "inflation" the French high
command decided early in 1917 that thereafter an airman would
need 10 victories, rather than 5, to make his début in the communiqué; by the time the war ended there were plans to raise the
number to 20. Similarly, the "price" of decorations went up. The

Pour le mérite was already hedged about with restrictions—it was conferred on officers only and was not given posthumously—but as the war progressed ever greater achievements were required in order to win it. In January 1916, Boelcke and Immelmann received it after their 8th victories, but later 12 were required, then 16, and by the end of the war it took more than 20. Even privately sponsored awards were affected by this inflation. By the end of the war the *Ehrenbecher* was awarded not for one aerial victory, but for eight or nine—and it was no longer made of silver.[21]

The spread of the ace system, and the preoccupation with "scoring," no doubt had an effect on the nature and the tempo of the air war, and certainly it had the effect of escalating the number of claims made. There was a tendency from the beginning for airmen to overestimate what they had seen and what they had done—this was noticed with the first reconnaissance and bombing operations; but now the tendency increased. A procedure was developed for confirming and crediting aerial victories—what the French called *homologation*—with official forms and attestations. The authorities insisted their verification was rigorous and scrupulous, and aviators constantly protested that it was too rigorous and too scrupulous, since it denied them legitimate victories. In fact the "rules" of evidence were too lax, and a whole range of considerations, from propaganda to pilot morale to tactical consequences, kept them that way. Particularly difficult was the matter of confirming victories on the other side of the line, but if credit were not granted with enough liberality fighter pilots would lack in aggressivity, preferring to wait for enemy planes to penetrate friendly airspace, where a "kill" was easier to verify. The French discovered this tendency in 1916, and *homologation* was accordingly liberalized.

So anxious were pilots to score victories that they claimed "kills" that were not dead. R.F.C. Form W3348, used for after-action reports, stipulated that enemy planes be listed as "destroyed," "driven down," or "driven down out of control," but ultimately these distinctions became blurred, as did the meaning of the German term *zur Landung gezwungen* (forced to land). Airmen dived out of an air battle with their ammunition exhausted or to evade pursuit, and then discovered some days later with considerable indignation that they had been added to an enemy pilot's score. A French pilot named André Quennehen reported that as he flew over the German lines he shut his engine off to listen to the firing: "The next day the Boches announced in their communiqué that they had brought me down." In every air service there were rumors of fraudulent claims that somehow got official validation; one such rumor involved Billy Bishop's report that he singlehandedly attacked a German fighter field, destroying German fighters as they rose to meet him; that claim, corroborated by no other witness but endorsed by Bishop's squadron commander, got him the Victoria Cross. Occasionally outright fraud was proved. On May 22, 1916, Adjudant Réservat of Escadrille N.65 destroyed a Drachen near Verdun, then was himself shot down and taken prisoner immediately afterward. Eventually Réservat escaped and rejoined his unit, where he found that Adjudant Barrault of Escadrille N.57 had taken credit for the Drachen. After an inquiry Réservat's claim was confirmed and Barrault was sent to the infantry.[22]

A pilot could count coup on virtually anything the enemy put in the air—airplanes, observation balloons, and airships. A much-envied French ace named Georges Lefevre had among his credits the German dirigible L-49. In some air services the rules were further liberalized so that full credit would be given to anyone who took part in bringing down an enemy. The Americans used this system, with the result that in two cases a single German airplane was downed and 16 American airmen—8 pilots and 8 observers—were each given credit for an enemy plane destroyed.

There was of course no way that an accurate count of air victories could be made at the time. One could only speculate on what the discrepancy would be between wartime victory counts and postwar statistics on the other side's losses. The discrepancy proved to be quite a large one. The British claimed 7,054 victories from June 1916 to the Armistice (earlier figures were not available); the French had 2,049 *homologués* but also another 1,901 that were "certain" though not officially confirmed. The Americans claimed 756, making a grand total of 11,760 air victories. According to German postwar calculations, the number of planes lost on the Western Front was 3,000. There was also a discrepancy, though not so large, between German claims and Allied losses.[23]

Taking the figures as they are, one must conclude that there was a small aristocracy of fighter pilots who garnered the lion's share of the aerial victories and the honors that they brought in their wake.[24] According to General Christienne's calculations, the aces were only about 4 percent of French pilots, yet they accounted for 50 percent of the officially accredited victories. This group and their counterparts in other countries were indeed the superheroes of the war. Their governments placed the highest value on their services, supplying them with the most advanced fighter aircraft (sometimes a "stable" of them) and freeing them from the more mundane duties so that they could gain even more victories; yet those selfsame authorities sometimes withdrew their aces from combat, fearing among other things the effect their deaths might have on the public's morale.

For the aces were the objects of a popular cult whose dimensions have yet to be measured. Their pictures and capsule biographics appeared in newspapers and magazines. Their wartime memoirs (written with official encouragement) took an honored place in bookstores and libraries; the first two editions of von Richthofen's *Der rote Kampfflieger* (The Red Air Fighter) ran to a half-million copies, and there was even a British edition in 1918. The merest detail of the ace's life was newsworthy: every Italian boy knew that Francesco Baracca flew a Spad, while Silvio Scaroni's "mount" was a Hanriot; Frenchmen repeated over their *apéritifs* the news that the shy and awkward Georges Guynemer had also scored in Paris—with the stage queen Yvonne Printemps. If the ace's life was a matter of national interest and his career a national triumph, his death was treated as a national tragedy. Oswald Boelcke received a funeral worthy of a field marshal. A crown prince and a procession of generals stood watch over the fallen captain's bier in Cambrai Cathedral, and that bier was adorned with a floral tribute from Kaiser Wilhelm II. The date of Boelcke's death, October 28, was designated *Boelcke Tag* (Boelcke Day) and observed for a time after the war.[25]

The aces seemed to dominate the air war like titans, and after the war was over their lives and combats came to dominate the literature about it; there was—and is—a kind of timeless fascination about them. Yet they can probably be best understood as simply the most salient personalities in a larger mass—that *confrérie* to which all fighter pilots belonged, both the famous and the obscure. They were all bound by their common profession, to be sure, but also by the way they regarded that profession. They believed that they were fighting a kind of war without precedent and without parallel, and in this they were correct. Many also believed—and on occasion argued—that theirs was the highest, the most demanding form of warfare.

Sholto Douglas, looking back over the war years, wrote: "Ours was a strain of a new and peculiar temper that even now is hard to analyze." To Douglas the fighter pilot's nerves were severely tested by the frequent and wrenching change from the comfort of the squadron mess to a fierce mêlée over the front lines, all within a few minutes—to it he attributed the ulcers, the nightmares, and the insomnia that plagued young pilots. The French fighter pilot Brindejonc des Moulinais, who had flown before the war, found combat flying far more demanding; he calculated that one year as a fighter pilot equalled three of normal life. Some British statistics from 1917 seem to support the contention that life in a fighter squadron was uniquely wearing: they showed that "the estimated average effective service" of an airman in observation units was four months, and that of a day-bombing pilot three and a half months, "while the effective service of a pilot in a single-seater fighter squadron was no longer than two and a half months." This does not mean that a fighter pilot's life expectancy at the front was two and a half months, as is sometimes said. All battle casualties played a part, including those who were wounded and recovered; in addition men were lost through "sickness," embracing both organic and emotional problems, and the latter were common. Still, in relative terms, the figures attest to the special demands placed on the fighter pilot.[26]

The man who flew a fighter flew alone, without the psychological comfort of an observer or machine gunner. As he flew alone, he also fought alone (though this happened less often after fighting in formation came into fashion), and this meant that he fought without the presence of a leader or comrades to sustain him and encourage him to do his best. "He is the absolute master of his destiny," wrote a French pilot, "free to seek out the adversary, to accept combat or decline it." He could, if he wished, simply look the other way when an enemy plane crossed his line of vision, or he could decide not to investigate that distant speck in the sky—and no one would be the wiser. Thus, the fighter pilot needed initiative, and what Wedgwood Benn called "nerve." Hubert Griffith recalled an example of this nerve on a photographic mission he flew one day: he was given a single fighter to accompany him, and at a certain point the fighter pilot saw two German fighters cruising above; instantly he started up to meet them—and to meet what Griffith felt would be "certain death." Sure enough, within seconds the British fighter came spiraling down in flames. Griffith felt he had witnessed "V.C. heroism at its highest."[27]

Since the demands were great, it was only fitting that the rewards should be commensurate with the risk. "We were hoping for glory," said a French pilot, "why not admit it?" And to him and to many of his comrades, glory came in the form of a red ribbon or one's name in the fine print of a communiqué. Today it has become fashionable to regard such things with a certain cynicism, but it is unquestionable that in the Great War men fought to get them, and quite often got themselves killed in the process. In the German military there was a term, *Kreuzschmerzen,* for men who "ached" for the Iron Cross; Billy Bishop's biographer makes it clear that the Canadian ached for the Victoria Cross— probably the ultimate decoration for valor—and knew no rest until he had it. Even a citation in the communiqué or the *Heeres-bericht* was no small matter to those involved: a German pilot confessed that when his name appeared the first time he was unable to close his eyes the entire night. The day that Manfred von Richthofen's name first appeared, a neighbor came running to his parent's house, breathless with the news. When a decoration came through in the Royal Flying Corps—which was infrequent—the entire squadron celebrated. After the news came that one of his squadron mates would get the Military Cross, Arthur Lee exulted: "At long last the squadron has won a decoration!" Lee wrote his wife, "The inevitable binge is to be held tomorrow evening, as today's bar stock isn't large enough for a real occasion." And then there was the fabled *Pour le mérite,* the *nec plus ultra* of the German Air Service. Hans Buddecke recalled in his memoirs how he had returned from an air battle over the Dardanelles and was relaxing with friends at a remote Turkish airfield: "And then a soldier brought me a yellow telegram. Whoever had taken it down was no master of the German language. I couldn't make out any of it except for three words at the end that were in French: *Pour le mérite.* There it was, the Blue Max."[28]

To the fighter pilot was also reserved a reward unknown to any other category of combatant: he could draw pleasure from his work, a pleasure in some cases intense and quite probably addictive. All airmen could enjoy flying, but the fighter pilot could and did enjoy fighting. Not all fighter pilots were emotionally equipped to find that enjoyment, and in others it was largely overridden by anguish and fear—but the pleasure was incontestably there to be had. A French pilot wrote that aerial combat offered to its initiates "uncommon" pleasures: "The fighter pilot must love it for itself, for the strong and cruel joys that it reserves to its chosen." A British aviator sounded the same note: "Given a certain temperament and a certain mood, an air fight is the greatest form of sport on earth. Every atom of personality, mental and physical, is conscripted into the task." The French and Germans were right to borrow the concept of the hunt when they designated the fighter function *la chasse,* and *die Jagd,* for the anticipation and the excitement of the chase were there. Silvio Scaroni knew those emotions when he saw an Austrian plane drone towards him: "The idea of our inevitable encounter brought me to a pitch of excitement (*orgasmo*) that I fought to control." Hans Buddecke claimed that the moment at which one began the attack was "the most precious of a fighter pilot's life," for it came after hours of fruitlessly searching the whole sky, while "the neck is rubbed raw from turning and twisting and the eyes stay filled with tears from the constant looking and searching." But many pilots said they experienced a feeling of exhilaration during an air battle. One of these was Sholto Douglas. "Because of the nature of my temperament," he wrote, "I did not know the wilder sense of exhilaration that was experienced by some." Yet he "knew a certain sense of elation, almost of inspiration"; and he goes on: "As I twisted and turned and dived and zoomed and fired and was shot at, I sometimes found myself shouting absurd battle cries, and even singing at the top of my voice."[29]

Did the fighter pilot know the same keenness of pleasure the hunter does when he sees his quarry go down? Here the answer is more equivocal. There were some who professed to find such a pleasure; one of them was Mick Mannock, of whom someone said, "Fighting wasn't enough for him—he needed to kill." But Mannock professed a hatred of the Germans that was uncommon in the air—or in the trenches, for that matter. Karl Degelow said that in the French and British formations that his *Staffel* met in battle there was often one timorous, inept opponent who tried to leave the fight. "This deserter we called the *Pudelchen*" (little poodle). Degelow and his comrades always tried to "bag" the *Pudelchen.* Then occasionally a pilot might be "out for blood" for a time because a comrade had been killed. The French ace Deullin wrote a friend in 1916: "Peretti has been avenged. . . . I was able to catch a Fokker and put twenty-five shots into it at ten meters. The guy was so shot up that his blood sprayed over my cowling, my windshield, my cap, and my goggles. Needless to say it was a pleasure to watch him go down from 2,500 meters and I didn't miss a meter of it." Billy Bishop said in his wartime autobiography that "it wasn't like killing a man so much as just bringing down a bird in sport"; yet in a letter home he confessed he was haunted by one German airman he had shot down: "My bullets shattered his face and skull. I can't get that picture out of my mind." Then there was the German ace Karl Menckhoff: "For him the shooting down of an enemy plane left a bitter after-taste. After a victory in the air he often came back shaken."[30]

However he reacted, the fighter pilot never seems to have forgotten that destroying the enemy was his essential function—in the atmosphere that reigned in the fighter arm he was never allowed to forget it. The letters of new pilots who had yet to score are eloquent in this regard. Mario Fucini recalled, "but my first victory just wouldn't come! And yet I was flying a lot and enemy aviators weren't that hard to find." And a Bavarian pilot named Dannhuber noted in his diary in August 1917: "I'm in despair! I've been a fighter pilot for eight weeks, and no success. Should I shame myself before all my comrades, throw in the sponge, and ignominiously return to two-seaters?" When the long-sought victory finally came there really was no respite, for the pilot had a new goal: five victories. "You really have a hard time getting those first five planes," acknowledged French ace Maxime Lenoir, "and then once you're made an ace, maybe because of chance, maybe because of greater self-confidence, the victories come more easily; but it's that blasted number five that is the hardest to get." Once a man was an ace, he was in open competition with others; the first rivalry of this sort was probably the one between Boelcke and Immelmann. For men who were strongly competitive—and such men were drawn to the fighter arm because of the competition—the quest never ended. Billy Bishop, who has been described as having "a fiercely competitive spirit," became Britain's top-scoring fighter pilot and then was withdrawn from the front and eventually lost his "title." But he returned and in a frenzy of activity—25 victories credited in 12 days—he regained his place. Albert Ball was driven by an even more ambitious hope: to outscore any other British or French pilot and beat the record of the dead Oswald Boelcke as well: "Only three more to be got before I am top of England and France again. In order to whack the German man I'd love to get about ten more."[31]

It would be wrong to conclude that this was the dominant urge in all or even in most fighter pilots. They were impelled as all airmen were—and all ground soldiers, for that matter—by their sense of duty, by their dedication to and their solidarity with their comrades in arms. But the compulsion to excel in that bizarre game in which one competed with both the enemy and one's comrades in arms—that must be seen as an additive that drove the fighter pilot and gave sometimes reckless impulsion to his course. Billy Bishop's biographer said his career came to resemble the ride of a man on a careening roller coaster; and Bishop himself said, "I find myself shuddering at chances I didn't think of taking six weeks ago." Yet these men would not willingly get off the roller coaster; they fought until they were *abgekämpft* and beyond, and when they were withdrawn from the fighting they moved heaven and earth to get back to it. The American ace Elliot White Springs spoke for them all when he wrote: "I don't want to quit. My nerves are all gone and I can't stop." In all too many cases the outcome was fatal. On May 3, 1917, Albert Ball, then two months away from his twenty-first birthday, wrote his parents: "am feeling very old just now." Three days later, over the town of Lens, he met Lothar von Richthofen and fought his last battle. And Major Brocard had this tribute for France's most popular ace: "Guynemer was only a powerful idea in a very frail body, and I lived near him with the secret sorrow of knowing that some day the idea would slay its container."[32]

Those who find it difficult to believe this self-destructive tendency among the great aces of World War I should consider this paradox: Those who were the very best at aerial combat had the poorest survival rates. The reader is already familiar with the vague allusions to horrendous casualties in the air war, but for two of the belligerents there are recent figures that bear keeping in mind. Statistical compilations recently done in the Historical Service of the French Air Force indicate that 16 percent of French pilots lost their lives in combat—about one pilot in six (this compares very favorably with the infantry, which lost just under 25 percent). And the losses of Canadian airmen—who made up 15 percent of the R.A.F. at the Armistice—are known with great exactitude, thanks to researches carried out for the recent *Official History of the Royal Canadian Air Force*. The figures show that just over 10 percent of the 13,000 Canadian airmen lost their lives. The loss rates for the aces are appreciably higher: for the French aces and the German *Pour le mérite* recipients they are 25 percent, for the Austrian aces 28 percent, and for the Italian aces 30 percent.[33]

There is a final question to be answered. In this world of relentless hunters and driven men was there any place for the chivalry so often associated with aerial combat? Strangely enough there was, though there has been considerable dispute about the forms it took and the frequency with which it manifested itself. General Porro wrote that the aviators were rightly called "the cavaliers of the skies," for among them knightly forms and gestures were far more common than in any of the other services; Silvio Scaroni, on the other hand, has written that chivalry rarely made its appearance in the air war, and that this was true "on all the fronts, from France to Russia, from Serbia to Mesopotamia."[31]

What sometimes passed for chivalry was simply the aviators' way of observing the rules of war. Rather than passing the names of enemy airmen killed or taken prisoner to the International Red Cross for transmission to the other side, they simply dropped messages, usually over an enemy airfield. This practice began very early in the war. On October 12, 1914, Oberleutnant Hans Steffens flew over Paris, dropping some small bombs and a note listing the names of four captured French officers and asking that their families be informed that they were well. The note concluded "I'm very sorry about the bombs but *c'est la guerre*." In time this custom led to others; when an enemy aviator had been buried, photos of the funeral were sometimes dropped; on other occasions letters to or from captured airmen were transmitted this way. Wedgwood Benn recorded that once an Austrian plane appeared above his squadron's field in Italy—presumably to photograph it—and one of the British pilots succeeded in shooting it down. When they examined the wreckage they were mortified to find letters from captured squadron-mates which the Austrian pilot had simply come to deliver.[35]

The general respect held for airmen of the opposing side was reflected in the messages of condolence or even the funeral wreaths dropped when an enemy aviator of note had been killed. If the aeronautical press is representative of the views of the flying fraternity, then the admiration of enemy aces was sincere and widespread. Both British and French aviation journals published capsule biographies of aces such as Boelcke and Immelmann and often gave their ranking and number of victories. Only rarely do their readers seem to have objected; one Frenchman did protest over an article which La guerre aérienne published about Boelcke, whom the reader called an "assassin," and a member of "the vile race that has condemned to death millions of decent people."

Within the Royal Flying Corps there was something of a cult of von Richthofen. In squadron messes toasts were drunk to him or to his memory. In July 1917 *The Aeroplane* noted that there had been a heavy demand for photographs of the Baron and his "Circus" from officers of the R.F.C.; toward the end of the war a captured British pilot was found to be carrying a tiny patch of fabric that had come from the dead ace's wrecked plane (the plane had been completely stripped by souvenir hunters).[36]

Probably no other action more exemplified the chivalrous spirit than the issuing of individual challenges. Silvio Scaroni recorded the case of a French pilot named David who had had to leave an air battle when his gun jammed. Fearful that his opponents would think him a coward, he later dropped a note on the enemy airfield saying "I will be over Vauquois at noon on June 15, 1915." Sergeant David kept his rendezvous, but no enemy appeared to accept his challenge. Scaroni said that he knew of several cases on the Italian Front in which the gauntlet was thrown down in this fashion. Then there was the plan devised in the R.F.C.'s No. 11 Squadron late in 1915, to challenge Max Immelmann to single combat. A note was prepared, apparently with approval at wing level, that was straight from the *code duello:*

> A British officer pilot is anxious to meet the redoutable Captain Immelmann in fair fight.
>
> The suggested rendezvous is a point above the first line trenches just east of Hébuterne.
>
> The British officer will be there from 10 A.M. to 11 A.M. daily from November 15th till 30th, weather permitting.
>
> It is understood that only one aeroplane can be sent to meet this challenge, and that anti-aircraft guns may fire at either combatant.

For reasons that are obscure, the challenge was never delivered. This seems to have been the outcome in almost all such efforts at prearranged combat (they were not frequent); for one reason or another the duel never took place.[37]

It might be well to remember that chivalrous gestures were not unknown in the war on the ground. Prisoners were generally well treated and the enemy's dead given proper burial when that was possible. There was also communication of a sort across no-man's land, with truces and cease-fires arranged for the removal of the wounded, for cutting the grass in no-man's land, or even occasionally for the purpose of sunbathing. The infantryman, like the airman, got to know his opponent and most often to respect him. A recent analysis of World War I letters revealed very few cases of indifference or resentment against the enemy. The analyst noted: "It is probably not by chance that artillerymen who do not see their opponent at close range were more inclined to forget the human implications of war."[38]

One could even argue that if the soldiers in the trenches had been left to themselves they would have negotiated agreements that would have brought all fighting to a stop. With fighter pilots, despite relative lack of supervision, this was never a possibility. One finds in the literature episodes in which a pilot lets an enemy escape because the enemy's machine gun is jammed—the most famous case perhaps being Ernst Udet's account of how Guynemer spared his life. But such cases were probably very rare, because they went against the basic urge to enhance one's score. The American ace Douglas Campbell told an oral history interviewer that he knew of no such case, and that he had himself shot down a German photoreconnaissance plane knowing full well its machine gunner had run out of ammunition: "In my own case with that number five, your instinct was to—well, this isn't cricket—to shoot the guy that has no ammunition, but what the hell, are you going to let him take the pictures home? War isn't like that. And they'd probably shoot at us, so. . . ."[39]

Nor could there have been many instances in which a pilot gave up the advantage of surprise, advertising his presence before attacking an enemy. A favorite tactic, after all, was to attack from behind, at an angle which made the attacker invisible. Pilots sometimes commented ruefully on this kind of stratagem. "No credit to me," confessed an American aviator, "I just murdered him. He never saw me." One day, when Georges Guynemer almost struck a woman with his car and she shouted at him "Assassin!," Guynemer replied, "Madame, you don't know how right you are!" By the same token pilots didn't like to send an enemy down in flames. Baracca wrote his mother that he had sent down three "flamers," and that he thought he might stop using incendiary ammunition—but it is doubtful that he or others did so.[40]

Pilots sometimes worried about using incendiary rounds because, if they were captured with them, the enemy might judge them guilty of violating the laws of war, the Hague Convention having outlawed bullets that maimed or caused undue suffering. Captured German pilots who had been using incendiaries would sometimes produce "authorizations" certifying they were really hunting observation balloons. There was also much concern about explosive bullets, which each side suspected its "chivalrous" foe was using. The British actually did use explosive Pomeroy and Brock bullets, and there is a warning from General Trenchard in Air Council minutes that British airmen should be careful "not to be taken with bullets in their possession." And each side believed that the other would not scruple at using captured aircraft to approach and make easy kills. Periodically there were alerts about phantom Spads or Albatrosses with enemy airmen at the controls.[41]

Still, the chivalrous impulsion was undeniably present in the air war, and its manifestations were many. Sometimes they were comical: One day a German pilot brought his fighter down on an Allied field with its fuel tank empty. He asked for a full tank and a five minutes' start, and was taken aback when his request was refused. Then there was the touching case of Jaques Herbelin and the German pilot he shot down, Joachim Leopold. The two became friends and the friendship continued after the war. Then came World War II. Leopold came to Paris as an important functionary of the administration of Gross-Paris, and Herbelin became active in the Resistance. One day Leopold learned the Gestapo was going to arrest Herbelin, and he got a message to his friend that saved his life.[42]

To some, then, the code was real. But was it relevant? André Boulenger was returning from a cemetery where he had saluted the grave of a fallen German pilot when he encountered a ragged, muddy regiment of infantry headed up to the line:

> And I was ashamed, really I blushed at the romantic gesture I had just made. It seemed to me affected, theatrical, in bad taste. And I was also disgusted by the knightly courtesy of the German squadron. That sort of elegance is all too easy for us, I said to myself, we who wear clean clothes and spend our nights in beds with a solid roof over our heads. Maybe we die more often than they do, but we don't suffer, and our work is even a sport: *La guerre en dentelles*, how out of place in this filthy war![43]

=10=

The War on Other Fronts

The glamor and the public fascination that attached to the struggle in the air were phenomena largely limited to the Western Front. No one was more aware of this than the airmen who flew and fought in other theaters. They had the impression that they were not only out of the public eye, but also excluded from the highest priorities of their political and military leaders and accorded only a secondary importance. They were not wrong if we judge by the way the major belligerents allocated their aircraft. At the time of the Armistice the French Air Service had over 90 percent of its front line planes concentrated between the Swiss frontier and the English Channel; of the 2,690 machines the British had on all fronts, 1,799 were in France. For the German Air Service the situation at war's end is not quite so clear, but there is little doubt that the Western Front rather than the Eastern attracted the great bulk of Germany's air strength. In August 1914 she put only four *Fliegerabteilungen* facing the Russians; of the 3,128 planes the Germans acknowledged losing over the following four years, only 189 of those were listed as having been destroyed on the Eastern Front.[1]

The war in the east was characterized by a level of air activity far less intense than in the west. The heavy allocation of German resources in the west is only part of the explanation. The two other major belligerents in the east, Austria-Hungary and Russia, simply had fewer resources to commit. A recent estimate places Austro-Hungarian aircraft production during the war years at just over 5,000, a little more than a tenth of Germany's production. The Russian figure is placed by the same source at 5,600 planes. There was also the geographical factor, since the armies and the aircraft that flew on their behalf were spread over immense areas.[2]

On the Eastern Front the air war also evolved more slowly; new planes and new procedures tended to appear later than in the West. The Germans were in a sense responsible, since they gave priority to the fighting in France, where their adversaries were more formidable. But the Allies too, saw that modern matériel flowed first to the Western Front, then to their Russian Allies. In fact neither Russia nor Austria-Hungary had the industrial base or the technology to support a serious air effort without help. So the Germans provided this support to Austria-Hungary, and France undertook the same obligation toward the Russians. Generally what went east was what could be spared in the west. Aircraft outmoded in France still flew in Poland; and the dirigible, no longer seen in the West, could still take to the less dangerous skies of Eastern Europe.

Austria-Hungary made a gallant but futile effort to achieve self-sufficiency in the air. She had the misfortune of having to fight on three separate fronts when, as John Morrow says, she had a production base insufficient to support an air war on one. The aircraft industry rested in large part on the experience gained in the automotive industry—this was above all true of engine manufacture. But Austria-Hungary's auto industry was embryonic at best. Then, too, to keep airplanes serviced and repaired the best pool of technical expertise came from the automobile service sector—and this too was largely lacking in most eastern countries. When late in the war the emphasis shifted to the greater use of metals in airframes, the Austro-Hungarians were once again left behind. It is some measure of the country's deficiencies that she tried to buy Russian aviation matériel after Lenin took that country out of the war.[3]

The vicissitudes of the Russian Air Service have been chronicled by the Soviet historian Duz. His work follows a custom long practiced in Soviet historiography of contrasting the intelligence, skill, and valor of the Russian people with the criminal ineptitude of the Tsarist regime, but the basic handicaps of an underdeveloped country fighting a "high-tech" war are no less apparent. The Russians were never able to free themselves of foreign engine designs, and indeed sought to import powerplants in considerable quantities. The domestic manufacture of wireless sets for aircraft began only at the end of 1916, but "positive results . . . could not be achieved even towards the end of the war." The Russian Air Service remained dependent on imported sets, but through 1916 observers' reports were still being dropped in message bags, and aerial artillery spotters were landing near the battery they were working with to correct its fire. Only in August of that year was a special training program created for artillery observers.[4]

Through March 1916, Russian air units had received only 100 machine guns; as of April 1, 1917, there were only seven fighter craft of Russian make that had synchronizing mechanisms for firing a machine gun through the propeller arc. The government had solicited bids for the manufacture of airplane gunsights, but no domestic firm had come forward to take up a contract. Statistics published in the Soviet Union in 1925 give some idea of the dimensions of the supply problem. As of January 1, 1916, the Russians had 553 aircraft; their projected needs for the next year and a half were 5,201—10 times the number on hand. Contracts had been placed with Russian firms for 1,472 planes, and another 400 had been ordered from the Allies. By the end of 1916 the Tsar's government had placed massive orders abroad for planes, motors, observation balloons, parachutes, machine guns, ammunition, and wireless sets. The chief suppliers of military hardware were the British and the French, but sizable orders had also been placed in Italy, the United States, and Japan.[5]

During interrogation, captured Russian aviators complained about Russian-made aircraft, with the exception of the Sikorsky Ilya Muromets. Many French models they flew had been discarded by the Western Allies for one reason or the other. Among these was the bizarre Spad A 2 of 1915, which had a sinister reputation. The propeller was in the middle of the fuselage, behind the observer and in front of the pilot. In the event of a nose-over, the observer was "doomed to inescapable death"; there were also cases in which the propeller caught the observer's scarf and strangled him to death. Even when imported aircraft were well designed, lack of spare parts could keep most of the planes in a unit grounded. Repair personnel were in extremely short supply; in some units the planes were maintained by captured Austro-Hungarian mechanics.[6]

Along with technical deficiencies, the Russians struggled with conceptual and organizational problems that had already been resolved elsewhere. Well into the war there were debates over whether a single, multi-purpose airplane would suffice, or if different types were needed. Not until the end of 1915 was there a commander for all air units at the front; for the balance of the war the air service did not have a chief of its own. The composition of air units on the basis of their specialty was slow to jell. In mid-July 1917, there were still mixed units of observation planes and fighters.[7]

Flying on the Eastern Front offered some unique challenges; German pilots who flew on both fronts said it was simply harder in the east. The simple act of orienting oneself was made more difficult by the scarcity of reference points such as cities and rail lines. In the case of an emergency landing there were fewer places to bring a plane down safely. In certain sectors of the Eastern Front, flat and well-drained ground suitable for landing fields was difficult to find close to transportation facilities such as a railroad or a highway. A French pilot who flew with the Russians in the Carpathians said that he reacted with "intense stupefaction" when he discovered that his airfield was 80 kilometers from the front lines. Each mission thus entailed a flight of 200 kilometers "in a glacial cold" unknown in France.[8]

Observation and reconnaissance missions were by far the most numerous and the most important. Both sides carried out very deep strategic reconnaissance flights, especially while planning offensives (the Russians using the Ilya Muromets). Photographic work assumed a far greater importance in the east since in many areas—the Carpathians, for example—there were no maps worthy of the name, and the general staff relied heavily on photographs and maps made from them. Bombing was of distinctly secondary importance, though the transportation system was more vulnerable than in the west, chiefly because the rail network was far less dense. Rail junctions and railway stations were generally high on the bombers' priority list, and when they were hit the effects on the enemy's movement were immediate.

Aerial combat was far less frequent than in the skies over

France and Belgium; this was the opinion of pilots who fought on both fronts (the French and Russians had a pilot "exchange" to demonstrate their solidarity). Of the 7,425 aerial victories that German aviators claimed during the war, only 358 were chalked up in the east (Soviet contentions that over 2,000 German planes were destroyed seem highly suspect). Certain it is that German fighter pilots, anxious to build reputations for themselves, did their best to avoid service in the east; what is more, when German fighter units were moved from east to west to help in the Somme battle, they soon showed a lack of combat experience when compared with units that had been stationed in France.[9]

Russian pilots were involved in ramming incidents with sufficient frequency for that action to be considered as a tactic of sorts, some of them apparently believing that the airplane itself could be a weapon in aerial combat. There were clearly cases in which the Russian pilot expected to be killed; a Captain named Andreievich clearly had that in mind when he provoked his own death and that of an Austro-Hungarian pilot over Przemysl; he left behind an updated will and a last letter to his family. However, Nesterov—who also died in a ramming incident—may not have intended suicide, since earlier he had flown with a knife blade attached to the tail of his plane, and also experimented with a grapnel (there was a tendency to believe all mid-air collisions with enemy aircraft were the result of deliberate ramming).[10]

Despite such desperation measures as ramming, the air war in the east seems to have been fought with much the same decorum and "chivalry" as that prevailing in the west. Captain Walter Schroeder, who was with the German Air Service in Poland for a while, recorded that when a German plane did not come back, the Russians dropped messages for three consecutive days to announce that the plane's pilot and observer were safe and unwounded, and that the Russian airmen looked forward to welcoming more German prisoners soon. Shortly afterward Russian planes dropped letters from the prisoners themselves. "This sporting comradeship of opposing airmen is a fine thing," Schroeder concluded, "We dropped an acknowledgement to say that we had received their messages, for which we thanked them." These amenities were observed only among airmen, of course; ground troops were another matter. A German observation plane flying behind the Russian lines at 1,500 feet was suddenly hit by a volley of shots that cut a control cable, broke a strut and bracing wires, and wounded both pilot and observer. The plane started a slow, inexorable descent, its crew alarmed that they might not make the German lines. Their alarm increased when they noticed a squadron of Cossacks galloping after them like a pack of dogs after a crippled bird. Miraculously, the shattered plane managed to skim across the German forward positions; as it did so the pilot shouted triumphantly to his pursuers *"do svidanie!"*[11]

The battles in the air soon spread south into the Balkans; in March 1915 the French sent two escadrilles to help the hard-pressed Serbs. In the end the Serbs were overwhelmed, but the Allies managed to hold a bridgehead at Salonika, and in October the French sent eight more escadrilles for service there; they were supplemented by British units and ultimately by Italian units as well. Germany sent air units to help her ally, Bulgaria. Halberstadts and BE 2s and Voisins begun to people the skies over Salonika, though never as thickly as they did in France. Early in 1915 still another "sideshow" opened when the Allies tried to force the Dardanelles, and then landed troops there on the Gallipoli Peninsula in April (only to evacuate them in January 1916). The war in the Balkans expanded further with Greece and Rumania on the Allied side.

Aerial operations in the Balkans were at first done with air units belonging to the major belligerents, but since they all had Balkan allies, there was a general tendency to encourage them to create services of their own, their efforts being of course supported with matériel and technical expertise. All of the belligerents in the recent Balkan Wars had utilized small numbers of pilots and planes, but could scarcely be said to have created air services. That was certainly the case with Turkey, which became Germany's ally in October 1914. The Turks asked for air assistance immediately in the form of two Fliegerabteilungen. The German government called for volunteer aviators; those accepted made their way through the Balkans. The airplanes were not so easy to send, since they could not be flown to Turkey and could not be legally shipped through then neutral Rumania and Bulgaria. They were in fact shipped in crates labelled as Red Cross supplies and "circus equipment." Bombs for the German units went through as medical supplies. Ultimately the German Army's Air Service activated six-*Fliegerabteilungen* in Turkey (Nos. 300–305), while the German Navy sent a *Sonder-Kommando* (special squad) of seaplanes which operated out of three air stations on the Turkish coast.[12]

Voisin 5 bomber. Succeeding models of the Voisin served as the workhorse of French bombing squadrons for much of the war. The bottom photograph shows the variety of aerial bombs used by the French in 1915; the larger bombs are artillery shells fitted with tail fins. *Service Historique de l'Armée de l'Air.*

Franz and Emil. Their names are not known, but in the German Air Service it was customary to call an observer Emil and a pilot Franz. Here the officer observer is on the left, and his "Franz" is a sergeant. Their plane is an L.V.G. C.IV, and the picture was taken about 1916. *National Air and Space Museum, Smithsonian Institution.*

The Fokker Eindecker. The top photograph shows Eindeckers being assembled in a German factory, while the drawing "The Deadly Fokker," which appeared in *Flight* early in 1916 satirized the fearsome reputation the German fighter had acquired among the Allies. *Peter M. Grosz Collection; Flight International.*

Eh! Pingouin, au bureau avec ton barda, et vivement!

Au revoir, les copains! A bientôt! sur mon appareil!

EN PASSANT PAR PANAM!
Pour élève pilote, nous faisons le même vert-pomme, gris souris ou chocolat brûlé.

GARE DE LYON
Sûrement elles me prennent pour Guynemer!!!

The series of cartoons, which appeared in *La Guerre Aérienne*, traced "the story of an ace"; here the front-line soldier is delighted to receive his transfer to the air service, then hastens to get a new uniform. The bottom photo shows a student pilot at the controls of his "penguin." *La Guerre Aérienne; National Air and Space Museum, Smithsonian Institution.*

Four aces: Albert Ball (upper left), whose meteoric career brought forty-four victories, death at the age of twenty, and a posthumous Victoria Cross; Bruno Lörzer (middle photo), shown wearing his Pour le mérite, survived the conflict with forty-one victories and later became a Luftwaffe general; Raoul Lufbery, of French and American parentage, flew with the Lafayette Escadrille and the U.S. Air Service and had seventeen victories when he was shot down in May 1918; Francesco Baracca (bottom), Italy's top ace, had thirty-four enemy planes to his credit when he crashed in flames in June 1918. *National Air and Space Museum, Smithsonian Institution; Peter M. Grosz Collection; National Air and Space Museum, Smithsonian Institution; Museo Aeronautico Caproni.*

Kaiser Wilhelm II visiting a German airfield. The Kaiser played a major role in making aviators the most lionized figures in the war. *National Archives.*

The funeral of Captain Oswald Boelcke in the cathedral at Cambrai, October 31, 1916; Boelcke's death prompted a national outpouring of grief in Germany. *Karl Schneide Collection.*

Group portrait of the Turkish Air Service, including a number of German aviators; Oswald Boelcke is the seated figure above number one, and on his left is Major Erich Serno, who commanded the Turkish service. *Kivanc Hurturk.*

The Sopwith Cuckoo, the carrier-borne torpedo plane that was becoming operational at the end of the war; It heralded a new era in naval aviation. *National Air and Space Museum, Smithsonian Institution.*

The six-engined Tarrant Tabor, a British bomber built at the end of the war for the bombing of Berlin. Though the prototype nosed over in its takeoff attempt, killing both pilots, it announced a new era of the strategic bomber. *National Air and Space Museum, Smithsonian Institution.*

During the Balkan Wars Turkey had acquired 10 airplanes; but when Captain Erich Serno toured the Turkish air field at San Stefano, in January 1915, he found only two planes that were airworthy. Nothing daunted, he set about creating the Ottoman Air Force, whose first flying unit was formed in March of that year. Not surprisingly, the Turkish air service closely resembled the German. Its flight units had the organization and even the name of the German Fliegerabteilungen. Captain Serno, head of the service, enjoyed at the same time the rank of major in the Turkish Army. The airmen wore German uniforms, complimented by the kalpak, a lamb's wool cap, and "wings" distinctive to the Turkish service. Initially the personnel was heavily German, but that changed as increasing numbers of Turks learned to fly. For a considerable time the expansion of the service was limited by lack of airplanes, but supply problems eased when Bulgaria swung to the side of the Central Powers and those powers overran Rumania. (No planes were built in Turkey during the war, though local artisans were very adept at making replacement parts.) By the end of the war the Ottoman Air Force was a modest but viable service, and perhaps the best developed in the Balkans. At the time of the Armistice it was composed of 15 Fliegerabteilungen and its personnel was largely Turkish.[13]

Bulgaria's entry into the German camp afforded the opportunity to arm still another ally in the air, but in the case of Bulgaria success was more limited. The Bulgarians themselves had made a start, since in 1914–15 they had designed and built two aircraft of their own, one of which proved to be a success. In September 1915 the Bulgarian Engineers created an "Air Squad" composed of 6 pilots, 7 observers, and 100 or so ground personnel; that same month the Bulgarian Army opened a flight school. In Bulgaria there was no equivalent to Captain Serno, since the Bulgarians retained effective control of their infant service, relying on the Germans chiefly for airplanes and technical advice; the Germans obliged with, among other things, several small shipments of L.V.G. aircraft. By the end of the war the Bulgarians had two air squads, modelled on the Fliegerabteilung.[14]

For their part the Allies did what they could to endow their Balkan allies with aerial armament, the French usually taking the lead in fostering army aviation, while the British gave assistance in creating naval air units. In Macedonia the French organized several Franco-Serb escadrilles, and supplied technical assistance for the formation of two Rumanian aviation *grupuls;* these efforts were part of a much broader program of military assistance that eventually drew both Yugoslavia and Rumania into the French alliance system of the postwar period.

The Greeks had at least the nucleus of an air service at the beginning of the war, this in the form of two flyable Farman airplanes left over from the Balkan conflicts of 1912–13. With the outbreak of the war, however, neutrals such as Greece could no longer obtain aircraft, and even gasoline became scarce; by early 1916 the Greek Air Service had only one airworthy machine. Only one pilot was graduated from flight school that summer, his classmates being sent back to the ground units they had come from. Then in 1917, after considerable internal tumult, Greece cast her lot with the Allies. A French officer, Major Denain, drew up a new plan for the Greek Air Service, and the French and their Greek allies set to work, sending a first contingent of 36 air cadets to France for flight training at Chartres. In December an all-Greek reconnaissance and bombing escadrille came into existence, and three other units were organized before war's end. While the French were building up the Greek Army's air service, the Royal Navy was rendering the same service to the Greek Navy. The airminded British Admiral Mark Kerr showed a keen interest in this work and took Greek naval aviation under his wing.[15]

The air war in the Balkans in some ways resembled that on the Eastern Front. The resources committed were modest and the operations of low intensity. A German Fliegerabteilung in Macedonia could expect to be assigned a sector 60 to 80 kilometers wide and from 100 to 200 kilometers deep. A single reconnaissance unit might have to supply the needs of eight or nine divisions. The tempo of operations we may guess from the statistics compiled by the historian of the Bulgarian Air Service: for the years 1917 and 1918 the Bulgarians were engaged in some 60 air battles; their combat losses were five pilots and two observers. In nine months of aerial activity at Gallipoli, German and Turkish airmen made 150 flights and dropped 200 bombs.[16]

Though planes were few and the conditions in which they operated were difficult, they were often strikingly effective in reconnaissance. Captain Serno and a German naval officer named Schneider went aloft on the morning of March 18, 1915, and flew over the Dardanelles; by a stroke of luck they happened to catch the Allied fleet—no fewer than 18 warships—steaming for the Straits in a critical move to silence the Turkish forts in the Narrows. The airmen hurried back to their base at Chanak-Kale where they jumped on horses and rode to spread the alarm. In a far less dramatic way the airplane did signal service for an Italian army operating on the Albanian front in 1916. According to General Porro, the three squadriglie employed there were invaluable: "In this zone, which lacked proper topographical maps and passable roads, each day the contribution of aviation became more valuable and more advantageous to our troops." What maps there were of many Balkan areas were often inaccurate: a town indicated as being on the banks of a river could be ten miles away, for example. Tactical reconnaissance suffered accordingly until aerial photographs could be turned into maps.[17]

Photographic reconnaissance was thus of special value, but it also had to be carried out in especially challenging conditions. In many of the air services modern equipment and competent personnel were in short supply. The photographic section of the Bulgarian Air Service seems to have had only two aerial cameras, and its darkroom was mounted on a two-wheeled cart. In the first months of operations the Bulgarians took fewer than 100 photographs, and these were "weak and unclear." One day in March 1916 a Bulgarian pilot took an aerial observer named Lieutenant Sotirov on a reconnaissance mission in the region of Mount Chengel. Sotirov saw what appeared to be the tents of a sizable bivouac on the south slope of the mountain and he took pictures of it. His report created consternation at Bulgarian Army headquarters; the photographs were quickly developed but they were so poor in quality that they told nothing. There was nothing to do but to send a second aerial observer to corroborate the findings of the first, and this was done. The second observer returned to report—to the immense relief of the Bulgarian General Staff—that what had appeared to be tents were in fact the houses of an abandoned village. Only then was it discovered that Lieutenant Sotirov was nearsighted. "He was prevailed upon to abandon aviation."[18]

Artillery spotting seems not to have been done as effectively as on the Western Front, for there are numerous complaints about its lack of effectiveness. Part of the explanation lies in lack of equipment, for the British did not have wireless sets generally available for their observation planes until the end of 1916. Then too, quite often the observers were called upon to direct naval gunfire, as at Gallipoli, and this type of operation was still in the pioneering stage. On the other hand the airplane served as a communications link in a way unknown on the Western Front. In rugged country without a telephone network and with abominable roads, the airplane became a courier of sorts between the major elements of an army—a role that had been envisaged for it well before 1914.[19]

Aerial combat never developed much in the Balkan fighting, in part because of the small number of planes involved and the strong priority given to the observation-reconnaissance function. Hans Buddecke wrote that when he arrived in the Dardanelles, he and two other German pilots flying Fokkers effectively achieved air superiority in the region. Buddecke was able to launch his career as an ace while there, and a few other pilots managed to make names for themselves. There was Lieutenant von Eschwege, who got the title "Eagle of the Aegean" for his relentless destruction of Allied observation balloons on the Salonika front (it was his plane that was blown out of the sky by means of an observation balloon carrying a dummy observer and a heavy charge of high explosives). Then there was the French ace at Salonika, Dieudonné Costes, who scored eight victories—in a thousand hours of flying. The Balkan countries had their heroes too: Lieutenant Mura, the first Turkish pilot to down an enemy plane, and Aristides Moraitines, a hero of Greek naval aviation who vanished on a flight from Salonika to Athens.[20]

Aerial bombing is frequently mentioned, but seems to have had very little impact on the Balkan fighting. The tendency there was for the air units to be "maids of all work," playing any number of roles in turn, and bombing accuracy suffered accordingly. Save for the brief appearance of the German Bombengeschwader I, bombing remained at the amateur level. For the Allies particularly, the bomber could have paid very large dividends. Turkey's lifeline was the rail line from Berlin, and if it were cut for any appreciable length of time, the consequences for the Turkish war effort would have been very serious indeed. The Royal Naval Air Service tried several times to hit a bridge on the line, but without success. Similarly unsuccessful were bombing attempts on a long railway bridge near Aleppo, whose destruction would also have been catastrophic for the Turks.[21]

If the vast expanse of territory was the chief geographical feature of the Eastern Front, then the mountains were the chief feature of the Balkans, and one of particular significance to aviators. Crests and ridges of 3,000 or 4,000 feet could be serious obstacles, particularly since violent winds played about many of them. The ruggedness of the terrain made any emergency landing a dangerous enterprise. In the Serbian campaign of 1915 the six German Fliegerabteilungen committed lost a total of 96 planes, and only one of them is thought to have been as a result of enemy action. All but three were wrecked in emergency landings, and two others were thought to have crashed because of violent winds. Since terrain suitable for airfields was hard to come by, aviators often had to fly considerable distances. The bombing of airfields was a fairly common occurrence, perhaps because there were few of them and everyone knew where they were.[22]

The topography and the lack of good roads made supply a constant problem, and air units were far less mobile than elsewhere because their ground elements could not be easily displaced. In the Serbian campaign of 1915 supply columns did well to move four kilometers a day, and aviation gasoline was moved by ox cart. Where there were rail lines their operation was inefficient, and the lines run by the Hungarians were the object of special complaint. One German unit had a gasoline tank car "lost" on the Hungarian railways. It was eventually found in a remote siding where it was serving as a water container. Airfield facilities were generally primitive. In their letters aviators would mention, almost in passing, that they were living in the packing crate their airplane had arrived in (such quarters could be more commodious than one might think: the crate for a Maurice Farman was 47 feet long; it was often partitioned by its occupants).[23]

The climate posed further problems. At Mudros, a British air base in the Gallipoli campaign, we are told that "all flying other than in emergencies was done in the early morning, stopping at about 10 A.M. and starting again after about 4 P.M." In the middle of the day it was simply too hot. Motors overheated even when equipped with extra radiators. Photography became impossible when the temperature reached a certain point, because the gelatin layer on the photographic plates came loose from the glass and "threw up blisters." In the darkrooms the developer and fixing bath had to be kept on ice. At the Dardanelles there was also a fine dust that found its way into mechanisms and shortened the life of engines. Parts of the Balkans were "fever country"; airmen in Macedonia frequently came down with malaria.[24]

The problems of simply coping seem to have been a central theme for the airmen who served in the other, even smaller and more remote "sideshows": in Palestine, where the contest was over the Suez Canal; in Iraq, where it was the oil fields of the Persian Gulf; and in German East Africa, where the German General von Lettow-Vorbeck conducted such a brilliant defense. In these areas too, the numbers of airplanes committed were very small and their usefulness almost entirely limited to reconnaissance.[25]

The most remote sideshow of all was the tiny German enclave of Tsingtau, on the coast of China. It had a garrison of 1,300 men, six field pieces, a few fortress cannon, and one flyable Rumpler Taube. In the fall of 1914 the little colony was assaulted by 60,000 British and Japanese troops, backed by the big guns of a powerful naval force. The Taube flew reconnaissance missions during the entire siege. Its pilot "could not carry an observer because of the weight problem, so he was forced to steer with his feet while taking notes." He also attacked a Japanese ship, dropping two small bombs that missed. The defenders of Tsingtau eventually surrendered. But they were undaunted and the conviction was universal: "If only we'd had more airplanes!"

=11=

Maritime Aviation

A historian has suggested that if Napoleon Bonaparte had somehow been restored to life in 1914, he could probably have done a creditable job of leading an army, for land warfare had not changed all that much; but if Napoleon's contemporary, Lord Nelson, had found himself in command of the British fleet of 1914, he would have been incapable of directing it intelligently. A naval revolution had come with the late nineteenth century, and indeed was continuing when the Great War broke out. Much has been made of naval conservatism, and one does not have to reach far for turn-of-the-century naval authorities who had seen quite enough of rapid changes. An exasperated naval commentator wrote in *La Vie Maritime* in June 1910 that, while the French Navy was still agog over the submarine, "there is now a new gimcrack, the airplane!" It was time, said the author, to call a halt to an "abominable farce: Though France is rich, she is not rich enough to waste her wealth on the wares of toymakers."[1]

But as the second decade of the century began, navies found in their ranks an increasing number of partisans of aeronautics; some were highly placed, men such as Winston Churchill, who served as First Lord of the British Admiralty from 1911 to 1915; and Rear Admiral Bradley A. Fiske, of the United States Navy. More obscure but also far more numerous were the young naval officers who believed their service should have wings, men such as René Daveluy and Paul Teste in France, and Alessandro Guidoni and Mario Caldarera in Italy.[2]

The weight of the argument gradually shifted to the side

of innovation, not because the innovators were more numerous or more eloquent, but because the airplane eventually proved itself. Much has been made of the 1908 pronouncement by the British Admiralty that "aeroplanes would not be of any practical use in the naval service"; but the Lords of the Admiralty happened to be right—in 1908 and for a time thereafter it was not possible to make "practical use" of the airplane at sea. Then in 1909 Blériot conquered the Channel; in 1910 another Frenchman, Henri Fabre, made the first take off and landing on water, and an American, Eugene Ely, flew a plane off a platform installed on an American warship. In 1911 Ely made his first shipboard landing, and his fellow countryman Glenn Curtiss unveiled a practicable seaplane.[3]

Initially naval circles had shown considerable interest in lighter-than-air craft. The German Navy in particular began investing in dirigibles, following the Army's lead. The Royal Navy took the same path, building the R. 1 or *Mayfly;* but that craft was soon lost in an accident, and mishaps also claimed the German naval airships L. 1 and L. 2; these calamities helped redirect interest toward the airplane. That interest was already manifest in other navies: in 1910 the Le Pord Commission was created to advise the French Navy on the wisdom of acquiring airships; instead, the Commission recommended that "before anything else the Navy should focus its efforts on aviation." A General Board of the U.S. Navy produced a similar recommendation: "The value of airplanes for use in naval warfare should be investigated without delay."[4]

Within a year the U.S. Navy acquired its first three airplanes. In 1912 the British government gave the Royal Navy an air service: the Naval Wing of the Royal Flying Corps. That same year the French Navy acquired its Aviation Maritime, and the German Navy purchased its first planes. In 1913 the Italian government decreed the creation of the Aeronautica della Regia Marina and the U.S. Navy decided to build its first air station at Pensacola. When war came a year later, the navies of the major belligerents each had anywhere from 20 to 100 aircraft; the new air services each had a home base of sorts: Eastchurch (Great Britain), Helgoland (Germany), Saint Raphaël (France); the Italians chose Venice, and directly across the Adriatic the Austro-Hungarian naval air arm established itself at Pola. In most navies a ship was found that could be converted into an "aeroplane carrier"; these were usually old vessels like the Italian cruiser *Elba* and the French torpedo boat tender *Foudre.* (The German Navy was an exception, for it designated no vessel for work with seaplanes prior to 1914.)

The launching of British naval aviation was somewhat unusual in that the Royal Flying Corps was to supply the air needs of both services through its military and naval wings. In practice the two wings drifted so far apart that in 1914 there was nothing to do but to transfer the Naval Wing outright to the Royal Navy under the name Royal Naval Air Service; the Military Wing then assumed the title of Royal Flying Corps. This short-lived experiment rested on what seemed a sound assumption in 1912: each of the wings could if necessary serve as a reserve to the other, since their work was similar. Indeed the duties which the naval aviators would perform in war were thought to be essentially those expected of army airmen. First and foremost was the possibility that the airplane—and the airship—could serve as the eyes of the fleet, eyes that could see much more than the fast cruisers that normally did naval reconnaissance. The airplane was faster, cheaper, and offered a much smaller target. Once it was capable of wireless transmission—a technique in which the navies showed great interest in 1914—it would be unbeatable as a scout. Experiments with tethered balloons conducted at the turn of the century had revealed that the navy stood to gain even more from aerial reconnaissance. While the lookout in the crow's nest of a cruiser would be lucky if he spotted an enemy vessel "hull down" a dozen miles away, at 3,000 feet the horizon retreated to something like 60 miles. Aerial observation seemed to offer other dividends as well, such as the ability to spot mines and submarines that were completely submerged; early trials had been encouraging in this regard. In a more general way the airplane had demonstrated its practical value as an information gatherer, having performed creditably in the British, French, and German naval maneuvers of 1913.[5]

Like its army counterpart, the naval air arm also had something to offer as an adjunct to the powerful ordnance of the era. Naval gunnery had evolved rapidly, with new "big guns" that had flat trajectories and great ranges, so that the battleship of the day could often fire much further than its fire control could see. Artillery "spotting" for the navies was foreseen by 1914, though practical implementation was less advanced than in the land forces. Then too, there was the possibility of using the air weapon offensively at sea. Here initially speculation centered on the dirigible because of its load-bearing capacity; aerial bombs were held to be particularly effective against ships since it was thought that even a near miss would drive a wall of water against a ship's hull and possibly crush it. Another concept which had already moved from the drawing board to practical experimentation was the torpedo-plane; the chief obstacle to its development was the great weight of the marine torpedo, a half ton or more.[6]

If the navy's commitment to air power before 1914 was somewhat slower and more limited than that of the army, part of the explanation lies in the additional obstacle the sea service had to overcome in order to find craft that were at home on the water as well as in the air. What naval airmen would have preferred was a seaworthy machine that could fly, one that could regard any body of water as a suitable landing field. A British naval expert explained at the beginning of the war that "what the Navy is seeking is a machine capable of making an oversea voyage in moderately rough weather, able to ascend or descend as required without damage to its engine from immersion, or to its body from the buffeting of the waves."[7]

By 1914 there were two distinct lines of development; one had produced the flying boat, whose fuselage was also a hull, and other the float-type seaplane, which carried pontoons instead of landing gear. Preference between the two varied from one air service to the next, with differing tastes well defined by 1914. The French and the Austro-Hungarians showed a marked predilection for flying boats, perhaps because they had developed early and successful craft of this type, the French Donnet-Lévêque and the Austrian Lohner. The German Navy made early and disappointing trials with the flying boat and abandoned it for the aircraft carrying double pontoons. The Americans, after much experimentation, came to favor the float plane with a single central pontoon and smaller ones located on the wing tips—probably because that configuration lent itself to catapult launching, in which the U.S. Navy pioneered. The flying boat tended to evolve into a large, multiengine craft with greater range (and the luxury of an enclosed cabin). The German Navy, which relied on dirigibles for long distance reconnaissance, had no need for such craft until the end of the war, when airship losses led to the steel and aluminum Zeppelin/Dornier RS IV. The flying boat was an expensive machine that the navy had to develop on its own; for that reason there was a certain attraction in simply adapting a land airplane to naval purposes by the addition of floats. By this means the Sopwith

Baby, the Bréguet XIV and any number of other planes were mobilized for sea service.

In 1914 the belief was widespread that on the sea, as on the land, the opponents would join battle quickly in massive and decisive engagements. The German Navy expected the British fleet to cross the North Sea in great force. From the first hours of the war German seaplanes flew out of Helgoland with orders to "reconnoitre seaward to the limit of their capabilities." For the first few days they flew incessantly; "each flying officer hoped to be the one to first bring the news 'They're here'!" But the British had decided on a policy of blockade, closing the Channel to the German High Seas Fleet and placing the Grand Fleet at Scapa Flow in the Orkneys, where it could guard the northern stretch of sea. The fleet's commander, Admiral Sir John Jellicoe, was disinclined to take risks; Churchill had said of him that he was "the only man on either side who could lose the war in an afternoon."[8]

The British and German fleets were destined to meet only once, at the battle of Jutland, in May 1916; it was a sharp, bruising encounter in which the Germans gave better than they got, but it brought them no long-term advantage and the blockade continued as before. Occasionally there was other action as detachments of cruisers and destroyers probed and feinted in the waters of the North Sea and collided, as in the Heligo Bight in August 1914 and at Dogger Bank in January 1915. Both sides remained on the *qui vive* to the end, with ships, dirigibles, and airplanes charged with the tasks of surveillance.

In the Mediterranean many naval analysts were predicting a desperate struggle between the French fleet on the one hand, and the naval forces of the Italians and the Austro-Hungarians on the other. But when war came Italy at first proclaimed her neutrality, and then in May 1915 cast her lot with the Allies, giving them a lopsided preponderance in the Mediterranean. The Austro-Hungarian fleet, which was modest in size, prudently spent the war in the fortified port of Pola. The only excitement in the early days of the war was the unsuccessful Allied hunt for the German battle cruiser *Goeben* and her light cruiser escort the *Breslau*, which the declarations of war had surprised in the Mediterranean. The *Goeben* was subjected at various times to Allied mine fields, shelling by Russian ships, and several hundred aerial bombs, but she survived the war. The Mediterranean was an Allied lake for the balance of the conflict, an advantage which enabled them to launch and support operations at Gallipoli and later on the Salonika front. There would be no Mediterranean Jutland, and the chief threat the Allies faced there would come from German submarines.[9]

In the very limited number of engagements involving capital ships, both in the North Seas and the Mediterranean, the role played by air power was at best very limited. German airships were fairly effective in seeing that the seas were clear before forays by the Kaiser's cruisers and destroyers, but prior to the sortie that led to Jutland, German Admiral Reinhard Scheer relied chiefly on U-boats to keep the British fleet at Scapa Flow under surveillance; a Zeppelin reconnaissance had to be cancelled because of adverse winds. Early on the morning of June 1, 1916, the airship L 12 did locate Jellicoe's Grand Fleet, whose position it reported. The dirigible continued to shadow the fleet for over an hour, but by then the battle was over. As for the British, their seaplane carrier *Engadine* put one plane into the air during the battle. Its crew successfully scouted the enemy fleet before being forced down by a broken fuel line; their report seems not to have reached Admiral Jellicoe.[10]

For the first part of the war, at least, naval aircraft lacked the range for anything more than reconnaissance at the tactical level, with the possible exception of in the narrow Adriatic. There Austro-Hungarian Lohner seaplanes were able to keep Italian ports under fairly constant surveillance. On July 16, 1915, an Austrian seaplane reported the departure of three Italian cruisers from Brindisi; based on this information an Austro-Hungarian submarine took up position off the coast of Ragusa, where it torpedoed the *Garibaldi*. But in the northern seas one has the clear impression that knowledge of enemy ship movements came chiefly from scouting units on the surface, submarine pickets, and the monitoring of enemy wireless traffic. There neither the seaplane nor the dirigible could claim to be the eyes of the fleet.[11]

If observation planes had the reputation of "fair weather machines" on land, they were even more deserving of that title in the navy. They could not fly when there was adverse weather—this had been the problem for the Zeppelins at Jutland—but even when conditions were suitable for flying they could be unsuitable for a seaplane to take off. For a float plane or flying boat to take off or alight successfully, a calm sea was a necessity. Floats and seaplane hulls were fragile affairs of plywood and canvas; what is more, a spinning propeller could be counted on to shatter if it struck a wave or swell. Sometimes, when the state of the sea was marginal, a seaplane could place itself in the calmer water to be found in the wind-shadow of its mother ship and accomplish a take off that way—a risky enterprise since it involved flying directly at and then over the mother ship. But in the North Sea particularly, the state of the sea often ruled out seaplane operations. On 6 days out of 10 the sea was at least at state three, fairly turbulent, and on 1 day out of 5 it was state four or worse. At Jutland a bad swell had prevented the *Engadine* from continuing flying operations, and in truth the calm seas that favored seaplane operations were rarely encountered.[12]

Admiral Jellicoe wrote after Jutland: "It was apparent that little improvement could be expected so long as we are dependent on the machines rising from the water." In fact, the limitations of the seaplane had been foreseen well before the war. A report prepared for the French Navy in 1912–13 warned that the successful use of aircraft on the high seas was "intimately bound up with solving the problem of a departure from on board." The war brought quick confirmation: on five separate occasions the Royal Navy took seaplanes off the German coast, intending to launch them for a raid on the Norddeich wireless station; each time the operation had to be cancelled, due to fog, sea state, but mostly to the "crippling limitations of the machines themselves." The war also presented a new hazard to seaplane launching and recovery operations. The seaplane carrier was obliged to come to a stop, or nearly so, when it put a plane into the water or recovered it, and in waters increasingly infested with submarines such halts were dangerous.[13]

The ultimate solution to the problem of taking air power to the high seas had been offered by the French aviation pioneer Clément Ader, writing in the 1890s (his work was not published until 1909). Ader's answer was a flush deck aircraft carrier which would store its planes below decks, bring them to the flight deck by means of an elevator, and steam into the wind for launch and recovery operations. The carrier planes would have folding wings, and would be equipped with wheels. Ader prudently recommended the fuselage behind the pilot's position be left open, so that the airman could make a quick exit "in case of a fall into the water."[14]

From Ader's vision to the modern aircraft carrier the path was neither smooth nor direct. Take-off platforms began to appear experimentally, then became a fixed feature of wartime seaplane carriers. From these platforms seaplanes occasionally took off mounted on detachable wheeled dollies; then later the platforms were used by land aircraft, whose pilots simply "ditched" their planes when their mission was completed. There were other, more bizarre schemes, some of which never got beyond the drawing board: landing decks which sloped upward to slow a plane's progress, and take-off platforms that resembled ski jumps. The French navy considered a scheme for a "tangential" takeoff, in which a tethered plane flew around a mast until it built up flying speed and was released. Another technique tested by the French was to hoist a plane up on a high boom projecting over the ship's side. On a given signal the pilot revved his engine to the maximum—and the plane was dropped. These various experiments finally led to the first true "flat top," HMS *Argus*, which joined the Royal Navy in September 1918.[15]

If the wartime evolution of maritime aeronautics is a confused story, this is partly because the naval air arm was obliged to meet several pressing challenges at once; waging war is after all largely a matter of crisis management. And for the Allies there was no greater crisis than the one the Germans presented with their intensive submarine campaign in 1917 and 1918. The diminutive U-boat demonstrated its powers of destruction very early in the war. On September 22, 1914, the U-9 torpedoed the British cruiser *Aboukir*, and when her sister ships *Cressy* and *Hogue* slowed down to pick up survivors, the U-9 put torpedoes in them as well; all three cruisers went down with considerable loss of life. But at the beginning of the war Germany had only a score of submarines, considerably fewer than either Britain or France; moreover there was good reason for using the new weapon sparingly, avoiding attacks on vessels other than enemy warships: the submarine was controversial, some said barbarous, and neutrals like the United States were inclined to react very negatively when civilians died on torpedoed merchant ships.

But by late 1916 Germany had few other cards to play, and her now sizable fleet of 100 U-boats could work tremendous destruction on Allied shipping, particularly around the British Isles. Unrestricted submarine warfare would probably bring the Americans into the war on the Allied side, but if the German Navy's calculations were correct, Britain could be brought to her knees before American might weighed much in the balance. Such was the argument that the Kaiser's admirals presented, and which he in the end endorsed. For a time it seemed the calculations were accurate; by mid-1917 sinkings had reached catastrophic proportions: in the month of April alone, when the U.S. entered the war, the U-boats sent more than 350 ships to the bottom. The Allies responded with a number of measures. The convoy system was introduced and perfected, with merchantmen herded together and shepherded through dangerous waters under armed escort. The second tactic was to hunt down the U-boats, and for this purpose the Allies mobilized surface vessels, airplanes, dirigibles, tethered balloons, and even their own submarines. What is more, the Allies set up what they hoped would be deadly snares for the U-boat—elaborate complexes of nets and mines. The Dover Barrage was to deny the U-boats the use of the Channel, save at ruinous cost. The North Sea Barrage, which stretched from the Orkneys to Norwegian waters was a massive British effort, though it called for 100,000 American-supplied mines. Then there was the Otranto Barrage, a complex set up between the heel of the Italian boot and the coast of current-day Yugoslavia; it was a joint effort by the British, French, and Italians, and its purpose was to bottle up within the Adriatic the German and Austro-Hungarian submarines operating out of Pola and Cattaro. Then, too, the British tried to get at the source of their problem, launching a bombing campaign against the U-boat bases at Zeebrugge and Ostend (the Germans responded by putting their submarines in reinforced concrete shelters, as they would do again in the next war); and in perhaps the most aggressive and spectacular gesture of all, early in 1918 the British made a sudden descent on Zeebrugge and tried to block it up.[16]

Of all the countermeasures the convoy system is considered to have been the most effective. A U-boat that attacked a convoy could count on being stalked itself by patrol vessels armed with hydrophones and depth charges. Even if the U-boat commander was willing to take the risk, the convoy was not that much easier to locate than a single ship; in the intervals between convoys the ocean highways, especially the western approaches to the British Isles, were largely deserted. The submarines, whose cruising time was limited, found themselves hunting through an empty sea. The static anti-submarine defenses, the barrages, were probably the least successful measures, particularly considering the enormous resources committed. Formidable as they appeared to be, they were more hindrances than barriers (not until the summer of 1918 did the British succeed in closing the Channel to U-boats). Anti-submarine patrols by surface vessels, airplanes, and dirigibles—what today might be called search-and-destroy efforts—involved a staggering amount of searching and very little destruction. Even so, the patrolling, especially of the aerial variety, could be considered a successful operation; if it did not destroy the submarines, it effectively neutralized them. This was possible first of all because of the operational limitations of the early U-boats, and secondly because aerial observation proved to be of particular value in anti-submarine operations.[17]

The submarine of 1914 was, like the airplane, an essentially untried weapon. The U-boats of the German Navy had scarcely a decade of evolution behind them, having been added to the fleet in 1906. The U-boats of the "thirties" class, U 31 to U 41, which joined the fleet beginning in 1915, were good representatives of the type employed in 1917. They were of 675 tons surface displacement, about 200 feet long, and they carried 6 torpedoes which they fired through either bow or stern tubes. Properly speaking they were submersibles rather than submarines, designed to operate on the surface most of the time. There they had an efficient diesel propulsion system that could take them 4,400 miles at 8 knots before they needed refueling; in an emergency their diesels could push them along at 16 knots, twice the speed a merchantman would average. Once submerged, the U-boat had to rely on a much less satisfactory electric propulsion system; it could cover only 80 miles at its most economical speed, before it had to surface and recharge its batteries. Even at periscope depth the vessel had to use electrical power. Visibility through the periscope was limited (only toward the end of the war were there periscopes that could scan the skies). And of course once the ship was completely under it was also completely blind—and harmless. For a variety of reasons, then, the U-boat stayed on the surface as much as it could; it dived when it attacked, and when it was itself attacked or feared it would be seen.[18]

In some naval circles there had been high hopes before the war that an aerial observer would be able to spot submarines that had submerged to a considerable depth; however, the experience of the war was disappointing. On the high seas and in the

Channel and North Sea areas the submerged U-boat was essentially invisible. In the Bosporus, on the other hand, submerged craft were easily visible, and even naval mines could be seen to a depth of 18 feet. In the Mediterranean, when sea and atmospheric conditions were favorable, it was also possible to see submarines at considerable depth. On September 15, 1916, Austrian Lohner seaplanes spotted the French submarine *Foucault* at a depth of 80 feet. They attacked it, using bombs with pressure-sensitive detonators, and forced it to the surface, where its crew scuttled it. This was one of the very few instances in which the destruction of a submarine by air attack could be verified (scores of such sinkings were claimed, but the submarines actually destroyed at sea by aerial means could probably be counted on the fingers of one hand).[19]

Prewar trials and calculations indicated that an observer in an airplane or dirigible could spot a submarine on the surface at a distance of 10 miles, but wartime experience revealed the average sighting distance to be about 5 miles, varying with sea state, atmospheric conditions, and the amount of daylight. The submarine on the surface had its own lookouts, of course, and they almost invariably spotted the airplane first. The sighting generally triggered an immediate dive. "Aircraft were an infernal nuisance," one submarine veteran recalled, "You never can be certain if they have seen you or not and the tendency is to take it for granted that they have done so." Should plane and submarine see each other at the same instant, there was every chance the submarine would escape; even the U-boats of 1914 could go under in less than two minutes, and later models could do so in 25 seconds. And even should the airplane deliver an attack, its small bombs would rarely do any damage (to prevent patrol craft from attacking Allied submarines by mistake, these carried on their foredecks distinctive white markings whose design was changed every two weeks).[20]

The U-boats' hunting grounds were largely restricted to European waters, in part because the highest concentration of targets was there, and partly because the U-boat's effective range was limited. Later in the war U-boat "cruisers" with greater autonomy appeared, and in 1918 a few German submarines showed up on the east coast of the United States, but the major battlefields in the U-boat wars were the Mediterranean, and the waters around the British Isles, where two-thirds of all the sinkings occurred.

As the convoy system was perfected, the U-boats were compelled to do more of their hunting in British coastal waters, where the convoys dispersed and the individual ships made their way to their various destinations. This shift made it possible for land- or shore-based aircraft and dirigibles to play an even greater role in anti-submarine activities, for the chief limitation on their use was their range and autonomy, which were far less than was the case for patrolling surface vessels. In the six months from May, 1918, to the Armistice, the British supplemented their 4,000-odd surface vessels with 216 seaplanes, 190 land planes, 85 large flying boats, and 75 dirigibles.[21]

In the Mediterranean the Central Powers had only a half-dozen Austro-Hungarian submarines at the outset, but in the spring of 1915 the German Navy managed to send the U-21 through the Straits of Gibraltar; subsequently the Germans partially assembled and shipped by rail a number of the smaller boats. The Germans and Austro-Hungarians became active in the eastern Mediterranean in 1915, notably in the Dardanelles; with Turkish cooperation the Germans even pushed submarine operations into the Black Sea. By late 1916 sinkings began to rise alarmingly; the Otranto Barrage seems not to have been very effective. While the French were the dominant naval power in the Mediterranean, combatting submarines required the help of the British, Italians, Americans, and even the Japanese, who sent three destroyer flotillas. The French had also to cover the coast of Normandy and the Bay of Biscay; they eventually turned the latter jurisdiction over to the U.S. Navy, which made extensive use of seaplanes to keep the seas clear for the arrival of the American Expeditionary Force. The U.S. Marines' 1st Aeronautical Company got the task of flying anti-submarine patrols out of Punta Delgada, in the Azores.[22]

The airship, largely driven from land warfare by the middle of the war, made something of a comeback in the struggle against the U-boat. The British, who dedicated the most resources to the U-boat war, took the lead in using the naval dirigible, mostly in the form of the small, non-rigid design to which they gave the name "blimp." Admiral Sir John Fisher may well have had the idea first, for he wrote to Admiral Jellicoe, in February 1915, that he had hit upon the dirigible as a "submarine destroyer" and was ordering the construction of 50, even though "everyone thinks I'm mad!" The SS type (for Sea Scout) had the wingless fuselage of a BE 2c suspended below the envelope and could stay aloft for 8 hours; larger and more sophisticated models soon followed. At sea, where it was not exposed to enemy fighters or antiaircraft batteries, the dirigible proved an excellent vehicle for submarine patrols, capable of operating all day and carrying sufficient bombs to do real damage in the unlikely event it actually attacked a submarine. (In addition to its high visibility, the blimp had a top speed of only 40 miles per hour.)[23]

In all, the British produced over 200 dirigibles. They passed their designs to the French, who also developed models of their own—the Zodiac and Astra-Torres ships—some of which carried impressive armament: a 75mm cannon. The French Navy had 40 dirigibles at war's end; the Italian Navy had 10 of the Forlanini pattern. The United States Navy placed orders for 16 dirigibles in March 1917, and used them for antisubmarine patrols along the eastern seaboard.[24]

The flying boat also owed much of its popularity to its usefulness in the U-boat war. It grew in size during the conflict, with a vogue for twin-engine craft; the Felixstowe F.2A, the best of the British wartime boats, had a wingspan of nearly 100 feet and a crew of five. Germany's four-engined Zeppelin-Dornier RS IV, designed to replace the rigid airship for strategic reconnaissance, was an enormous plane with a loaded weight of over 11 tons. The French held to smaller craft, such as the F.B.A. and the Donnet-Denhaut. The best flying boat in the Mediterranean was probably the Austro-Hungarian Lohner; the Italian Navy did it the honor of copying it. Flying boats often carried heavy armament for use against U-boats; the French mounted 37/mm cannon, and the British used the Davis "recoilless" cannon, a long tube which fired a shell in the direction of the target and a bag of sand in the other direction. But in fact the flying boat had only a slightly better chance of doing battle with a submarine than a blimp did. Long before the aircraft was within range, the submarine would have "pulled the plug." Forcing submarines below the surface and keeping them there was achievement enough, however; the tendency in this type of antisubmarine warfare was to intensify patrolling to the point that a plane or dirigible came into view every 20 minutes or so, making it impossible for the sub to surface in the daytime. By the end of the war it was common for the patrol planes and blimps to carry no armament at all. If a submarine could be forced to run submerged for a distance of 60 miles—the width of the Otranto Barrage and the diameter of the octagonal "Spider's Web" search pattern British seaplanes maintained in the North Sea—the U-boat would likely exhaust its batteries.[25]

If in the land war aerial observers could bring artillery to bear on distant targets, at sea this function should have been even more important, given the great range of naval cannon and the small, precise targets "under the horizon" that an enemy fleet would represent. But there were scarcely any naval battles of major proportions, so the partnership of aerial observer and gunner did not have a chance to evolve as it did on land. On those occasions in which aerial observation was used for naval gunlaying, the objectives were usually on land. This was the case in the Dardanelles, where naval gunfire was directed—not very effectively— at Turkish positions. The airmen's help was not always welcomed by Royal Navy gunners. Admiral Davies recalled that at Gallipoli "ships varied very much in their readiness to accept the air reports of fall of shot." Another source indicates that "the Navy in the Aegean as a rule refused to take its spotting from aircraft," and that German wireless operators exacerbated the situation further by getting on the R.N.A.S. observers' frequency and sending the ships "rude messages."[26]

In Flanders, curiously, German naval guns sometimes fired from land to sea. The German Army made use of a number of naval cannon of the 280–300-mm variety along the Belgian coast, guns with a range of nearly 20 miles. They were usually employed in support of the army, but on occasions when British ships steamed in to shell U-boat installations, the guns were trained out to sea. Their fire was directed by specially trained aerial observers, and so effectively that the British ships soon withdrew. Perhaps the most remarkable instance of air-directed naval gunfire involved the German light cruiser *Königsberg*, which was in African waters at the outbreak of the war. She took refuge up the Rafiji River in German East Africa, and the British sent out two shallow-draft monitors to destroy her. With the help of a hastily formed team of air observers, the monitors got the *Königsberg's* range and battered her into a hulk; two airplane crews shared in the prize money. Then there was the curious case of the German commerce raider *Wolf*, which had a long and eventful cruise in the latter half of the war. The ship carried a single Friedrichshafen seaplane nicknamed *Wölfchen*, which "spotted" for the raider in an unusual way. The seaplane would take off and scout over the horizon: when it located an Allied merchantman it would make menacing passes, perhaps release a bomb or two, and drop a message in approximate but unambiguous English: "Steer south to German cruiser and do not use wireless. If not obeying orders you will be shelled by bombs."[27]

Naval aviators pushed research in several other directions to make the airplane an offensive weapon at sea. Given the continued unreliability of the seaplane for operations on the high seas, there was in the end only one solution—to convert the seaplane carrier into a portable airfield; that is to say, an aircraft carrier. The conversion was not complete in HMS. *Furious* since she had a flight deck forward of the bridge but the conformation of a cruiser from bridge to stern. As Hugh Popham described her, "like some latterday chimera, or a species caught in mid-evolution, she had the hindquarters of the past and the forequarters of the future." Take-offs from her flight deck had become routine, but landing on it, flying alongside the bridge, then slipping sideways onto the flight deck, was hazardous in the extreme, and was abandoned after one pilot was killed in the maneuver. Consequently, when the *Furious* left port in July 1918 for the first carrier strike in history, the pilots of the seven Sopwith Camels she carried were under orders to ditch their planes upon returning from their mission. That mission, flown at dawn of July 19 off Schleswig, was to bomb the German dirigible sheds at Tondern, at the mouth of the Elbe. The attack was a brilliant success, since the L 54 and L 60 were destroyed in their sheds. Richard Bell Davies, who was Senior Flying Officer on the *Furious* that day, wrote later that "the Tondern raid did a great deal more than eliminate one airship base. It finally removed the belief held by many senior officers that attacks by shipborne aircraft on shore and harbour targets were no good." The aircraft carrier had found its *raison d' être*.[28]

The torpedo plane, clearly envisaged before 1914, made its appearance as a practical weapon toward the end of the war and probably would have had considerable use had the fighting continued another year. Research was particularly active in Great Britain, Germany, and Italy. The British Short seaplane was an early candidate for torpedo-dropping. Aptly described as a "spindly, entomological-looking" machine, the Short had the same handicap as most aircraft of the early war years: it lacked the power to transport a torpedo-sized load. Even so, it is recorded that, in July 1915, "Flight Lieutenant Edmunds persuaded a Short seaplane to lift a torpedo over the Gallipoli Peninsula and sank a Turkish transport." The British scored several other successes in the Dardanelles, enough to stimulate partisans of the torpedo plane. Admiral Bradley Fiske argued that "the torpedo plane, under favorable conditions, would make the $20,000 airplane a worthy match for a $20,000,000 ship." The British Admiralty ordered an improved torpedo plane, the Sopwith Cuckoo, which was becoming operational when the war ended.[29]

Development also continued in Italy, where the navy borrowed two army Capronis, rigged them for half-ton torpedoes, and practiced torpedo runs in the summer of 1917. They staged two bombing raids on Pola on the night of October 2–3, with a Caproni torpedo plane taking advantage of the confusion to make a run at an Austro-Hungarian cruiser. The drop was unsuccessful, but the Italian Navy continued its experiments and created its first torpedo bomber unit, the Squadriglia San Marco, in March, 1918. The Germans too, turned to the bomber as torpedo carrier, mobilizing the Gotha for that purpose. They sank several ships in the Channel in the course of 1917. The missions were relatively few, since a successful attack required just the right combination of weather and sea conditions.[30]

With the increasing concentration of aircraft over certain bodies of water, notably the North Sea, it was unevitable that aerial combat should develop there, and with it the naval fighter. The British experimented with taking fighters to sea as early as 1915, when the Zeppelin menace first appeared. As naval air stations sprang up at Felixstowe and Great Yarmouth, at Dunkirk and St. Pol, and at Zeebrugge and Helgoland, naval aircraft found a battlefield over the Channel and the North Sea. Each side needed to keep track of enemy ship activity and at the same time shield its own harbors and coastlines from hostile observers. It was important to see where enemy minelayers or minesweepers were at work, and equally important to keep the enemy from knowing one's own mining and minesweeping operations.

In the North Sea, reconnaissance planes required escort as early as 1916, and torpedo planes likewise needed protection. The arming of seaplanes became general; Britain's Felixstowe F. 2a flying boat was armed with no fewer than four machine guns. German seaplanes that, like the Felixstowe F. 2a, were designed eventually as naval fighters included the Hansa Brandenburg W. 12 and W. 29 created by Dr. Ernst Heinkel. French naval airmen, who flew smaller and more lightly armed flying boats, were especially vulnerable to the Brandenburgs. Early in 1917 the French began to lose a flying boat a week; then on May 26 four of their F.B.A.'s, flying in close formation, were all shot down. The Brandenburgs would sometimes alight on a calm sea to conserve gas, and sit like so many ducks, waiting for an Allied plane to appear.[31]

The seaplane, however well designed, could rarely match the performance of the land plane. As a result, the tendency on both sides was to introduce land planes into the struggle for air supremacy at sea. By 1918 aerial reconnaissance of British ports had to be done by German naval aviators flying army aircraft. And the Brandenburg monoplanes met their match and more in British Camels and in Sopwith triplanes flown by French naval pilots. The Germans, for their part, created a number of land-based naval fighter units.

The practice of using land planes for naval purposes had serious consequences in wartime, for it increased the demand for a commodity already in short supply, and it aggravated interservice quarrels in which the navy was more often than not the loser. The navy also found it difficult to secure production of planes specifically needed for sea service—flying boats and aircraft with folding wings, for example—because the army had tied up resources or manufacturing capacity. In Germany at one point the two services were bidding against each other for the output of the Fokker firm. Major Wilhelm Siegert cited at least one instance in which the German Army put a cordon of troops around an airplane factory to keep *Kriegsmarine* pilots from taking the planes as they rolled out of the factory. In Britain a series of governmental boards had the thankless task of trying to harmonize the matériel needs of military and naval air services.[32]

Engines too were a bone of contention. In Britain they caused a "bitter enmity" between the two services. In Germany the army gained control of engine output; the navy complained that the trickle of powerplants was so slight that at times it could commit no more than 10 or 15 fighters to the struggle for air supremacy over the North Sea. Naval authorities everywhere protested that their development programs were delayed because of the land service. Their special needs ranged from high-endurance aircraft engines to wireless sets with greater range, to self-starters (the difficulties of climbing down and spinning the prop of a float plane bobbing on the high seas can well be imagined).[33]

But the quarrels went beyond matters of procurement. When the chief of the German Army's air service suggested to his naval counterpart that an exhausted army fighter unit at the front might temporarily change places with a naval fighter unit that was seeing little action on the North Sea, the suggestion got no response. For a long time the two services did not have mutually agreed-upon recognition signals for their aircraft; what is more they did not share the data generated by their respective intelligence services. Then there were "turf wars" of sorts. The U.S. Army vetoed a plan to place a Marine air unit on the Western Front in association with the U.S. Marine Brigade of the First Division. The Royal Flying Corps successfully resisted the detaching of its units for the Gallipoli expedition, so the early air support had to be handled by the R.N.A.S. French naval air units also found themselves earmarked for campaigns in out-of-the-way places; their float planes operated somewhat incongruously over the Sinai desert.[34]

Back in 1912, when the Royal Navy was fighting the idea of a common air service, its spokesmen argued that the functions of the naval aviator would be so different that "officers with a naval training and experience could alone perform these duties with any success." The experience of the war bore out the wisdom of this argument, for naval airmen had to cope with hazards and dangers unknown to army aviators, and to face them the men who flew over the sea needed additional skills. Navigation was of course one of these, and a more thorough knowledge of the mechanical side of flying was another. The crew of a flying boat forced down with a dead engine often had no recourse but to make the repairs themselves. Then there were the special tricks one learned, such as bringing a seaplane down in heavy fog. This was the method used by flying boats operating out of Great Yarmouth: "They carried a long stick, which was fitted, before alighting, in a socket, vertically outside the hull, and was coupled to the control column. When the end of the stick dragged in the water it pulled the column back and the boat sat down."[35]

A special drawback of patrol flying was the mind-numbing tedium, as the plane or blimp droned over empty sea. "Patrols were always dull," recalled one airman who flew the Spider's Web;

"we had given up any hope of being able to see and attack an enemy submarine. . . ." The statistics on patrol operations are eloquent in this regard: German seaplanes averaged 400 hours of flying for each contact with the enemy. British blimps spotted a total of 49 U-boats between June 1917 and October 1918; in that time they had flown a million and a half miles.[36]

The deadliest enemy was the sea. In the early days of the war, when planes flew singly and without radio, if they failed to return searches were almost always fruitless. When planes acquired wireless transmitters they could at least signal their positions if forced down; then, patrolling in pairs was introduced, and this provided a certain sense of security, plus the advantage of two wireless sets in the event one failed to function. If one plane were forced down, the other hovered overhead, though if the plane on the water got into further difficulty, the airmen overhead felt a strong urge to alight and give what help they could. From time to time rescue parties found neither plane, and the assumption was that one had gone to the assistance of the other, and the sea had claimed them both.

"Ditching" a land plane was at best a risky enterprise. The Sopwith Camel tended to pitch forward violently; its pilot could almost count on a blow to his head, and deem himself lucky if he were not knocked unconscious; flotation bags would presumably keep the plane afloat for a time, and the D.H. 6 was highly regarded for sea service since "it floated well." Float planes, which rode high on the water, had a bad habit of tipping over backwards and capsizing; when that happened the crew tied themselves to the pontoons. Flying boats rode so low that with any kind of sea running at all, they began to ship water; when that happened the crew set to bailing. The buffeting of the waves often produced acute seasickness.

There were standard procedures for the crews of downed planes; one of the first steps was to put out a sea anchor so as to keep the plane pointed into the wind. If they had been forced down by engine failure, they tried to make repairs; if the engine could be made to run at all and the state of the sea permitted it, it might be possible to taxi home. Seaplanes usually carried pigeons, and these could be released with messages; flare pistols were also standard equipment.

Downed airmen could survive for a week or more if the plane remained seaworthy and they had water (if the engine were liquid-cooled the crew could drink the water in the radiator). There were cases of seaplanes drifting across the Channel, and one case in which the Mistral blew a French plane and its crew from off Marseilles all the way to Corsica. There were incredible rescues: a French airman had drifted for 27 hours in a blinding snowstorm in the middle of the English Channel when a British packet came knifing by so close he could touch it. Captain Friedrich Christiansen, a legendary figure among German naval flyers, found himself clinging to his downed and badly damaged plane on a dark and stormy North Sea night; after nine hours he was waiting for death when the submarine U-10 popped to the surface beside him.[37]

In the fall of 1917 U.S. Navy aviators had begun antisubmarine patrols over the Bay of Biscay, using French Tellier flying boats. The first submarine alert at the Le Croisic air station came on the morning of November 22. Eager and with little thought of preparation, Lieutenant Kenneth Smith and his mechanic and observer took-off in their Tellier and vanished out to sea. They had taken neither a flare pistol nor a sea anchor, nor a supply of food and water. They did have pigeons, and these arrived periodically over the next three days; the messages said the plane was down with engine trouble somewhere in the Bay of Biscay, then in the rough seas it was beginning to break up. Then the last pigeon came in with a final message; it would probably have passed into history had Lieutenant Smith and his companions not been found by a French torpedo boat minutes before their battered flying boat sank. But the last words in Lieutenant Smith's message could well serve as the epitaph of all the airmen the sea did claim. They were: "Please tell friends that we died game to the end."[38]

=12=

The Final Battles

At 4:40 A.M. on March 21, 1918, some six thousand German guns suddenly opened fire in what the Germans called the *Kaiserschlacht*, the great battle they hoped would bring the war to a rapid and successful conclusion. The idea had come from General Erich Ludendorff, then the dominant figure in the High Command; he took an active role in planning the offensive, which carried the code name Michael. The German preparations were carried out with elaborate precautions so that the buildup would go undetected. Cannon and munitions were concealed with great care; the massive concentration of troops took place at virtually the last moment. Men and supplies moved forward only at night, so that Allied aerial observers would see normal levels of traffic in their daily reconnaissances. It was therefore with some consternation that two days before the attack, German troops in at least one forward position found themselves showered with leaflets from a British plane wishing them "best of luck for your attack on March 21."[1]

Whatever the inspiration for the leaflets, it is nonetheless true that the Allied High Command did not know exactly where or when the Germans would attack, though they understood quite well that some offensive action was imminent. By 1918 aerial reconnaissance had become one of the best means of finding out the where and when; in the case of previous offensives it had invariably provided both sides with solid clues to the enemy's preparations. So reliable was the "eye in the sky" that one French general recalled: "All of our past experience had shown us the impossibility, indeed the futility of any attempt at surprise. The enemy's preparations, which lasted for months, had not escaped investigation by our reconnaissance planes." But before the great assault launched against the British Army in the St. Quentin sector that March, Allied air intelligence had failed to detect the menace— partly because of the Germans' painstakingly thorough efforts at concealment, partly because of a bout of bad weather just before the attack, and partly because the Allies lacked reconnaissance planes that could penetrate sufficiently deep in the enemy's rear to detect the massed reserves.[2]

The German air service had an important role in the preparation of Michael. There was first of all the task of photographing every square foot of the British lines for a stretch of fifty miles— this without a significant increase in aerial activity that might arouse the enemy's suspicions. The photographs became the basis for exceedingly detailed maps of the British positions for use by the German infantry and artillery. German fighter forces were also under orders to avoid increased aerial activity even if it meant allowing British reconnaissance planes to range widely over the German side of the lines. "In no case must an attempt be made to conceal preparations by means of strong defensive patrols, as the enemy can break through them, no matter how strong." And finally, artillery and spotting planes were to do no registration before the battle, since this too could alert the British. The guns were to be put on target by means of tailored firing tables that took into account the individual gun's characteristics, as determined on firing ranges far behind the lines. The tables, prepared by professional mathematicians, also made allowances for temperature, humidity, wind direction and force, and in some cases even the earth's rotation. In all, Ludendorff amassed 730 aircraft for the offensive, over a third of the German front-line strength. Some models, like the high-flying Rumpler Rubild with supercompressed engine, were new models that would make their debut in the coming battles.[3]

The March offensive was extremely successful. The German advance rolled over much of the old Somme battlefield, and the contrast with the French and British efforts of 1916 was telling. Then the Allies had conquered 95 square miles in the space of 140 days at a cost of 500,000 casualties; in the first twenty-four hours of Michael the German infantry took 140 square miles at a cost of 40,000 casualties. The German success was in part attributable to new weapons such as the light machine gun, which enabled advancing troops to carry greater firepower with them; but even more important was a new tactical recipe that called for specially trained storm troops, infiltration of the enemy lines, an elaborate firing plan for the artillery, and a high degree of coordination between footsoldiers and the big guns. (The recipe had been developed and refined on the Eastern Front and against the Italians at Caporetto in October 1917.)[4]

Michael lost momentum and ended in April, having given the German Army possession of a thousand square miles of France. There were succeeding German drives interspersed with periods of relative stability on into July. Then the pendulum swung, and it was the Allies who mounted a series of successful offensives on down to the Armistice. The final months of the war then, saw a kind of fighting far different from the "battlefield constipation" that had so long characterized the Western Front. Though the airplane had not played a major role in the tactical revolution, it was able to adapt itself fairly quickly. Both sides made lavish commitments of aircraft: the Allies, in order to discover and hopefully to block the enemy's axes of advance; the Germans, to track the movement and direction of reserves the British and French were bringing forward and, if possible, to delay them—by systematic bombardment of rail lines, for example. Casualties mounted quickly with the new tempo of activity: in the two months of January and February, 1918 the RFC had losses of 96 and 91 airmen killed or missing on the Western Front, but the monthly average rose in March–June to 215. For the French, killed and missing averaged 66 in January–February, 114 in March–April, and 216 in May–June. For all three belligerents the year 1918 would be by far the worst year for air losses.[5]

The war of movement placed new demands on the air services. The traditional pattern of artillery spotting was disrupted, for "both the artillery and the airmen had operated under conditions of static warfare far too long and new methods could not be learnt so quickly." The reconnaissance mission was also affected, for now the enemy often had to be located. Jean Puistienne recalled that his fighter escadrille was pressed into service for reconnaissance and ground attack and sent on its missions with vague orders: "Departure 3:30, region Mondidier, Roye, Chaulnes. The enemy should be there somewhere; find him, attack his troops with machine guns, bring back the most precise information you can."[6]

With the battle lines more fluid it became more difficult to tell friendly territory from that of the enemy, and a solution was found by the frequent issue of updated maps indicating where the lines ran. By this means the airmen were kept well informed about how things were going in the land battles. André Duvau recalled that from May 31 to June 2 his bomber escadrille flew seven missions and that "it was time to get busy because on the ground things weren't going well at all. The Boches were advancing rapidly; each time we took off they gave us a new drawing of the lines." Even with updated maps the aviators made errors; the instances in which aircraft attacked friendly troops multiplied. The airmen themselves could also be victims of a rapidly shifting situation on the ground. They would land at a familiar airfield and find themselves prisoners. Units were uprooted from fields that had been their homes for months and even years. The new style of war turned Jean Puistienne's escadrille into aerial vagabonds. He recalled moving from one field to another, the fuselage of his Spad crammed with his clothes, a bundle of his belongings lashed to the plane's landing gear. Occasionally the enemy advance was so rapid that evacuation was impossible; the airmen set fire to their planes and joined the columns of retreating ground troops.[7]

Along with its challenges, the campaign of 1918 offered new opportunities for the use of air power. Hardly had the *Kaiserschlacht* begun when the commander of the hard-pressed British Fifth Army called for reinforcements. Ground troops sent to the threatened sector could only trickle in, moving over rail lines that were under German bombardment; but aircraft from the neighboring British Second Army were on the scene within half an hour. Later on in the summer, when it was the Germans who were threatened in one sector and then in another, they too made use of the airplane's extreme mobility. When heavy fighting was raging near Cambrai, the High Command brought several *staffeln* of ground-attack planes in from the Laon region some seventy miles away, and then sent them back to their home base that same evening to face a threat developing there. Then there were occasions when the airmen came to the rescue of friendly ground troops. As armies surged back and forth, units were sometimes isolated and surrounded. A French battalion found itself in that predicament at the Château of Vandières in July; for two days flights of Breguet bombers kept the outpost supplied until French ground forces could fight through to its defenders.[8]

The changed conditions of warfare had the effect of hastening the emergence of a fourth category of warplane, one destined for the ground-attack mission, or to use the modern term, close air support. In this guise the airplane was to participate directly and actively in the land battle, not as an aerial observation platform but as an offensive weapon. The genesis of ground-attack aviation was the infantry contact patrol plane, charged with following the progress of friendly infantry in battle, filling in the communications gap that often developed on the battlefield. The nature of their work took airmen in contact patrol work quite close to the battlefield; sometimes it was necessary to descend as low as 800 feet to distinguish friendly troops from hostile ones. Since they could often identify enemy positions, they took to dropping messages to their own advancing infantry, and since the planes used were usually armed two-seaters, it was not long before they were themselves attacking the enemy resistance points. As with bombing and aerial fighting, these interventions seem to have begun through individual initiative. Low-level aerial attack of battlefield objectives received official sanction at the Battle of the Somme. For the opening of the battle the R.F.C. assigned eighteen contact planes to "trench fights" with the dual purpose of "close reconnaissance and destructive bombardment." The battles of 1917 saw further use of the low-flying planes.[9]

But it was the Germans who hit upon the idea of special ground-attack units, the *Schlachtstaffeln*, which they formed from pre-existing *Schutzstaffeln*, two-seaters which served as armed escorts for the contact patrol planes. The new units received a special "Instruction" a month before the opening of the *Kaiserschlacht*; there they were described as "a powerful weapon which should be employed at the *decisive* point of the attack." They were not to be unleashed to roam freely over the battlefield, as British and French planes were, but to intervene when and where ground authorities felt they would have maximum effect. Coordination with ground operations was developed as much as the primitive communications equipment would permit. The ground-attack planes could only carry the lightest of armament, machine guns, and small anti-personnel bombs; not surprisingly the German instructions stressed the role of "shattering the enemy's nerve," and for this purpose formation flying at minimal altitude was strongly recommended.[10]

In the campaign of 1918, with troops out of their trenches and on the roads, the possibilities for ground-attack aircraft increased, and the breed began to proliferate. On the very first day of Michael, German Schlachtstaffeln attacked British troops in and around the town of Roupy, softening it up in preparation for an assault by German infantry. The Allies learned very quickly that when the enemy had achieved a breakthrough, air attacks on his columns could slow his advance while new ground defenses were being cobbled together. On June 4, French intelligence learned that a large number of German troops were massed for an assault east of the forest of Villers-Cotterets, where they were sheltered in a deep ravine, out of reach of French artillery. The French Air Service despatched 120 Breguet XIV bombers which made several passes from a height of only 600 meters, dropping 7,000 bombs. The German assault never took place.[11]

In the summer of 1918 the British added another refinement to the rapidly emerging art of ground attack, a partnership between the airplane and the tank. While the British were now employing tanks in considerable numbers and with no little success, the tank proved highly vulnerable when it encountered enemy artillery. The artillerymen usually saw the tank first and got in the first shot—with often fatal consequences. The British solution was to have low-flying planes scout ahead of the tanks and attack enemy artillery that might be lying in wait. The collaboration was reasonably successful and would have been more so if the partners had been in radio contact, but they were reduced to flares and other visual signals.[12]

Effective as ground-attack operations proved to be in 1918, they were not without their hazards. Such missions became more costly to those who flew them as enemy troops lost their initial fear of low-flying planes and fired at them with increasing effect. The Germans sometimes strung cables through the air in sectors where low-flying Allied planes were expected. In the fighting in October 1918 the U.S. Air Service organized an interception system for the Schlachtstaffeln; keeping fighters on patrol between 200 and 800 feet, they claimed ten German planes for every American fighter lost. What fragmentary figures survive suggest that ground-attack was becoming an increasingly risky operation. John Slessor cites the case of No. 80 Squadron, which was employed in close air support work almost continuously from March 1918 until the end of the war: "Their average strength was 22 officers, and in the last 10 months of the war no less than 168 officers were struck off the strength from all causes—an average of about 75 percent per month, of whom little less than half were killed."[13]

While tactical air weapons were refined in that last year of the war, strategic air power seemed to take a new lease on life. April saw the emergence of a British Air Ministry and of the Royal Air Force, a part of whose resources were pledged to an "independent" bombing force, charged with carrying the war to the cities of Germany: the bombing force came into existence under General Trenchard in June, but British bombers had begun sprinkling high explosives in the Ruhr some months before. The Germans too were carrying the war to an enemy metropolis— Paris. There was a preliminary raid to test the city's defenses on the night of January 30–31, with thirty G planes sent against the northern part of "Festung Paris." Franz Schlenstedt, then with Bombengeschwader 7, recalled that his unit's particular target was the vast munitions plant at Sevran. Though few of the specific objectives were ever damaged, the bombers found the French air defensives ineffective. The raids began in earnest in March, and before the war ended the night bombers had come forty-four times. The French authorities kept a scrupulous record of the attacks; according to their figures the bombers dropped in all 25,000 kilos of explosives, with bombs up to three hundred kilos in weight. The French met them with searchlights, anti-aircraft guns, night fighters, and a cordon of barrage balloons that forced the bombers to come in over 3000 meters—a height that ruled out any bombing accuracy.[14]

Though the raids on Paris were described as *Vergeltungsmass-nahmen*—reprisal measures for Allied attacks on "open cities" such as Mannheim and Freiburg, there is little doubt that they had another purpose. The pattern of raids complemented the daytime shelling by the "Paris guns," which also began in March. It is clear that they and the shelling were designed to deliver a shock to the heart of France at the same time she was suffering reverses in the field—the sort of "one-two punch" that had been planned against the British the year before. In Paris the greatest wave of shock and indignation came on Good Friday, when one of the giant cannon shells struck the Church of Saint-Gervais, bringing down a part of the vault and killing nearly a hundred worshipers. By late summer the night bombers had at their disposal a weapon even more terrible than the Paris guns: a small incendiary known as the Elektron, which burned at between 2000° and 3000° Fahrenheit. According to careful estimates, a single raid with Elektrons— "little things," the German air crews called them—might destroy a third of the City of Lights. The Elektrons were never used, though it is questionable whether they would have had any major adverse effect on French morale. For it was September before they were ready in any number, and by September the French and their allies sensed that the hour of victory—and of retribution—was approaching.[15]

For the sands were running out for Germany and her allies. In the air war the signs of the shift in fortunes were not always dramatic that summer, but they were unmistakable. First of all German airmen had the impression of being increasingly overwhelmed by the sheer number of their adversaries. Rudolf Berthold recorded in his diary on June 10 that he had gotten his thirty-third and thirty-fourth air victories, but that he had picked his victims out of a mass of one hundred enemy planes: "Never until now have I seen so many opponents at once." When the German Army advanced in the spring and summer, the flying units went forward with them, occupying airfields that had been hastily abandoned by the French or British. There German airmen were struck by the evidence of "inexhaustible supplies of matériel" which stood in stark contrast to their own dwindling resources. First of all, the Allies seemed to have plentiful stocks of fuel, while the German air service was having to practice strict economy, reserving the best fuels for fighter craft, and using benzol, alcohol, and kerosene mixtures for less critical flying.[15]

The Allies examined all German aircraft that fell into their hands, looking for deterioration in quality and evidence of shortages in critical commodities. The signs were everywhere: rubber had virtually disappeared from German aircraft, as had brass and copper. Wheels were frequently made of wood, or were curious steel rims cushioned with metal springs. Wood was in short supply, judging from the amount of splicing used; only plywood seemed plentiful. In German observation balloons, fabric was being replaced by goldbeater's skin, a membrane taken from the intestines

of oxen. A captured German memorandum of June 1, 1918, reproduced by the R.A.F. as *Confidential Communication Order No. 6*,
called for greater efforts in salvaging downed aircraft because
"our aeroplane industry is more and more reduced to relying
on the working up of motors and instruments saved from destroyed
aeroplanes. . . . The supply of material to the front has become
essentially dependent on the return of waste material from the
front." Even more interesting, the German memorandum called
for salvaging Allied wireless sets; the Allies had perfected a continuous wave apparatus which German scientists had been unable
to match. Until German apparatus was available they planned
to use the enemy equipment.[17]

If in the realm of matériel the situation of the Allies was
infinitely better—and in fact improving—much of the credit went
to their newest ally, the United States. The Americans were shipping aviation gasoline from their refineries and spruce from the
forests of the Northwest, and they were undertaking to solve the
castor oil shortage by planting a hundred thousand acres in castor
beans. In the short term, the American effort counted for embar-
rassingly little, or at least it seemed to after the resounding declarations the nation had made on entering the war. The United States
pledged—"almost gaily in our ignorance," as a contemporary put
it—to maintain a force of 4,500 aircraft and 5,000 pilots at the
front by June, 1918. Congress voted $640,000,000 for that pur-
pose, but a year after our declaration of war we had yet to take
our place in the skies over the Western Front. There was a considerable hue and cry within the country, and our allies could not
resist ironic references to an aerial armament effort "launched
upon the world with the blaring of trumpets and the clashing of
cymbals." In Germany the *Frankfurter Zeitung* noted on the first
anniversary of the American entry into the war that "up to the
present we have encountered no American air unit, no American
plane, and no American motor."[18]

That same month the first U.S. Air Service pilot downed a
German plane; by the end of May the Service had its first ace.
In June it began bombing operations, and in September the Ameri-
cans directed a massive aerial effort that helped wipe out the St.
Mihiel salient. By the time of the Armistice there were forty-five
American squadrons assigned to the armies on the Western Front,
and though most of the 740 planes were French, they were manned
by some 1200 American airmen, and they constituted a far from

negligible force. And in addition to their numbers, the Americans brought a new spirit, a bracing confidence in early victory. War Department instructions stressed that "immature, highstrung, over confident, impatient candidates are not desired," but the instructions seem not to have been followed. The Americans brought to the war an eagerness and a zest all their own. After Elliott White Springs returned from his first aerial combat he dashed off a note to his sister back in South Carolina: "God, it was great! Sherman was all wrong. He was unlucky enough to be in the wrong branch of the service." Sholto Douglas, who saw a good bit of American aviators, wrote that "they were never lacking in guts, and they went about their fighting with an enthusiasm that won the admiration and respect of all those who ever came into contact with them." A German pilot, contrasting them with the French, said that the Frenchman was "cautious" in his engagements while the American was "more attack-happy."[19]

Had the war continued into 1919, as many thought it would, the American contribution in the air would have been a massive one. In the last week before the Armistice the Americans were building 500 planes a week, while engine production was approaching that of Britain and France combined. By April 1919 production was to reach a rate of 40,000 aircraft per year. Add this to the fleet of heavy bombers the British and French were building, the three hundred Sopwith Cuckoo torpedo planes that would be available for a massive carrier-borne strike at the Kaiser's fleet, and the new night fighter units, and the armored ground strafers—and one can understand why the campaign of 1919 was to offer a resounding demonstration of what air power could do. But it was not to be. On the morning of November 11, 1918, the guns fell silent and the Great War was over.

=13=

An End and a
Beginning

The final battles of a war are usually followed in short order
by the opening skirmishes among historians, as they struggle
to explain why and how it all came about. The First World War
was no exception. When Air Marshal Trenchard submitted his
final report on the activities of his independent bombing force
early in 1919, an analyst in *Flight* deduced from it that the force
had clearly tilted the scales in favor of the Allies, though "by
what period it actually did shorten the war it is impossible to
say." But the British Army's official history judged the aerial bombing campaign of 1918 to have been "without important results."
In the more general accounts and analyses the airplane and the
dirigible have not occupied places of prominence. Writers of military history have tended to regard battle as the essence of warfare
and to assign the principal roles in their narratives to the combat
arms that meet in major engagements. In the great land battles
of 1914–1918 they found aviation playing no such role. To them
it appeared as an auxiliary, preparing and supporting the main
action without itself being center stage. And so like the engineers,
the signal corps, and others in that role, at best aviation got a
supporting actor's modest billing. Historians of air power have
attempted to redress the balance, though in doing so they tended
to place heavy stress on aviation's autonomous role rather than
its contributions to the land campaigns. Basil Collier's well re-

217

garded *History of Air Power* is fairly representative: some seventeen pages of its chapter on World War I are allotted to the airplane's contribution in the land war; approximately the same number of pages is dedicated to strategic bombing efforts, which could not have accounted for ten percent of the energies and resources that the belligerents committed to the air war.[1]

What conclusions can we draw from the present study, brief and broad as it is? First of all, the history of military aeronautics must be dated before 1914. In the years leading up to Sarajevo it was assumed that air power would have a place in any major war to come, though this view may have been more firmly fixed in the mind of the tabloid-reading public than in the thinking of the general staffs. In the case of aerial reconnaissance, by 1914 the expectations rested on several years of trials and maneuvers, as well as on experience gained in a series of minor wars; as a consequence, the exploitation of aerial reconnaissance during the war brought no big surprises, and certainly no bad ones.

In 1914 the idea of aerial combat remained a speculative one; the few scenarios sketched out before the conflict bore more resemblance to Jules Verne than to the realities of the fighter war that emerge in 1915–18. When the fighter function did appear, it evolved "according to the needs of battle more than according to a doctrine or in some deliberately chosen direction." The wartime evolution of the ground-attack mission seems to have proceeded in the same fashion, unencumbered by preconceptions. On the other hand, a great deal was expected of aerial bombing, and once again the expectations were probably greatest in nonmilitary circles. When the bomber did appear, in the guise of both the airplane and the dirigible, its generally disappointing performance seemed to confirm the skeptics' view that aerial bombing's proper place was in science fiction.[2]

In this connection it must be said that military aeronautics was conceived and born in a less hostile environment than is often represented. From the very beginning aeronautics—military or otherwise—captured the public's imagination and enjoyed broad support; what is more, it almost always had friends in high places. Military conservatism was certainly there and it did not lack for spokesmen—men like the British admiral who exclaimed on seeing his first dirigible "this is the work of a lunatic!" But whatever the shortcomings of the early twentieth-century military, they were not blind to technological innovation and its impact on the art of war; they had already seen too much—smokeless powder, the wireless, internal combustion engines, rapid-fire cannon, and the like. On reflection, it is hard to quarrel with John Terraine's assertion about the generals of the Great War: "the truth is that those ruddy-cheeked, bristling moustached, heavy jawed, frequently inarticulate generals rose to challenge after challenge, absorbed weapon after weapon into their battle systems, adapted themselves to constant change with astonishing address." If anything, they tended to err in introducing new weaponry too hastily, rather than too slowly, armor and chemical warfare being two cases in point. On close examination, then, it is impossible to conclude that aeronautics was the Cinderella of the wartime services; its phenomenal growth during the conflict proves just the opposite. Georges Huisman was right when he wrote "here is another myth to be demolished, despite all that is done to have it accepted—that of a high command hostile to aviation."[3]

One could make the argument that military aeronautics suffered almost as much from the attentions of its partisans as from the attacks of its enemies—this because its partisans rather consistently oversold it. The journalists and the pulp writers with their apocalyptic scenarios were not the only ones at fault. There was Joynson Hicks, a political figure of considerable standing, who argued in 1912 that Germany had moderated her foreign policy out of fear that the French might launch "a cloud" of planes against her. And there were responsible military and naval figures, Admiral Bradley Fiske, for example, who wanted to defend the Philippines from Japanese attack by building four airfields and placing a hundred airplanes on each—this in 1911. There was General Billy Mitchell, who in October 1918 tried to convince General Pershing that parachuting an entire American division behind German lines was "perfectly feasible." A British historian has suggested that "the inspiration of a minority of far-seeing enthusiasts has been vitiated over and over again by inadequate technology or conventional thinking." An American historian put it more bluntly: "The aviators envisaged and promised great things, but their aircraft continually let them down. . . ."[4]

In justice to the airmen, it must be said that their visions of air power were simply premature more often than they were wrong. Admiral Henri Noumy of the French Navy suggested that the differences between the aviators and the military and naval establishments of which they were a part amounted to nothing more than a "lovers' quarrel," since both parties were really seeking the same thing, an air service that could make the maximum contributions to victory. Noumy felt obliged to remind the partisans of aviation that it took time to fit new weapons into complicated battle systems; in the preface to a book on naval aviation, he wrote, "the Navy is a large, powerful machine; it cannot execute hairpin turns."[5]

If we turn from perceptions of the air weapon to the fundamental matter of its role in the Great War, we must say that the role was not a major one. Neither the airplane nor the dirigible figured for anything in the development of the positional warfare system on the Western Front, and in the last months of the war, the airplane was not a basic ingredient in the breakup of that system. One could go further; after reviewing the aviators' contribution to the conflict, Malcolm Smith has recently written: "One would search in vain to discover instances in which they dramatically affected the course of battle or campaign."[6]

For the balance of the war the most important role of the airplane, aided by the tethered balloon, was purely and simply observation. It put an end to the *bataille de rencontre*, in which two armies collide blindly; it warned of any movement or change in the enemy camp, and with few exceptions it foretold the enemy's offensive and helped guarantee that it would fail. But the essence of war is weaponry and the death and destruction it metes out. What was the airplane's contribution here? In a way that contribution was immense. The supreme killing device in the Great War was neither the rifle bullet nor that fired by the machine gun; nor was it poison gas or any of the other weapons born in the war. It was the exploding artillery shell, which blew its shards of steel across the battlefield like a deadly hail. Surgeons in the dressing stations saw the evidence every day, and later the systematically conducted postmortems confirmed that three wounds out of four were inflicted by the artillery—a complete reversal from previous wars, in which small-arms fire claimed by far the largest number of victims. The men in the trenches didn't know the statistics, but they knew who their most dangerous enemy was. "This is a cowering war," wrote one American soldier the day before a German shell took his life, "pigmy man huddles in little holes and caves praying to escape the blows of the giant who pounds the earth with blind hammers." But the hammers were not really blind. They were guided by the tiny, fragile machine turning overhead.[7]

Aerial artillery spotting, like the other reconnaissance functions, had the effect of inhibiting movement, of keeping the armies in their earthworks, and thus of contributing to the defensive side of warfare, and indeed it has been argued that air power used in this way "was a decisive factor in creating and maintaining the stalemate which was characteristic of the Great War." The fighter plane, which was called into being by a preoccupation with reconnaissance, played something of an ambivalent role. As an escort to the observation plane it contributed mostly to the defensive; as a destroyer of such planes it tended to facilitate the offensive. The bomber's role was ambivalent too, but it found its most profitable work as an extension of the artillery, attacking communications lines and concentrations of matériel and reserves—the sort of activity that makes an offensive more difficult to mount.[8]

Only strategic air power seemed to offer a real alternative to the bloody, indecisive collisions along a static front: the swift, deep, surgically precise stroke at just the right objective—what Clausewitz called the enemy's center of gravity—that would ensure his rapid collapse. Both the French and Italians probed the possibilities quite early, only to give up the idea: in their circumstances a duel between strategic bombing forces could only work to their disadvantage. The British and the Germans persisted but got only mediocre results. They could not produce the physical damage needed; they consistently overestimated the damage to enemy morale they could inflict, and recent studies of the British strategic effort of 1917–18 suggest it served primarily "as a token to satisfy public demands for reprisals." Still the allure of the strategic bomber would persist. It would become the central element in the thought of Giulio Douhet and Hugh Trenchard.[9]

On the other hand, the close air support function which had been the last to evolve would vanish almost completely after the war. The Canadian official history notes that "it disappeared quickly and completely from the corpus of doctrine upon which R.A.F. procurement and training was based." The chief reason for its disappearance in Britain and elsewhere was apparently the heavy casualties involved. When the issue came up again in 1939, the Air Staff reminded British Army leaders of the 30 percent losses per day that "trench flights" had cost its squadrons at Cambrai in November 1917: "The air force have never been unwilling to face heavy loses; but it must be realized that highly trained pilots cannot be replaced with the same ease as infantry soldiers."[10]

Curiously, ground-attack aviation did have an attraction for the U.S. Air Service. In the postwar period it was the only military power which maintained a special "attack" wing whose mission was close support of the ground forces. While it has been a habit in these pages to treat the air services in common, and the practice has seemed justified, the Americans were not the only exception to the rule. There was, in fact, a considerable range of differences among the belligerents: Austria-Hungary, Russia, the Balkan countries, and to some degree Italy were incapable of matching the French, British, and Germans in the air for lack of the scientific-technical-industrial base that such sophisticated warfare called for. At the time there was a tendency to minimize such shortcomings, for the European military were still repeating Napoleon's cele-brated dictum that in war the moral is to the physical as three is to one—this being taken to mean that the motivation of fighting men is far more crucial than their numbers or their armament. Even if the Napoleonic equation were valid in the Emperor's own day, the increasing importance of the purely mechanical in "high tech" warfare was bound to call it into question. How much courage, how much confidence in victory on the part of a pilot would compensate for a really inferior airplane?

If there was a single air service which stood apart from all the others in 1918, it was the Royal Air Force. There were subtle distinctions between the British airmen and those of other belliger-ents. If the German aviator fought cleanly, it was attributed to his sense of *Ritterlichkeit* or chivalry; the Frenchman admired the *beau geste;* but the British airman fought that way because he was a good sportsman and war was something of a game. Both the French and the Germans commented on the British preoccupa-tion with sport. "They were very sporting," said one German airman, "we were much more military." And in combat the British aviator was remarked for a specific quality. Over and over again German aviators used the same word to describe their British opponents: *Zähigkeit,* tenacity.

If we examine the composition of the major air services, the contrast is striking; in 1918 over half the front-line aircraft in the French and German services were reconnaissance planes. In the R.A.F., on the other hand, 58 percent of the planes were fighters. The systematic employment of deep, offensive fighter patrols was distinctly British; the French tried it only briefly in 1917 and the Germans not at all. The policy has been much criticized over the years and with some cause. One of its avowed purposes was to shake the opponent's morale, but as far as German aviators were concerned, it does not seem to have achieved its purpose. In July 1918 James McCudden wrote of the men he was fighting: "The more I fight them, the more I respect them for their fighting qualities." There is a wealth of other testimony that the Germans too, were game to the end. In the fighter battles behind the German lines those German pilots who survived when their planes were downed—and this would be a clear majority—would soon be in the air again; British pilots forced down would be on their way to a prison camp. German airmen commented on the number of green replacement pilots in the British fighter squadrons opposing them, a weakness that may have fed upon itself as the war continued.[11]

In the British service reconnaissance was less important numerically, and there is evidence that it was deficient in other ways. Well into the war it seems to have been the pilot who did much of the observation work, rather than the observer. Formal, specialized training for observers developed later than for most of the other belligerents. The British approach toward training in general was distinctive, relying heavily on personal motivation and initiative, hopefully aided by a certain flair for the job at hand. This was not necessarily the best way to procure highly trained specialists; in the case of flight training, if we may give credence to some of the statistics on training accidents, such methods were wasteful of life.

It has been customary to attribute these differences to the vagaries of leadership. Thus the offensive-mindedness of British fighter pilots is said to reflect the thinking of Trenchard, who enjoyed a rather free hand in directing the British air effort in France. But the same ideas were espoused by Trenchard's predecessor, Sir David Henderson, and they also found expression the fighting doctrine of the Royal Naval Air Service. By the same token the evolution of aeronautics in the French Army was said to be influenced by the fact that while Joffre was ignorant of aerial matters, he was also open-minded. It has been asserted recently that the employment of aviation in the A.E.F. was affected down to corps and divisions levels because General Pershing "gave little attention" to his air service, having been disappointed with the way airplanes performed in his operations along the Mexican border.[12]

In one of the more provocative books on the Great War to appear in recent years, historian Tim Travers has suggested that the distinctions visible in the military machines of the various belligerents are not traceable to individuals so much as they are to a kind of cultural-institutional mindset that varied from one country to the next. Specifically Travers argues that the British military were so imbued with notions of the offensive and of the "psychological battlefield"—the Napoleonic equation—that they were not able to use new weaponry as effectively as others, notably the Germans. Travers found that while British officers accepted new weapons readily enough, they had "emotional difficulty in coming to mental grips with the tactical and command changes implied by the new or improved technology."[13]

Travers has very little to say about the use of air power. This is unfortunate since the approach is a fresh one and could provide some new insights as to why the airplane was not ultimately incorporated into the battle system as other new weapons were. Part of the explanation no doubt lies in the airplane's "technical peculiarities," as someone called them, but part probably lies in its uniqueness and the implications thereof. Most new weapons could be related to existing ones, and used—or misused—accordingly; thus the machine gun was for a time considered artillery and the tank a fortress that could be moved about on the battlefield. But the airplane was totally new and like nothing else in the panoply of war; its use required thinking—literally—in a new dimension. Moreover its employment was hedged about by all sorts of technological limitations that could not be ignored or overridden, matters of speed, range, carrying capacity, etc. On the "psychological battlefield" soldiers would be inspired to fight for hours with empty stomachs; when a plane's fuel tank was empty, its flying and fighting stopped. Then, too, the plane's action was difficult or impossible to coordinate with that of other arms, for coordination implies communication and the air-ground links were inadequate. Faced with these daunting complexities, a corps or army commander who knew little of aviation had two choices: he could turn to the nearest officer with an airman's wings on his tunic and ask, "what can you do?" or he could treat the airplane as he sometimes did other devices that threatened to change the battlefield he knew—he could simply ignore it.

But the airplane also challenged and ultimately altered attitudes, especially among the men who flew. There is evidence that the aviator had to come to grips emotionally with what was in essence a kind of partnership with a machine. In the end the partnership was viable because the aviator considered himself the master, the senior partner. The laurels and the victory credits came to him. While his altimeter told him his altitude so would his eyes, and it often pleased him to trust the latter. Wedgewood Benn, who reflected on this man-machine relationship, concluded that the aviator conceived of himself as an artist. He put his trust in his talent, in his "flair," and disdained gadgetry. For that reason he flew without reference to his instruments and he dropped bombs without using his bombsight. Some efficiency was no doubt lost thereby, but the ego was preserved and man remained the master.[14]

Yet the machine changed the man. There was something about the partnership and about the miracle of flight it made possible that transformed those who flew and set them apart from all others. The aviators themselves acknowledged this. A German flyer recalled that "during the war the idea often came up that flyers were a new kind of race, called into being by new physical and moral demands." Many years afterward General Carl Spaatz reflected: "I guess we considered ourselves a different breed of cat, right in the beginning. We flew through the air and other people walked on the ground. It was as simple as that."[15]

The British may have been right in speaking of a "temper of the air"; if it existed, two of its traits were undoubtedly a confidence in the air arm and what it could do and a strong faith in its future. Alan Bott was convinced that before the war was over the fighting in the air would be "as decisive as hostilities on land and sea." In a brief essay he wrote a few days before he was killed, James McCudden made a similar prophesy. Sefton Branker wrote in 1917 that the Royal Flying Corps had attained "a position of almost predominant importance." Outside of the air services this talk passed for boastfulness; Malcolm Cooper has described British airmen of the era as having "overdeveloped professional pride." That, along with their strong, and sometimes headstrong personalities, made it impossible for them to "work easily within established service hierarchy." To those on the ground, the airman's view of the air war would continue to carry "a charge of aspiration if not boastfulness."[16]

Other traits were no doubt initiative, enterprise, and an independent streak, understandable in a service in which men were often left to fly and fight on their own, and traceable to the airman's fundamental and unending desire to be in the air. A general with aircraft at his disposal might ignore them, but neither they nor their pilots would languish in idleness; the airmen would find a way to get into the air and once there they would find a way to get into the action. We have seen that such initiative and enterprise led to aerial combat and ground attack, and counted for more than a little in the practical origins of aerial bombing. The war provided at least two major examples of air services virtually writing their own orders when none came from above. The first was the Royal Naval Air service, which undertook some very ambitious operations when given its head in 1914–15. The other was the U.S. Air Service; left largely to its own devices during the Meuse-Argonne campaign, "it tended to operate as an independent element, engaging in bombardments of the enemy's rear, in pursuit, and in observation." In the end one is left to wonder which consideration kept aviation from fitting neatly into an army's order of battle. Was it the special, distinctive nature of the airplane or the special, distinctive nature of the man who flew it?[17]

Whatever the origin of the difference—indeed the cleavage between the air service and its parent—the war increased it, even as it enhanced the functions and stature of aviation. While the role of the air weapon in the Great War was a modest one, the role of the Great War in the rise of air power was anything but modest. Toward the end of the conflict Sefton Branker observed that "the war has been the making of aviation," and the assertion was emphatically true. There was the accelerated technical development, of course, but also the spreading conviction that if the airplane had not replaced the footsoldier or the artillery piece as the central cog in the military machine of 1918, its role could only continue to grow as it continued to evolve. In their postwar reflections generals of the Great War—men like Ludendorff and Foch—hinted the plane might be the weapon of choice in wars to come; at the same time it loomed large in the visions of such postwar military theorists as Hans Ritter and B. H. Liddell-Hart. And the enhanced image of aviation brought with it a heightened sense of identity, of distinctiveness, putting the air service at greater distance from the rest of the army.

If the war years guaranteed the future of military aviation, they also endowed it with a past that was rich and storied, for all its brevity. The aviators had stocked their pantheon with heroes, and the war left them a harvest of totems and traditions to be honored. The rampant black horse that had adorned Baracca's Spad came to mark the planes of the 91st Fighter Squadriglia—and the automobiles of Enzo Ferrari. In a custom now three-quarters of a century old, each September 11 the officers and men of the French Air Force assemble to hear the reading of Georges Guynemer's last citation.

The burden of the past, like the promise of the future, tended to set the airman apart. During the war French pilots had developed the custom of the flyover for various ceremonies, and they were angered when aircraft were banned from the great victory parade held on the Champs Elysées on July 14, 1919. They were consequently delighted—and the authorities furious—when a few days later a French pilot flew his fighter *through* the Arc de Triomphe. German airmen took it as a tribute to their prowess when the Versailles Treaty banned military aviation in their country. Wilhelm Siegert and other air power partisans liked to say that on November 11, 1918, the German Air Service was the only fighting force still engaged in offensive operations, a claim that rankled in some German military circles. In Britain the Royal Air Force used its newfound independence to shed some of the trappings of the past. It adopted a new and distinctive uniform and invented for its general officers the title of air marshal, which humorists in the sister services said sounded like an encroachment on the preserve of the Almighty.[18]

The public took little notice of these broils unless they made dramatic headlines, as the Billy Mitchell court-martial did. Then they were inclined to be supportive of the airmen. What people remembered of the air war were the bright or awesome images and stirring, dramatic episodes. There was first of all the struggle for the mastery of the air, the glamorous fighter pilots' war, and secondly the war the bomber waged against civilians like themselves. In these episodes the airmen appeared to be waging their own war quite removed from the struggle on land: to the public mind such operations lent substance to the airmen's argument that they ought to be independent.

But there was another reason for the public's favor: the end of the war marked the beginning of a new era of enthusiasm for the airplane, an era often called "the Golden Age of Flight." While the other weapons of the Great War, the tanks and the submarines, faded from view, the warplanes put on civilian guise and became more popular than ever. In Europe, Gotha and Handley Page bombers were refurbished to haul the first airline passengers and their luggage; in America the Curtiss "Jenny," built by the thousands to train pilots for the U.S. Air Service, had another long and illustrious career bringing the miracle of flight to county fairs and cow pasture airfields.

The airmen of the Great War, those of them who survived, found themselves lionized; while everyone tried to forget the hell of the trenches, the air war lived on in song and story, in folklore and myth. A youth named Charles Lindbergh, captivated by accounts of the air war, would make flying the cornerstone of his life. A budding writer named William Faulkner responded to adventure's call and joined the Royal Air Force, getting as far as a flight training school in Canada when the war ended. Thereafter he fashioned for himself a glamorous fantasy-life in the best devil-may-care tradition of the aviator: "I took up a rotary-motored Spad with a crock of Bourbon in the cockpit, gave diligent attention to both. . . ." For years afterward he alluded to dogfights in the skies over France, to crashes and war wounds; for a time he affected a limp. Faulkner was far from being the only bogus veteran of the air war in post-1918 America. The Lafayette Escadrille had only 38 Americans and 4 Frenchmen among its flying personnel, but Philip Flammer has estimated that through the years more than 4,000 other Americans claimed membership.[19]

For many in that elite fraternity who really did fly and fight in Great War, the fascination with flying persisted; Elliott White Springs said "it got into the blood like wine." Of the 146 French aces who survived the war, 66 continued an active interest in aviation. For others, the memory of their wartime experiences remained warm and vivid. Cecil Lewis described how he had watched twelve F.E. 2Bs take off two decades before. "We stood on the tarmac watching them go. And still after twenty years my heart swells at the sight. I can hear the strong engines and smell the tang of burnt oil."[20]

For those who could write, the market for reminiscences and even fiction on the air war was a lucrative one. In 1923 Joseph Kessel's *L'équipage* was a runaway best seller in France with 82 editions in 30 months. In 1926 Elliott White Springs had similar success with *War Birds*. Of all the airmen's memoirs in English, Cecil Lewis' *Sagittarius Rising* (1936) is surely the most beautifully written. But many others less talented and more prolific fed the public's taste: Haupt Heydemarck in Germany, Jacques Mortane in France. In 1927 Floyd Gibbons brought out his *Red Knight of Germany*. In vivid, vigorous prose that would inspire a generation of pulp writers on aviation, Gibbons paid tribute to a Manfred von Richthofen who "grinned at grim death in a hundred duels above the clouds."

By the 1920s, then, the aviators of the Great War were on their way to that cloudland of myth from which this book has sought to draw them. What final word can be said about them? That if they and their deeds do not figure very prominently in the cold military annals of the Great War—and, when objectively considered, they should not—their names should be writ large in the social and cultural history of their era. In his eulogy of the fallen Guynemer, Georges Clemenceau said with unabashed frankness, "the people needs legends." It fell to those who flew to provide those legends, to do shining deeds in a world darkened by war and to incarnate the best of human virtues in the worst of times. It does not seem surprising that when their work was over they should have been hailed as a new breed of heroes. Nor, when one knows them, does it seem inappropriate.

Endnotes

1. The Dawn of Air Power

1. Russell J. Parkinson, "Aeronautics at the Hague Conference of 1899," *Airpower Historian* VII, 2 (April 1960), 106.

2. Jean de Bloch [Ivan S. Bliokh], *La Guerre* (6 vols., Paris, 1898–1900), I, 201, 203.

3. Parkinson, "Aeronautics," p. 109.

4. *Ibid.*

5. Charles Christienne, Pierre Lissarrague, Alain Degardin, Patrick Facon, Patrice Buffotot and Marcellin Hodeir, *Histoire de l'aviation militaire française* (Paris and Limoges, 1980), pp. 19–20; C. F. S. Snowden Gamble, *The Air Weapon: Being Some Account of the Growth of British Military Aeronautics from the Beginnings in the Year 1783 until the End of the Year 1929.* Vol. I: *November 1783–August 1914* (London, 1931), p. 76.

6. W. N. Hutchinson, *The Navigable Balloon in War and Peace* (London, 1888), p. 82.

7. H. W. L. Mödebeck, *Handbuch der Luftschiffahrt, mit besonderer Berücksichtigung über militärischen Verwendung* (Leipzig, 1886), p. 190.

8. Christienne *et al.*, *Aviation*, pp. 20–25; "Schwarz, David," *Encyclopedia Judaica*, *XIV*, 1023–24.

9. Kriegswissenschaftliche Abteilung der Luftwaffe, *Die Militärluftfahrt bis zum Beginn des Weltkrieges 1914*, zweite, überarbeitete Auflage, herausgegeben vom Militärgeschichtlichen Forschungsamt (3 vols., Frankfurt am Mein, 1966), I, 24; II, 34–37.

10. Christienne *et al.*, *Aviation*, p. 25; René Chambe, *Histoire de l'aviation* (Paris, 1972), pp. 92–93.

11. *New York Times*, October 19, 1914.

12. James Brown Scott, ed., *The Proceedings of the Hague Peace Conferences. Translations of the Official Texts* (5 vols., New York, 1920–21), IV, 148.

13. *Militärluftfahrt*, I, 102.

14. *Ibid.*, 12.

15. Hugh Popham, *Into Wind: A History of British Naval Flying* (London, 1969), p. 2.

16. Alfred Gollin, *No Longer an Island. Britain and the Wright Brothers, 1902–1909* (Stanford, 1984), pp. 306–7; Charles Christienne, *L'Aviation française, 1890–1919: Un certain âge d'or* (Paris, 1988), pp. 66–70.

17. Christienne, *Age d'or,* pp. 74–76, *Militärluftfahrt,* III, 22; Angelo Lodi, *Storia delle origini dell'aeronautica militare, 1884–1915: Aerostieri, dirigibilisti, aviatori dell' esercito e della marina in Italia nel periodo pionieristico* (2 vols., Rome, 1976), I, 98.

18. Office of Air Force History, *History of the Greek Air Force* (2 vols., Athens, 1980), I, 12; Manuel Ruiz Romero, *La aviación durante la Revolución mexicana* (Mexico, 1988), p. 39.

19. *Militärluftfahrt,* I, 24, 44–45.

20. *Ibid.,* II, 86.

21. Alfred Gollin, "England Is No Longer an Island: the Phantom Airship Scare of 1909," *Albion,* XIII, 1 (Spring, 1981), 43–46.

22. "Current Status of Military Aeronautics," *Flight* I, 21 (May 22, 1909), 303.

23. John C. Cooper, *The Right to Fly* (New York, 1947), pp. 17–22.

24. Gollin, "Phantom Airship Scare," 43–57 passim; Neville Jones, *The Origins of Strategic Bombing, A Study of the Development of British Air Strategic Thought and Practice up to 1918* (London, 1973), pp. 26–39; *New York Times,* April 4, 1913.

25. Tom D. Crouch, *The Eagle Aloft. Two Centuries of the Balloon in America* (Washington, D.C., 1983), pp. 531–43 passim.

26. Editorial, *Aerial Age,* March 22, 1915, 18.

27. Charles Harvard Gibbs-Smith, *Aviation. An Historical Survey from its Origins to the End of World War II,* pp. 105–38 passim.

28. Gollin, *No Longer an Island,* p. 454.

29. Jürgen Eichler, "Die Militärluftschiffahrt in Deutschland 1911–1914 und ihre Rolle in der Kriegsplänen des deutschen Imperialismus," *Militärgeschichte* No. 4, 1985, 352–53.

30. Gollin, *No Longer an Island,* pp. 270–77; John Howard Morrow, Jr., *Building German Airpower, 1909–1914* (Knoxville, 1976), pp. 21, 93–94.

31. Snowden Gamble, *Air Weapon,* p. 121; Alex Imrie, *Pictorial History of the German Army Air Service 1914–1918* (Chicago, 1973), pp. 17–18; Christienne, *Age d'or,* pp. 79–80.

32. *History of the Greek Air Force,* I, 12; Lodi, *Storia,* II, 39; Florian Davatz, "The Swiss Air Force," *Aerospace Historian,* XVIII, (Winter, 1971), 172.

33. "L'Aéro-Cible Michelin," *Aérophile,* January 15, 1914, 44.

34. Vincenzo Lioy, *Cinquantennia dell' aviazione italiana. Contributo di pensiero, di speranza i di sacrificio in pace ed in guerra.* (Rome, 1954), pp. 8–11; Morrow, *Airpower,* pp. 17, 19, 21; "Aviation militaire en Suisse," *Revue Militaire Suisse,* XVIII, 11, (November, 1913), 790.

35. Peter Supf, *Das Buch der deutschen Fluggeschichte* (2 vols., Stuttgart, 1956–1958), I, 432–33.

36. Lioy, *Cinquantennia,* pp. 18–19; Jacques Mortane, *Les ailes de la mort (1914–1918–19??)* (Paris, 1932), p. 9.

37. David L. Woods, *A History of Tactical Communication Techniques* (Orlando, Fl., 1965), p. 250.

38. Lodi, *Storia,* I, 140–71 passim; Lioy, *Cinquantennia,* pp. 27–31.

39. Salvatore Pagano, *Stormi aerei e divisioni corazzati in cooperazione* (Rome, 1941), p. 10.

40. Sir Reginald Rankin, *The Inner History of the Balkan Wars* (2 vols., London, 1930), II, 656.

41. Henri Mirande and Louis Olivier, *Sur la bataille: Journal d'un aviateur français à l'Armée bulgare, au siège de Constantinople* (Paris, 1913), p. 136.

42. *New York Times*, November 2, December 5, 1912; E. Borel, "L'Aviation militaire," *Revue Militaire Suisse*, LIX, 11 (November, 1914), 645.

43. Lioy, *Cinquantennia*, p. 35.

44. Christienne, *Age d'or*, pp. 89–90.

45. Lee Kennett, *A History of Strategic Bombing* (New York, 1982), pp. 41–44.

46. Ferdinand Ferber, *L'Aviation: Ses débuts. Son développement. De crête à crête. De ville à ville. De continent à continent* (Paris and Nancy, 1908), p. 159.

47. Editorial, *New York Times*, November 2, 1912.

48. Edward C. Johnson, *Marine Corps Aviation: The Early Years 1912–1940* (Washington, 1977), p. 4; Felice Porro, *La guerra nell' aria*, 2nd. ed., riveduta e ampliata (Milan, 1935), p. 44.

2. The Eyes of the Army

1. L.Z. Soloviev, *Actual Experiences in War: Battle Action of the Infantry; Impressions of a Company Commander* (Washington, D.C., 1906), p. 41.

2. Peter Mead, *The Eye in the Air: History of Air Observation and Reconnaissance for the Army, 1785–1945* (London, 1983), p. 38.

3. Leonardo Crosara, *Gli aerostieri, notizie storiche degli aerostieri militari dal 1793 al 1919* (Rome, 1924), pp. 36–38; Georg Paul Neumann, Ed., *Die deutschen Luftstreitkräfte im Weltkriege. Unter Mitwirkung von 29 Offizieren und Beamten der Heeres- und Marine-Luftfahrt nach amtlichen Quellen* (Berlin, 1920), p. 580; R. Giacomelli, "Il pallone osservatorio italiano," *L'Aeronautica*, May, 1920, 135–44.

4. Mead, *Eye*, p. 104.

5. Mead, *Eye*, p. 9.

6. Chef de Bataillon Renaux, "L'Aérostation d'observation dans l'Armée allemande pendant la guerre 1914–1918," *Revue de l'aéronautique militaire*, March–April, 1922, 29.

7. Crosara, *Aerostieri*, p. 46; Joseph Branche, *Le ballon d'observation* (n.p., 1977), p. 43.

8. Branche, *Ballon*, p. 54; Renaux, "Aérostation," p. 32; Mead, *Eye*, p. 104–5.

9. Max Erhardt, *Im Ballon vor dem Feinde* (Stuttgart, 1918), p. 32; "L'attaque des drachen–ballons," *La guerre aérienne*, March 1, 1917, 246; Crosara, *Aerostieri*, p. 43.

10. Crosara, *Aerostieri*, p. 41.

11. Crosara, *Aerostieri*, p. 67; Giacomelli, "Pallone," p. 143.

12. Branche, *Ballon*, p. 159; Crosara, *Aerostieri*, p. 59; "Parlons d' ailes: un palmarès pour tous les héros," *La guerre aérienne*, January 14, 1912, 482.

13. Jacques Boulenger, *En escadrille* (Paris, 1930), p. 67.

14. Ernst von Höppner, *Deutschlands Krieg in der Luft; ein Rückblick auf die Entwicklung und die Leistungen unserer Heeres-Luftstreitkräfte im Weltkriege* (Leipzig, 1921), p. 3; Capitaine Pichot-Duclos, *Reconnaissances en aéroplane. Theorie. Cas concrets. Propositions* (Paris and Nancy, 1912), p. 12.

15. "Aircraft Work at the Front," *Flight*, October 9, 1914, 1017.

16. Mortane, *Ailes*, p. 46; Muscarà, F., *Storia dell'osservazione aerea dell'Esercito* (Rome, 1974), p. 194.

17. Höppner, *Krieg*, p. 8.

18. Baron von Löwenstern, "Die Tätigkeit der Flieger der deutschen 8. Armee vor and während der Schlacht bei Tannenberg," *Militär-Wochenblatt*, Jg. 124, No. 9 (1939), 541–6. I. Mosolov, "Boevoe Soderzhestvo russkikh i frantsuzkikh letchikov v pervoi mirovoi voine," *Voenno-Istoricheskii Zhurnal*, 1973, no. 6, 93; General Armengaud, *Le renseignement aérien, sauvegarde des armées* (Paris, 1934), p. 83; Höppner, *Krieg*, p. 11.

19. "The Work of the Royal Flying Corps," *Aeronautics*, January 5, 1916, 18.

20. Mortane, *Ailes*, p. 10.

21. *Ibid.*, 11.

22. Hans Schroeder, *An Airman Remembers*. Translated by Claud W. Sykes (London, n.d.), p. 174; Norbert Welkoborsky, *Vom Fliegen, Siegen und Sterben einer Feldflieger-Abteilung. Kriegstagebuchblätter der Feldflieger-Abteilung A Nr. 263 (ehem. Feldflieger-Abtlg. 32)* (Berlin, 1939), p. 33; M. Molfese, *L'Aviazione da ricognizione italiana durante la guerra europea* (Rome, 1925), p. 143.

23. Mead, *Eye*, pp. 78–79.

24. Welkoborsky, *Fliegen, passim*.

25. Walter Zuerl, *Pour le mérite-Flieger; Heldentaten und Erlebnisse unserer Kriegsflieger* (Munich, 1938), p. 333.

26. Philip M. Flammer, *The Vivid Air. The Lafayette Escadrille* (Athens, Ga., 1980), p. 22; Captain W. Wedgwood Benn, *In the Side Shows* (London, 1919), p. 140.

27. Crosara, *Aerostieri*, p. 91; Mead, *Eye*, p. 76.

28. André H. Carlier, *La photographie aérienne pendant la guerre* (Paris, 1921), pp. 16–40 passim.

29. Harold B. Porter, *Aerial Observation* (New York and London, 1921), p. 41; Porro, *Guerra*, p. 181; Neumann, *Luftstreitkräfte*, p. 490.

30. Simone Pesquiès-Corbier, Ed., "L'Aéronautique militaire française, 1914–1918," *Icare*, no. 58, 28.

31. H. G. [Hubert Freeling Griffith], *R.A.F. Occasions* (London, 1941), p. 14; Capitaine Canonne, "L'avion d'infanterie," *Revue de l'aéronautique militaire*, March–April, 1922, 25–27.

32. Flying Officer T. Mason, *The History of 9 Squadron, Royal Air Force* (London, 1965), p. 10.

33. John W. Stuart Gilchrist, *An Aerial Observer in World War I* (Richmond, Va., 1966), p. 49.

34. Porter, *Observation*, p. 20; H. G., *Occasions*, p. 47.

35. Raleigh and Jones, *War in the Air*, I, 213.

3. The Emergence of the Bomber

1. Transcript of oral history interview with Major General Benjamin Foulois, December 9, 1965, U.S.A.F.H.R.C., Maxwell AFB, p. 43.

2. Kennett, *History,* p. 17.

3. *Ibid.,* pp. 22–3.

4. J. A. Chamier, *The Birth of the Royal Air Force: The Early History and Experiences of the Flying Services* (London, 1943), p. 44; Jean-Marc Marill, "1914–1918, l'Aéronautique Militaire Française, naissance de la cinquième arme," thesis, doctorat de troisième cycle, University of Paris IV, 1981, p. 2; Porro, *Guerra,* 388–90; Neumann, *Luftstreitkräfte,* p. 428.

5. Peter Pletschacher, *Die Königliche bayerischen Fliegertruppen 1912–1919* (Stuttgart, 1978), p. 30.

6. E. Joynson Hicks, "Command of the Air," *The National Review,* April, 1912, 353.

7. Gollin, *Island,* p. 457; Lieutenant breveté Poutrin, "Les aéroplanes dans la guerre future," *Revue générale de l'aéronautique militaire, théorique et pratique,* I (1911), 382–5; René Martel, *L'Aviation française de bombardement V. 1, Des origines à la fin de 1915* (Lille, 1937), pp. 6–10.

8. Poutrin, "Aéroplanes," 384; Riley E. Scott, "Can the Panama Canal be bombed from the Air?" *Sunset,* April 1914, 784.

9. Lioy, *Cinquantennia,* p. 32; Martel, *Bombardement,* p. 14; Jones, *Origins,* p. 44.

10. Porro, *Guerra,* p. 66–7; Lt. Col. B. Roustam-Bek [Boris Leonidovich Tageev], *Aerial Russia: The Romance of the Great Aeroplane* (London and New York, 1916), pp. 90–93.

11. Pletschacher, *Fliegertruppen,* p. 31; Douglas Robinson, *The Zeppelin in Combat; a History of the German Naval Airship Division, 1912–1918,* 2d Ed. (Seattle, 1980), p. 24.

12. Christienne *et al., Aviation,* p. 69.

13. Mortane, *Ailes,* p. 23; Welkoborsky, *Fliegen,* p. 36.

14. Mead, *Eye,* p. 78, note 5; Welkoborsky, *Fliegen,* p. 41; Raleigh and Jones, *War in the Air,* II, 463.

15. Instruction sur l'organisation et l'emploi des groupes de bombardement, February 1, 1915, document communicated by the Service Historique de l'Armée de l'Air (S.H.A.A.).

16. Raleigh and Jones, *War in the Air,* III, 94; Mead, *Eye,* p. 89.

17. Supf, *Buch,* II, 269.

18. Order of General Joffre, November 1, 1914, communicated by S.H.A.A.; Schroeder, *Airman,* p. 88.

19. Jones, *Origins,* pp. 6–11; Christienne, *Age d'or,* p. 128.

20. M. de Brunoff, Ed., *L'Aéronautique pendant la guerre mondiale* (Paris, 1920), pp. 150–53.

21. Raleigh and Jones, *War in the Air,* II, 117.

22. John Slessor, *The Central Blue; Recollections and Reflections* (London, 1956), p. 18. Jacques Mortane, *Histoire illustrée de la guerre aérienne* (2 vols., Paris, 1922), II, 35.

23. Raleigh and Jones, *War in the Air*, II, 461; Christienne, *Age d'or*, p. 130.

24. Oberst (E) Freiherr von Bülow, *Geschichte der Luftwaffe. Eine kurze Darstellung der Entwicklung des dritten Wehrmachtteils* (Frankfurt, 1937), p. 53.

25. Bülow, *Luftwaffe*, p. 64.

26. Neumann, *Luftstreitkräfte*, p. 429.

27. *Ibid.*, p. 434.

28. Franz Schlenstedt, *Vollgas! Ein Fliegerleben, aufgezeichnet von Georg Böse* (Berlin, 1939), p. 47; Squadron Leader C. P. O. Bartlett, *Bomber Pilot 1916–1918,* ed. by Chaz Bowyer (London, 1974), p. 32.

29. Note sur l'emploi du bombardement, December 18, 1917, document communicated by the S.H.A.A., p. 1.

30. *Ibid.*, 3–4.

31. *Ibid.*, 4.

32. *New York Times*, October 9, 1914.

33. Note, December 18, 1917, p. 4.

34. *Le Figaro*, January 11, 1916; January 31, 1916.

35. Porro, *Guerra*, pp. 106, 390.

36. *Militärluftfahrt*, II, 89; Ernest Dudley, *Monsters of the Purple Twilight: the True Story of the Life and Death of the Zeppelins, First Menace from the Skies* (London, 1960), p. 34.

37. Zuerl, *Flieger*, p. 107.

38. Robinson, *Zeppelin*, p. 78; Cate Haste, *Keep the Home Fires Burning. Propaganda in the First World War* (London, 1977), pp. 95–96.

39. Dudley, *Monsters*, p. 190; Robinson, *Zeppelin*, p. 77.

40. Porro, *Guerra*, p. 110.

41. G. W. Haddow and Peter M. Grosz, *The German Giants: The Story of the R-Planes 1914–1918* (London, 1962), passim.

42. C. M. White, *The Gotha Summer: The German Daytime Air Raids on England, May to August, 1917* (London, 1986), p. 42.

43. *Ibid.*, 91.

44. White. *Gotha*, 132, 194; Raleigh and Jones, *War in the Air*, IV, 86–87.

45. White, *Gotha*, 126.

46. John Slessor, *Air Power and Armies* (London, 1936), p. 65.

47. Thomas Lumsden, "Treatment of War Psychoses," *The Lancet*, November 24, 1917, 804.

48. "The Metropolitan Hospitals and the Air Raid," *The Lancet*, July 14, 1917, 59–60; "Air Raid Psychology and Air Raid Perils," *The Lancet*, October 6, 1917, 540.

4. The Development of Aerial Combat

1. G. Sensever and L. Baillif, *Le combat aérien* (Paris, 1914), p. 9.

2. Patrick Facon, "L'armée française et l'aviation, 1891–1914," unpublished paper communicated by the author, p. 23; Jones, *Origins*, p. 46.

3. Ferber, *L'Aviation*, p. 159; Mead, *Eye*, p. 46.

4. Erich Olszewski and Helmrich von Elgott, *Das Flugzeug in Heer und Marine,*

Handbuch über das gesamte Gebiet des Militärflugwesens (Berlin, 1912), pp. 87–89; Facon, "Armée," p. 24; Raleigh and Jones, *War in the Air*, I, 412.

5. W. H. B. Smith and Jos. E. Smith, *Small Arms of the World*, 7th ed. (New York, 1963), pp. 127–31.

6. Captain Charles De Forest Chandler, "The Lewis Aeroplane Gun," *Journal of the U.S. Artillery*, September–October, 1912, 221–23; Freddy Capron, *La couronne et les ailes* (Brussels, 1961), p. 34.

7. Walter von Eberhardt, *Unsere Luftstreitkräfte 1914–1918* (Berlin, 1930), p. 43; Lodi, *Stòria*, II, 62; Peter Lewis, *The British Fighter since 1912. Sixty-Seven Years of Design and Development* (London, 1979), pp. 25–31.

8. "Why There is Little Fighting," *The Aeroplane*, August 26, 1914, 191; Christienne, *Age d'or*, p. 114.

9. "Zusammentreffen deutscher und französischer Flieger," *Flugsport*, January 13, 1915, 20; Major Cochrane Patrick, "Fighting in the Air," *The Aeronautical Journal*, December, 1918, 391.

10. Marill, "Aéronautique," p. 100.

11. Patrick Facon, "Aperçus sur la doctrine d'emploi de l'aviation française, 1914–1918," unpublished paper communicated by the author, pp. 3, 8; Marill, "Aéronautique," p. 100.

12. *New York Times*, January 5, 1915; Pichot-Duclos, *Reconnaissances*, p. 33.

13. Zuerl, *Flieger*, p. 78.

14. Bülow, *Luftwaffe*, p. 64; Marill, "Aéronautique," p. 102; Jérôme Blanc, "L'Aviation de chasse française, 1916–1918," Mémoire de maitrise, University of Paris I, 1981–82, pp. 3–4.

15. Marill, "Aéronautique," p. 102; Pierre Belleroche, *Histoire du combat aérien* (Marseilles, 1941), p. 34.

16. Bülow, *Luftwaffe*, pp. 66–71.

17. Blanc, "Chasse," pp. 4–7.

18. *Ibid.*

19. Bülow, *Luftwaffe*, p. 74.

20. Raleigh and Jones, *War in the Air*, III, 393–411.

21. Raleigh and Jones, *War in the Air*, III, 394; IV, Appendix XVII, passim.

22. G. Massenet de Marancour, *La chasse en avion* (Paris, 1921), p. 86.

23. Blanc, "Chasse," pp. 107–8.

24. Jean Puistienne, *Escadrille 155* (Paris, 1935), pp. 93–94.

25. Peter Simkins, *Air Fighting 1914–1918* (London, 1978), p. 52; Edward Ritter von Schleich, "Principien des Luftkampfes," in Ernst Jünger, Ed. *Luftfahrt ist Not* (Berlin, 1930), p. 259.

26. James McCudden, *Flying Fury: Five Years in the Royal Flying Corps*, Ed. Stanley M. Ulanoff (New York, 1968), pp. 187–88.

27. Porro, *Guerra*, p. 170; Zuerl, *Flieger*, p. 172; Massenet, *Chasse*, p. 26.

28. Massenet, *Chasse*, pp. 62–63; Zuerl, *Flieger*, p. 35.

29. Christienne *et al.*, *Aviation*, p. 114.

30. Blanc, "Chasse," 151–58.

31. Hans Joachim Buddecke, *El Shahin (der Jagdfalke). Aus meinem Fliegerleben* (Berlin, 1918), p. 100; Raleigh and Jones, *War in the Air*, III, 394.

32. Marill, "Aéronautique," p. 111; Patrick, "Fighting," 408.

33. Raleigh and Jones, *War in the Air*, III, 393.

34. Christienne *et al.*, *Aviation*, p. 115.

35. Edward H. Sims, *Fighter Tactics and Strategy* (New York, 1972), p. 54; Christopher Cole, *McCudden, V.C.* (London, 1967), p. 200.

36. Eberhardt, *Luftstreitkräfte*, pp. 287–92.

5. Harnessing Air Power

1. Richard P. Hallion, *The Rise of the Fighter Aircraft, 1914–1918* (Baltimore, 1984), p. 66; Porro, *Guerra*, p. 408.

2. Neumann, *Luftstreitkräfte*, p. 585; Etat numérique des pertes du personnel navigant pour la première guerre mondiale, typescript prepared and communicated by the Service Historique de l'Armée de l'Air.

3. Christienne *et al.*, *Aviation*, p. 184.

4. Hallion, *Fighter*, p. 66; Christienne *et al.*, *Aviation*, p. 157; Molfese, *Aviazione*, p. 129.

5. Eberhardt, *Luftstreitkräfte*, p. 39.

6. *Ibid.*

7. H. G., *Occasions*, p. 6. Simkins, *Fighting*, p. 5.

8. Morrow, *German*, p. 36; Mead, *Eye*, p. 79; Blanc, "Chasse," p. 16.

9. A. J. Insall, *Observer: Memoirs of the R.F.C., 1915–1918* (London, 1970), p. 19.

10. Neumann, *Luftstreitkräfte*, pp. 433–35.

11. Flammer, *Vivid Air*, p. 135; Bülow, *Luftwaffe*, p. 84.

12. Neumann, *Luftstreitkräfte*, pp. 286–91.

13. Neumann, *Luftstreitkräfte*, p. 305; Blanc, "Chasse," p. 116.

14. Raleigh and Jones, *War in the Air*, I, 260; Mead, *Eye*, p. 66; Flammer, *Vivid Air*, p. 42.

15. Bülow, *Luftwaffe*, pp. 65–68; Raleigh and Jones, III, 195–228 *passim*.

16. H. G., *Occasions*, p. 318; Bülow, *Luftwaffe*, p. 73.

17. Bülow, *Luftwaffe*, pp. 65–68.

18. Massenet, *Chasse*, p. 15; F.M. Cutlack, *The Australian Flying Corps* (Vol. VIII of *The Official History of Australia in the War of 1914–1918;* ed. by C. E. W. Bean) (Perth, 1933), p. 434.

19. Eberhardt, *Luftstreitkräfte*, pp. 46, 60.

20. Arthur Sweetser, *The American Air Service: a Record of its Problems, its Difficulties, its Failures, and its Final Achievements* (New York, 1919), p. 36.

21. Neumann, *Luftstreitkräfte*, pp. 116–17.

6. The Machines

1. Captain B. C. Hucks, R.F.C., "A Further Three Years' Flying Experience," *The Aeroplane*, June 13, 1917, 1554.

2. Jean-Pierre Lefevre-Garros, *Roland Garros* (Paris, 1988), p. 535.

3. Slessor, *Air Power*, p. 21.

4. R. Borlase Matthews, *The Aviation Pocket-Book for 1918* 6th ed. (London, 1918), p. 43; Christienne *et al.*, *Aviation*, Morrow, *German*, p. 202; Gastone Cammurati, "Aerei italiani 1914–1918," *Rivista Aeronautica*, June, 1972, 1034–35.

5. Philip S. Dickey, III, *The Liberty Engine 1918–1942* (Washington, 1968), pp. 8–38 *passim*.

6. Joseph A. Phelan, *Heroes and Aeroplanes of the Great War* (New York, 1968), p. 11; Neumann, *Luftstreitkräfte*, p. 148.

7. Christienne, *Age d'or*, p. 98; Howard Wolko, *In the Cause of Flight. Technologists of Aeronautics and Astronautics (Smithsonian Studies in Air and Space, No. 4)* (Washington, 1981), pp. 13, 16–19; Oliver Stewart, *Aviation: The Creative Ideas* (New York and Washington, 1966), p. 39.

8. Neumann, *Luftstreitkräfte*, p. 139.

9. "U.S. Army Aeroplane Specifications," *Journal of the U.S. Artillery*, January–February, 1913, 115; Pichot-Duclos, *Reconnaissances*, p. 34.

10. Morrow, *German*, p. 8.

11. Albert Étévé, *La victoire des cocardes. l'aviation française avant et pendant la Première Guerre mondiale* (Paris, 1970), p. 16.

12. Malcolm Cooper, *British Air Policy in the First World War* (London, 1986), pp. 4, 16.

13. Evan Hadingham, *The Fighting Triplanes* (London, 1968), p. 55.

14. Aloys von Griess, "Dreidecker gegen Zweidecker," *Technische Berichte*, October 15, 1917, 297.

15. Meeting of June 25, 1917, Minutes of the Air Board, Air Historical Branch, Ministry of Defense; Dickey, *Liberty Engine*, p. 38.

16. Neumann, *Luftstreitkräfte*, 146–48.

17. Kenneth Munson, *Aircraft of World War I* (London, 1967), pp. 82, 113.

18. Slessor, *Air Power*, p. 18; John Pudney, *Bristol Fashion. Some Account of the Early Days of Bristol Aviation* (London, 1960), p. 13.

19. "Un téléscopage miraculeux dans l'espace," *La guerre aérienne*, December 15, 1916, pp. 56–57; Sholto Douglas, *Combat and Command: The Story of an Airman in Two World Wars* (New York, 1966), p. 105.

20. Insall, *Observer*, p. 22.

21. Louis Coatalen, "Aircraft and Motor Car Design: Contrasted from the Standpoint of a Designer and Manufacturer in Both Types," *The Aeroplane*, May 16, 1917, 1254–64.

22. Matthews, *Pocket-Book*, pp. 112–40 *passim*.

23. *Ibid.*

24. Alfred Bodemer and Rober Langier, *Les moteurs à pistons aéronautiques français (1900/1960)*, vol. I. (Paris, n.d.), p. 156; Robert Schlaifer and S.D. Heron, *Development of Aircraft Engines and Fuels* (Boston, 1950), p. 578.

25. Louis Massinger, *Livre d'or de la Société Française Hispano-Suiza* (n.p., 1924), pp. 13–37 *passim*.

26. Schlaifer and Heron, *Engines and Fuels*, pp. 557–58. "L'Aéroplane et la cavalerie-Opinions allemandes," *Revue Générale de l'Aéronautique militaire théorique et pratique*, 1911, 179.

27. Puistienne, *Escadrille*, p. 27; Insall, *Observer*, p. 55.

28. F.W. Eddelbüttel, *Artillerie-Flieger* (n.p., 1918), p. 31.

29. "Alpha," "Notes on the Truing of Aeroplanes," *The Aeroplane*, Supplement VIII, May 2, 1917, 1134–36. Eddelbüttel, *Artillerie-Flieger*, p. 30.

30. L. A. Strange, *Recollections of an Airman* (London, 1933), p. 150; Air Board minutes, October 31, 1917, p. 3.

31. Lt. Col. Roy P. Grinker and Captain John P. Spiegel, M.C., *War Neuroses*

in North Africa. The Tunisian Campaign (New York, 1943), pp. 99–100; Arthur Lee, *No Parachute: a Fighter Pilot in World War I* (London, 1968), p. 155; Puistienne, *Escadrille*, p. 119; Schlenstedt, *Vollgas!*, pp. 53–54.

32. Lee, *No Parachute*, p. 50; *Flight*, March 20, 1916, 272.

33. Hadingham, *Triplanes*, pp. 27–28; Constance Babington Smith, *Testing Time: A Study of Man and Machine in the Test Flying Era* (London, 1961), p. 79.

34. *The New York Times*, January 27, 1916; *Le Figaro,* January 16, 1916.

35. Morrow, *German*, p. 42; Cooper, *Air Policy*, p. 20.

36. Cecil Lewis, *Sagittarius Rising* (London, 1936), p. 47.

37. Air Board Minutes, June 7, 1917.

7. The Men: Selection and Training

1. Boulenger, *Escadrille*, p. 8.

2. Christienne, *Age d'or*, p. 92; "Die Todesopfer der deutschen Fliegerei in den Jahren 1910–14," unpaginated appendix to Supf. *Buch*, I; Hanz J. Nowarra, *Heinkel and seine Flugzeuge* (Munich, 1975), p. 14.

3. "Safest Place for Soldier in an Aeroplane," *Aerial Age Weekly*, April 12, 1915, 83; Brigadier General Benjamin Foulois, "Early Flying Experience," *Air Power Historian*, April, 1956, 127; Christienne, *Age d'or*, p. 89.

4. Foulois, "Experiences," 127; Johnson, *Marine Aviation*, p. 4; Christienne, *Age d'or*, p. 88.

5. Pierre Perrin de Brichambaut, *Critères d'aptitude à vol en avion. Etude comparative des differentes méthodes employées en France, dans les pays alliés, chez les puissances centrales* (Paris, 1921), p. 63; Thomas Reimer, *Die Entwicklung der Flugmedizin in Deutschland* (Cologne, 1979), pp. 24, 40.

6. "Will Aviators Have Caisson Disease?" *The Literary Digest*, September 8, 1917, 26; Yandell Henderson, "The Physiology of the Aviator," *Science*, May 14, 1919, 433.

7. Captain T. S. Rippon and Lieutenant E. G. Manuel, "The Essential Characteristics of Successful and Unsuccessful Aviators, with Special Reference to Temperament," *The Lancet*, September 28, 1918, 411–15.

8. Wing Commander Martin Flack, "The Human Machine in Relation to Flying," *The Aeronautical Journal*, December, 1920, 660.

9. Wing Commander A. W. H. James, "Equitation as an Aid to Efficiency in the Royal Air Force," *Royal Air Force Quarterly*, July, 1930, 534–38; the estimates of arms of origin for German and French pilots are based on information supplied *passim* in Zuerl, *Flieger*, and Daniel Porret, *Les as français de la Grande Guerre* (2 vols.: Vincennes, 1983).

10. Slessor, *Air Power*, p. 2; Captain T. S. Rippon, "Medical Notes. The Wear and Tear of Flying," *Flying*, January 23, 1919, 108–9; Ernst Koschel, "Hygiene des Erstazes bei den Luftstreitkräften," in *Handbuch der ärztlichen Erfahrungen im Weltkriege 1914–1918*, ed. by Otto von Schjerning, Vol. 7, *Hygiene* (Leipzig, 1930), p. 20; Arnaud Teyssier, "Les origines de la Medicine aéronautique en France: l'expérience décisive de la Grande Guerre," unpublished paper communicated by its author, *passim*.

11. Sefton Branker, "The Teaching of Flying," *The Aeronautical Journal*, January–March, 1917, 19; Rippon, "Notes," 108.

12. Edwin C. Parsons, *I Flew with the Lafayette Escadrille* (New York, 1972), p. 313.

13. Rippon and Manuel, "Characteristics," 413–15.

14. Dennis Winter, *The First of the Few* (Athens, Ga.: 1985), pp. 19–20; Christienne, *Age d'or*, pp. 180, 181. Sidney Wise, *Canadian Airmen and World War I* (Ottowa, 1982), p. 638.

15. Welkoborsky, *Fliegen*, p. 10.

16. Marill, "Aéronautique," p. 149; *Synopsis of British Air Effort during the War (Papers by Command No. 100)*, p. 4.

17. André Duvau, *"BR 29." Souvenirs d'escadrille* (Vincennes 1976), pp. 5–6.

18. G.O.M., "With the Royal Flying Corps," *Royal Air Force Quarterly*, July, 1930, 719.

19. Muscarà, *Storia*, p. 37.

20. Schlenstedt, *Vollgas!*, p. 40.

21. *Synopsis*, p. 4.

22. Rudolf Requadt, *Im Kriegsflugzeug* (Berlin, 1916), p. 40; Sefton Branker, "Teaching," 16; Marill, "Aéronautique," p. 125.

23. Marill, "Aéronautique," p. 122.

24. Rippon and Manuel, "Characteristics," 412, 414.

25. Reginald Sinclaire, transcription of oral history interview conducted by Lieutenant Colonal Thomas A. Julian, USAF, November 21, 1969, call number K239.0512–780. United States Air Force Historical Research Center, Maxwell Air Force Base, Ala., p. 12.

26. *Ibid.*, 13–19.

27. Insall, *Observer*, p. 50; Requadt, *Kriegsflugzeuge*, p. 40; Porro, *Guerra*, pp. 90–92.

28. Insall, *Observer*, p. 35; Mario Fucini, *Voli sul nemico. Ricordi di un pilota della prima guerra Mondiale* (Rome, 1960), p. 18.

29. Branker, "Teaching," 26; Marill, *Aéronautique*, p. 127; Insall, *Observer*, p. 23.

30. Eddelbüttel, *Artillerie-Flieger* p. 11; Fucini, *Voli*, p. 19.

31. Insall, *Observer*, p. 44; Rippon and Manuel, "Characteristics," p. 414; Staff-Surgeon Hardy V. Wells, R.N., "Aeroplane Injuries and Diseases, with Notes on the Aviation Service," *Aeronautics*, November 8, 1916, 304.

32. Insall, *Observer*, p. 58; James R. McConnell, *Flying for France with the American Escadrille at Verdun* (Garden City, N.Y., 1917), pp. 25–26; Puistienne, *Escadrille*, p. 20.

33. Brunoff, *Aéronautique*, p. 101; "Debate on the Consolidated Funding Bill," *The Aeroplane*, April 11, 1917, 842.

34. Brunoff, *Aéronautique*, p. 101; Christienne *et al.*, *Aviation*, p. 157.

35. H. Graeme Anderson, "The Medical Aspects of Aeroplane Accidents," *Aeronautics*, February 13, 1918, 150–53; "Debate," 842.

36. Winter, *First of the Few*, p. 37; Raleigh and Jones, *War in the Air*, I, 425, 426; Wise, *Canadian Airmen*, p. 107; Neumann, *Luftstreitkräfte*, p. 586.

37. Fucini, *Voli*, p. 13; Wise, *Canadian Airmen*, p. 100.

38. Requadt, *Kriegsflugzeug*, pp. 21–22, 24; Puistienne, *Escadrille*, p. 19.

39. "Parlons d'ailes: 'Rigolos' et 'Bourreurs'," *La guerre aérienne*, July 12, 1917; *Air Ministry Weekly Orders, No. 515, Regulations for Pilots*, June 26, 1918,

passim; Wise, *Canadian Airmen,* p. 166; Eddelbüttel, *Artillerie-flieger,* p. 12.
    40. Raleigh and Jones, *War in the Air,* I, 209.

8. The Men: En Escadrille

1. H. G., *Occasions,* pp. 8, 9, 13; Fucini, *Voli,* p. 22; Daniel B. Jorgensen, *Air Force Chaplains,* Vol. 1, *The Service of Chaplains to Army Air Units 1917–1946* (Washington, 1961), p. 41.
    2. Edgar C. Middleton, *The Way of the Air* (London, 1917), p. 35.
    3. "The Attributes of a Successful Flying Officer," *The Lancet,* September 28, 1918, 425; Puistienne, *Escadrille,* p. 76; Boulenger, *Escadrille,* p. 25.
    4. "Contact" [Alan Bott], *An Airman's Outings* (London, 1917), pp. 178–79; Flammer, *Vivid Air,* p. 59; Harold Buckley, *Squadron 95* (Paris, 1933), p. 113; J. Mortane, "Les glorieuses, la F. 25," *La guerre aérienne,* July 5, 1917, 8.
    5. Flammer, *Vivid Air,* Preface, ix; Porret, *As français,* I, 43; H. G., *Occasions,* pp. 12, 23.
    6. Requadt, *Kriegsflugzeug,* p. 50–51.
    7. Insall, *Observer,* p. 111; H. G., *Occasions,* p. 18.
    8. Martel, *Bombardement,* p. 314.
    9. Stewart, *Creative Ideas,* p. 38.
    10. Insall, *Observer,* p. 87; Haupt Heydemarck, *Soldatendeutsch* (Berlin, 1934), p. 61; *Cinquante-Quatre Flying Corps Songs* (Cambridge, 1918), p. 10.
    11. H. G., *Occasions,* p. 73; "On Active Service Flying," *The Aeroplane,* April 18, 1917, p. 138; "Contact," *Outings,* p. 191; Duvau, *Souvenirs,* pp. 9–10.
    12. *New York Times,* March 10, 1915.
    13. Jorgensen, *Chaplains,* p. 28; *Weekly Orders, No. 517, The R.A.F. Salute,* June 26, 1918.
    14. G. O. M., "Royal Flying Corps," 719.
    15. Puistienne, *Escadrille,* pp. 94–95.
    16. *Historique du groupe de Chasse I/2. Les Cigognes (1914–1945)* (Vincennes, 1982), pp. 131–33.
    17. Boulenger, *Escadrille,* p. 87; H.G., *Occasions,* p. 25; Porret, *As français,* II, 229.
    18. *Almanacco delle Forze Armati 1927* (Rome, 1928), pp. 693–94; Porret, *As Français,* I, 53.
    19. "Our Variegated Foes," *The Aeroplane,* May 16, 1917, 1246.
    20. D. H. Robinson, *The Dangerous Sky; a History of Aviation Medicine* (Seattle, 1973), pp. 83–84; Flammer, *Vivid Air,* p. 30.
    21. Puistienne, *Escadrille,* pp. 86, 109.
    22. Puistienne, *Escadrille,* p. 119; Duvau, *Souvenirs,* p. 17; Zuerl, *Flieger,* p. 57.
    23. E. A. Sutherland, "Observations on the Medical Examination of Aviation Candidates," *The Lancet,* December 14, 1918, 809.
    24. Schlenstedt, *Vollgas!,* p. 89; "Le drame dans la carlingue," *La guerre aérienne,* June 7, 1917, 467.
    25. Eddelbüttel, *Artillerie-Flieger,* p. 31; H. G., *Occasions,* p. 20; Buddecke, *El Shahin,* p. 58.

26. Requadt, *Kriegsflugzeug*, pp. 190–92.

27. *Ibid.*, 193–97.

28. *Ibid.*, 200–203.

29. Puistienne, *Escadrille*, p. 196; Flammer, *Vivid Air*, p. 211, note 39.

30. Harold Rosher, *With the Flying Squadron, Being the War Letters of the Late Harold Rosher to his Family* (New York, 1916), p. 144.

31. Cecil Lewis, *Sagittarius Rising* (New York, 1936), unpaginated preface.

32. Haupt Heydemarck, *War Flying in Macedonia*, translated by Claud W. Sykes (London, 1935), p. 122.

33. Requadt, *Kriegsflugzeug*, p. 109.

34. H. G., *Occasions*, p. 3.

35. Porret, *As français*, I, 93.

36. Mortane, *Ailes*, p. 71.

9. A New Breed of Heroes

1. Lefèvre-Garros, *Garros*, pp. 506–14; P. Kritskii, *Podvigi russkikh aviatorov* (Yaroslavl, 1915), pp. 5–6.

2. "Notes on the Flying Corps," *The Aeroplane*, September 9, 1914, 230; *Flight*, November 13, 1914, 118; Kritskii, *Podvigi*, p. 3.

3. *The Aeroplane*, September 30, 1914, 294; "Parlons d'ailes: Appel à la légalité," *La guerre aérienne* January 17, 1918, 155; "Don de 10,000 francs aux aviateurs," *L'Aérophile*, August 1–15, 1916, 250.

4. Walter A. Briscoe and H. Russell Stannard, *Captain Ball, V.C., The Career of Flight Commander Ball, V.C., D.S.O.* (London, 1918), p. 218–20; "Chronique-éphémérides de la guerre aérienne," *L'Aérophile*, October 1–15, 1914, 384.

5. "Deutsche Flieger im Heeresbericht," *Flugsport*, no. 3, 1917, 78.

6. "The Morane Monoplane in War," *Aeronautics*, January 5, 1916, 12; "Les aviateurs cités dans des communiqués," *L'Aérophile*, January 1–15, 1916, 160.

7. "Statements in Parliament," July 19, 1916, 46, "Berkeley," "Tradition," *The Aeroplane*, May–June, 1917, 35; "Without the Limelight," *Aeronautics*, December 20, 1916, .

8. *Le Figaro*, March 29, 1916.

9. "Knight Errant of the Air," *Flight*, February 3, 1916, 97; *New York Times*, March 26, 1916; "Parlons d'ailes: Pilote et poilu," *La guerre aérienne*, December 21, 1916, 82; Boulenger, *Escadrille*, p. 2.

10. Zuerl, *Flieger*, p. 126; "Contact," *Outings*, pp. 175, 202.

11. Eric J. Leed, "From Experience to Ideology: an Analysis of the Images of War in German War Literature, 1914–1930," doctoral thesis, University of Rochester, 1972, p. 250; J. P. Dournel, "L'image de l'aviateur français en 1914–1918. Une étude du milieu des aviateurs d'après la revue: *"Le guerre aérienne illustrié*, III—Tensions et conflits à propos de l'aviation," *Revue Historique des Armées*, III, No. 7, (1976), 103.

12. Boulenger, *Escadrille*, p. 95.

13. Irene Guerrini and Marco Pluviano, "Dandismo e cavalleria nelle lettere

de Francesco Baracca," in *La Grande Guerra: Esperienza, memoria, immagine,* ed. by Diego Leoni and Camillo Zadra (Bologna, 1986), p. 39, Note 7; Neumann, *Luftstreitkräfte,* p. 386; Dournel, "Image," 101.

14. Porro, *Guerra,* p. 396; Dan McCaffery, *Billy Bishop, Canadian Hero* (Toronto, 1988), unpaginated Introduction.

15. Eric J. Leed, *No Man's Land: Combat and Identity in World War I* (Cambridge, England, 1979), p. 111.

16. Porter, *Observation,* pp. 1, 8; Jean Deçay, "nos as ignorés, les mitrailleurs," *La guerre aérienne,* March 24, 1917, p. 314.

17. "Parlons d'ailes: un palmarès pour tous des héros," *La guerre aérienne,* June 14, 1917, 452.

18. Douglas, *Combat,* p. 166; Charles B. Nordhoff, "Aerial Tactics," *Atlantic Monthly,* September, 1918, 415.

19. Gordon W. Callender, Jr. and Gordon W. Callender, Sr., Eds., *War in an Open Cockpit. The Wartime Letters of Captain Alvin Andrew Callender, R.A.F.* (West Roxbury, Mass., 1978), p. 72.

20. Porret, *As français,* II, 127–29.

21. *Ibid.,* Introduction, I, xi–xii.

22. "Nos morts: André Quennehan," *La guerre aérienne,* December 28, 1916, 123; McCaffery, *Bishop,* pp. 129–33; Porret, *As français,* II, 264.

23. Christienne *et al., Aviation,* p. 357; Neumann, *Luftstreitkräfte,* p. 588; *Synopsis,* p. 18; Historical Research Division, Aerospace Studies Institute, *U.S. Air Service Victory Credits. World War I (USAF Historical Study No. 133)* (Maxwell Air Force Base, Ala., 1969), p. 2.

24. Christienne *et al., Aviation,* p. 114.

25. "Flieger-Hauptmann Oswald Boelcke," *Deutsche Luftfahrer Zeitschrift,* November 22, 1916, 320–21.

26. Douglas, *Combat,* p. 196; Raleigh and Jones, *War in the Air,* V, 425.

27. Dournel, "Image," *Revue Historique des Armées* II, No. 4 (1975), 71; Benn, *Sideshows,* p. 202; H. G., *Occasions,* Preface, p. ix.

28. Boulenger, *Escadrille,* p. 26; Lee, *No Parachute,* p. 137; Buddecke, *El Shahin,* p. 91.

29. Dournel, "Image," *Revue Historique des Armées* II, No. 4 (1975), 71; "Contact," *Outings,* p. 245; Silvio Scaroni, "Paragoni impossibili. La 'cavalleria' nella guerra aerea," *Rivista Aeronautica,* December, 1972, 2044; Buddecke, *El Shahin,* p. 100; Douglas, *Combat,* p. 214.

30. Zuerl, *Flieger,* p. 326; Pesquiès-Courbier, "L'Aeronautique," 23; William A. Bishop, *Winged Warfare* (New York, 1918), p. 198; McCaffery, *Bishop,* p. 149.

31. Fucini, *Voli,* p. 99; "Tagebuchblätter," in *Bayerische Flieger in Weltkrieg* (Munich, 1919), p. 141; Maxime Lenoir, "Mes combats," *La guerre aérienne,* May 3, 1917, 394; McCaffery, *Bishop,* unpaginated Introduction; Briscoe and Stannard, *Ball,* p. 247.

32. McCaffery, *Bishop,* p. 146; Douglas, *Combat,* p. 248; Briscoe and Stannard, *Ball,* p. 253; Jacques Mortane, *Guynemer, the Ace of Aces,* trans. by Clifton Harby Levy (New York, 1918), p. 246.

33. Les pertes humaines dans l'aviation française, 1914–1918, typescript communicated by the Service Historique de l'Armée de l'Air; Wise, *Canadian Airmen,* pp. 645–49; Zuerl, *Flieger,* p. 544; Porro, *Guerra,* p. 415; Dr. Martin O'Connor,

Air Aces of the Austro-Hungarian Empire 1914–1918 (Mesa, Ariz., 1986), Appendix IV, p. 267.

34. Porro, *Guerra*, p. 406; Scaroni, "Paragoni," 2038.

35. Supf, *Buch*, II, 260; Benn, *Sideshows*, p. 247.

36. "A nos lecteurs," *La guerre aérienne*, November 23, 1916, 34.

37. Scaroni, "Paragoni," 2040; Insall, *Observer*, p. 75.

38. Hannah Hafkesbrink, *Unknown Germany. An Inner Chronicle of the First World War based on Letters and Diaries* (New Haven, 1948), p. 113.

39. Douglas Campbell, transcription of oral history interview conducted July 8, 1964, donation of the Society of World War I Aero Historians, U.S. Air Force Historical Research Center, Maxwell Air Force Base, p. 23.

40. Flammer, *Vivid Air*, p. 64; *Le Figaro*, September 29, 1917; Guerrini and Pluviano, "Dandismo," 142.

41. Air Council, Minutes, March 23, 1918.

42. Porret, *As français*, I, 208.

43. Boulenger, *Escadrille*, p. 127.

10. The War on Other Fronts

1. Christienne *et al.*, *Aviation*, p. 187; Neumann, *Luftstreitkräfte*, p. 588.

2. Olaf Groehler, *Geschichte des Luftkriegs 1910 bis 1970* (Berlin, 1975), p. 58.

3. Morrow, *German*, pp. 10–12.

4. P. D. Duz, "History of Aeronautics in the U.S.S.R.," typescript translation of *Russkie Aeronautiki vo vremia pervoi mirovoi voine* (Moscow, 1960), pp. 61, 110, 112. Typescript in the Aeronautics Department, National Air and Space Museum.

5. Duz, "History," pp. 48, 110; U.S.S.R., Tsentral'noe statisticheskoe upravlenie, otdel voinnoi statistike, *Rossia v mirovoi voine (v tsiffrakh)* (Moscow, 1925), pp. 52, 63–64.

6. Walter Oertel, "Die russischen Flieger," *Deutsche Luftfahrer Zeitschrift*, December 20, 1916, 362–63; Duz, "History," p. 88; Claude W. Cain, "Flying for the Czar. Alexander Riaboff and the Imperial Russian Air Service," *Cross and Cockade Journal*, Winter, 1970, 309.

7. Duz, "History," p. 36.

8. Lieutenant Stribik, "Chez les bolsheviks," *La guerre aérienne*, January 31, 1918, 64.

9. Neumann, *Luftstreitkräfte*, p. 588; Duz, "History," p. 138; Bülow, *Luftwaffe*, p. 76.

10. "Die russischen Flieger," *Flugsport*, January 27, 1915, 59; Duz, "History," p. 81.

11. Schroeder, *Airman*, p. 146; "Vor der russischen Grenze," *Flugsport*, December 26, 1914, 977.

12. Christienne *et al.*, *Aviation*, pp. 207–8; Carl Mühlmann, *Das Deutsch-türkische Waffenbundnis im Weltkriege* (Leipzig, n.d.), pp. 301–3.

13. Dr. Bryan P. Flanagan, Ed., "The History of the Ottoman Air Force in the Great War: The Reports of Major Erich Serno," *Cross and Cockade Journal*, Summer, 1970, 98–104.

14. Institute za Vojenna Istorija pri Generalnija Shtab na B.N.A., *Istorija na Vojennata Avijacija na Bilgarija* (Sofia, 1988), pp. 15–23.

15. Christienne *et al.*, *Aviation*, pp. 207–8.

16. Neumann, *Luftstreitkräfte*, p. 500; *Istorija*, p. 22; Karl Sterling Schneide, "Aviation in the Dardanelles Campaign," March 1915–January 1916, unpublished paper communicated by its author, p. 15.

17. Schneide, "Dardanelles," pp. 4–6; Porro, *Guerra*, p. 131.

18. *Istorija*, p. 13.

19. Cutlack, *Australian*, p. 427.

20. Porret, *As français*, II, 305; Schneide, "Dardanelles," p. 15.

21. Benn, *Side Shows*, pp. 137–38.

22. Neumann, *Luftstreitkräfte*, p. 497.

23. "La Guerre en Orient," in Mortane, *Histoire illustrée*, II, 213.

24. Hadingham, *Triplanes*, p. 33.

25. Charles B. Burdick, *The Japanese Siege of Tsingtau: World War I in Asia* (Hamden, Conn., 1976), p. 132.

11. Maritime Aviation

1. J. Muraccioli, *L'Aéronautique navale des origines à 1918* (Paris, 1985), p. 17.

2. David Wragg, *Wings over the Sea* (New York, 1979), pp. 9–25 *passim;* Admiral Barjot, *Histoire de la guerre aéro-navale* (Paris, 1961), pp. 11–21; Ferruccio Botti and Mario Cermelli, *La teoria della guerra aerea in Italia dalle origini alla seconda guerra mondiale* (Rome, 1989), pp. 85–7.

3. Popham, *Into Wind,* prologue, xvi.

4. Albert Vulliez, *Aéronavale (1915–1954)* (Paris, 1955), p. 47; Paolo E. Coletta, *Admiral Bradley A. Fiske and the American Navy* (Lawrence, Kansas, 1979), p. 93.

5. Crosara, *Aerostieri,* p. 127; *Militärluftfahrt,* I, 230.

6. Ferruccio Botti, "Aviazione navale in Italia agli inizi del secolo," *Rivista Marittima,* December, 1986, 72–73; *Militärluftfahrt,* I, 240.

7. "Modern Naval Warfare: IV, the Advent of the Air-Craft," *Illustrated London News,* September 9, 1914, 416.

8. Militärluftfahrt, I, 242; Groehler, *Luftkrieg,* p. 49; C.G. Grey, *Sea Flyers* (London, 1942), p. 37.

9. Neumann, *Luftstreitkräfte*, p. 546.

10. Geoffrey Bennett, *The Battle of Jutland* (Trowbridge and London, 1972), pp. 60, 74, 151–52.

11. Porro, *Guèrra,* p. 68.

12. *Militärluftfahrt,* I, 242.

13. Popham, *Into Wind,* p. 25; Francis Dousset, *Les porte-avions français des origines (1911) à nos jours* (Brest and Paris, 1978), p. 12.

14. Clément Ader, *L'aviation militaire* (Paris, 1909), p. 43.

15. Dousset, *porte-avions,* pp. 10–12; Popham, *Into Wind,* pp. 56–58.

16. Alfred Price, *Aircraft versus Submarine* (London, 1973), p. 10; Popham, *Into Wind,* pp. 46–49; Paul G. Halpern, *The Naval War in the Mediterranean* (Annapolis, 1987), pp. 276–83.

17. Barjot, *Aéro-navale,* pp. 33–50 *passim.*

18. Price, *Aircraft,* pp. 11–12; John Terraine, *The U-Boat Wars 1916–1945* (New York, 1989), pp. 19–21.

19. Halpern, *Mediterranean,* p. 277.

20. Price, *Aircraft,* p. 31.

21. *Ibid.,* 24, 25, 29.

22. Halpern, *Mediterranean,* p. 344; Johnson, *Marine,* p. 15.

23. Popham, *Into Wind,* p. 41; Robin Higham, *The British Rigid Airship, 1908–1931: A Study in Weapons Policy* (Westport, Conn., 1975), pp. 111–15.

24. Christienne, *Age d'or,* pp. 73–75; Giorgio Bompiani and Clemente Prepositi, *Le ali della guerra* (Milan, 1934), p. 318.

25. Owen Thetford, *British Naval Aircraft 1912–1958* (London, 1958), p. 582; John Killen, *History of Marine Aviation* (London, 1969), pp. 52–53.

26. Halpern, *Mediterranean,* p. 63; Vice-Admiral Richard Bell Davies, *Sailor in the Air* (London, 1967), p. 121; Grey, *Sea Flyers,* p. 97.

27. Edward Leiser, "The Loss of the Koenigsberg," *Cross and Cockade Journal,* Winter, 1972, 357–75; Peter M. Grosz, "The Cruise of the Wölfchen," *Cross and Cockade Journal,* Spring, 1973, 1–26.

28. Popham, *Into Wind,* p. 16; Davies, *Sailor,* p. 179.

29. Grey, *Sea Flyers,* p. 98; Coletta, *Fiske,* p. 184.

30. Carlo Unia, *Storia degli Aerosiluranti italiani* (Rome, 1974), pp. 6–8.

31. Grey, *Sea Flyers,* p. 114; Vulliez, *Aéronavale,* p. 70; Belleroche, *Combat,* p. 143.

32. Morrow, *German,* pp. 31–32; Neumann, *Luftstreitkräfte,* p. 308; Porro, *Guerra,* p. 138; Hadingham, *Triplanes,* p. 29.

33. Cooper, *Air Policy,* p. 50; Morrow, *German,* p. 32; *Essai historique de l'aéronautique navale* (Paris, 1944), p. 3.

34. Neumann, *Luftstreitkräfte,* pp. 309–10; Johnson, *Marine,* p. 15.

35. Popham, *Into Wind,* p. 5; Davies, *Sailor,* p. 169.

36. Higham, *Airship,* p. 123, footnote 2.

37. Zuerl, *Flieger,* p. 167.

38. Ralph D. Paine, *The First Yale Unit. A Story of Naval Aviation* (2 vols., Cambridge, Mass., 1925), II, 43.

12. The Final Battles

1. Martin Middlebrook, *The Kaiser's Battle: 21 March 1918: The First Day of the German Spring Offensive* (London, 1978), p. 63.

2. Armengaud, *Renseignement,* p. 162; General Voisin, "L'exploration aérienne en guerre de stabilisation, l'attente de l'offensive allemande (février-mars 1918)," *Revue des Forces Aériennes,* February, 1931, 132–143.

3. "Ludendorff's 'Breakthrough' Air Tactics. Secret German Manual of Position Warfare for Air Forces—Translated from the Original," *Aircraft Journal,* April 12, 1919, 1, 9–10; Bruce I. Gudmundsson, *Stormtroop Tactics: Innovation in the Germany Army, 1914–1918* (New York, 1989), pp. 161–62.

4. Gudmundsson, *Stormtroop Tactics* pp. 108–21; Rod Paschall, *The Defeat of Imperial Germany, 1917–1918* (Chapel Hill, 1989), p. 140.

5. Complete Casualties of the R.F.C. and R.A.F. on the Western Front,

June 1917–June 1918, Plans Archives, vol. 56, Air Staff Notes 1918–1928, Air Historical Branch, Ministry of Defence; SHAA, Etat numérique.

6. Middlebrook, *Battle*, p. 284; Puistienne, *Escadrille*, pp. 137, 141.

7. Duvau, *Souvenirs*, p. 15; Puistienne, *Escadrille*, p. 137.

8. Hoeppner, *Luftstreitkräfte*, pp. 172–73; Christienne *et al.*, *Aviation*, p. 152.

9. Raleigh and Jones, *War in the Air*, III, 378; General Maginel, "L'intervention de l'aviation dans la lutte terrestre," *Revue Militaire Générale*, October, 1938, 504–13.

10. "The Employment of Battle Flights," Raleigh and Jones, *War in the Air*, IV, 433–38.

11. Christienne *et al.*, *Aviation*, p. 152.

12. Brereton Greenhous, "Close Support Aircraft in World War I. The Counter Anti-Tank Role," *Aerospace Historian*, June 1974, 87–93; History of Tank and Aeroplane Co-operation, Air 1, 444, P.R.O.

13. J. C. Slessor, *Air Power and Armies* (London, 1936), p. 100; Raleigh and Jones, *War in the Air*, IV, 243, 247.

14. Schlenstedt, *Vollgas!*, p. 254.

15. Poirier, *Bombardements*, pp. 307–10; Zuerl, *Flieger*, pp. 254–47.

16. Zuerl, *Flieger*, p. 61; Schlenstedt, *Vollgas!*, p. 85.

17. "Salvage of Aeroplanes," *Communication Orders*, Collection in the Air Historical Branch, Ministry of Defence.

18. Sweetser, *Air Service*, p. 146; Theodore Knappen, *Wings of War; An Account of the Important Contribution of the United States to Aircraft Invention, Engineering, Development, and Production during the World War* (New York, 1920); Flammer, *Vivid Air*, p. 165; *Frankfurter Zeitung*, April 23, 1918.

19. Sweetser, *Air Service*, p. 101; Burke Davis, *Elliott White Springs, His Life and Times* (Chapel Hill, N.C., 1987), p. 60; Douglas, *Combat*, p. 246; Zuerl, *Flieger*, p. 329.

13. An End and a Beginning

1. "The Independent Air Force," *Flight*, January 9, 1919, 37; Mead, *Eye*, p. 142.

2. Marill, "Aéronautique," p. 136.

3. John Terraine, *The Smoke and the Fire* (London, 1981), p. 173; Georges Huisman, *Dans les coulisses de l'aviation 1914–1918* (Paris, n.d.), pp. 34–35.

4. Joynson Hicks, "Command of the Air," p. 13; Colletta, *Fiske*, p. 128; Isaac Don Levine, *Mitchell, Pioneer of Air Power* (Cleveland, 1943), p. 147; Johnson, *Marine*, p. 63.

5. Vulliez, *Aéronavale*, preface, p. iv.

6. Cooper, *Air Policy*, preface, p. xvi.

7. General Toubert, "Les pertes subies par les Armées françaises pendant la guerre 1914–1918, *Revue d'Infanterie*, September 15, 1921, 305–12; Leed, *No Man's Land*, p. 206.

8. Charles D. Bright, "Air Power in World War I: Sideshow or Decisive Factor?" *Aerospace Historian*, Summer, 1971, 58.

9. Cooper, *Air Policy*, p. 26.

10. Wise, *Canadian Airmen*, p. 575; Bomber Support for the Army. Memo by the Air Staff, November 21, 1939, Air 35–214, P.R.O.

11. Oberstleutnant Schwabedissen, *Der Kampffliegerverband*, vol. 1 of *Der Dienst in der Luftwaffe* (Berlin, n.d.), p. 13; Winter, *Few*, p. 16; McCudden, *Flying Fury*, p. 266.

12. Paul F. Braim, *The Test of Battle: The American Expeditionary Force in the Meuse-Argonne Campaign* (Newark, 1987), p. 158.

13. Tim Travers, *The Killing Ground. The British Army, the Western Front and the Emergence of Modern Warfare* (London, 1987), pp. 250–51, 253.

14. Benn, *Sideshows*, p. 202.

15. Requadt, *Kriegsflugzeug*, p. 91; James P. Tate, "The Army and its Air Corps: A Study of the Evolution of Army Policy toward Aviation, 1919–1941," Ph.D. Dissertation, Indiana University, 1976, p. 1.

16. Sefton Branker in "Contact," *Outing*, x; Cooper, *Air Policy*, pp. 21, 60; Kent Roberts Greenfield, "Air Power and Strategy," in *American Strategy in World War II: A Retrospective* (Baltimore, 1963), p. 78.

17. Braim, *Test of Battle*, p. 158.

18. Charles Godefroy, "Sous l'arc de triomphe en plein vol," *L'Aérophile* 1–15 August, 1919, 250; Neumann, *Luftstreitkräfte*, p. 118.

19. Frederick R. Karl, *William Faulkner: American Writer. A Biography* (New York, 1989), pp. 111–19, 123–5; Flammer, *Vivid Air*, preface, p. ix.

20. Davis, *Springs*, p. 8; Lewis, *Sagittarius*, pp. 23–4.

Essay on Sources

The notes appended to the chapters of this book refer to those works on various aspects of the air war that proved most helpful in its preparation, so it seems superfluous to list them all again. Yet the sources—and sometimes the dearth of them—call for some comment, particularly since that comment may be useful to others reading or researching in the field; it is chiefly to that end that this brief *tour d'horizon* is offered.

As the notes indicate, material for the book has been drawn above all from published materials, but the author was able to use a considerable variety of sources, and it might be useful to note them here. The archives of the Royal Flying Corps/Royal Air Force are preserved in the Public Record Office at Kew, where the author was able to work for a limited time. The collection of chief interest is Air 1, for which there is a useful card index in the Offices of the Air Historical Branch, Ministry of Defense, now located in Great Scotland Yard. Research was also done in the archives of the French Air Service, most of which are held by the Service Historique de l'Armée de l'Air, located in the Chateau de Vincennes; additional materials concerning aviation at the corps and division level were retained by the French Army and are available from its archival service, the Service Historique de l'Armée de Terre, also located in the Château de Vincennes. The major collection is Series A in the S.H.A.A. holdings, comprising something over 100 cartons; the collection was much reduced in size by the severe losses during World War II. Far more catastrophic were the losses in the Luftwaffe archives. They too suffered heavily at the end of the Second World War, and it has been estimated that less than one percent of the archives relating to the aerial effort in 1914–18 have survived. The author's visit to Freiburg, where German military archives are kept, yielded very little of use for the present work.

A very valuable non-published source is the oral history interview, and in several countries aerial veterans of the Great War have been interviewed and their remarks preserved. Perhaps the most ambitious effort in this regard is that of the United States Air Force Historical Research Center, Maxwell Air Force Base, Alabama. Its holdings are

251

listed in its recent *Catalog of the United States Air Force Oral History Collection*, edited by Maurice Maryanow (Maxwell Air Force Base, Ala., 1989). There are also oral history materials relating to the First World War in the Imperial War Museum, London, and in the S.H.A.A. in Vincennes, though neither of these collections was used in the preparation of this book. The S.H.A.A. interviews have not been transcribed, and so are available only in audio version.

When the researcher turns to published material on the air war from 1914 to 1918, he finds himself in a vast sea of literature, and it is a sea that is not well charted. The aeronautical journals of the era are a particularly rich source, and fortunately there is a guide to them in the *Bibliography of Aeronautics* which Paul Brockett edited periodically for the National Advisory Committee on Aeronautics from 1909 to 1932. The bibliography of books and articles is international in scope—for the period 1909–16 there were nearly 400 entries concerning aeronautics in France. A more recent compilation, which indexes English-language articles on aeronautics, including those of historical interest, is the *Air University Library Index to Military Periodicals*, which has appeared since 1949. Unfortunately there is no convenient index to the articles in the more popular journals that have sprung up in recent years to satisfy the interest of aficionados of World War I aviation: The American journal *Cross and Cockade* (1960–85); the British *Cross and Cockade* (1970–   ) and the American *Over the Front* (1986–   ). Though the articles are usually neither by nor for professional historians, they are often exhaustively researched and of considerable value. Among the one-volume bibliographies of value for the World War I period are Karl Köhler, *Bibliographie zur Luftkriegsgeschichte* (Frankfurt, 1966); Myron J. Smith, *World War I in the Air: A Bibliography and Chronology* (Metuchen, N.J., 1977), and James Philip Noffsinger, *World War I Aviation Books in English: An Annotated Bibliography* (Metuchen, N.J., 1987).

There are also bibliographies at the national level that are very useful. The first of these to appear was Giuseppe Boffito, *Biblioteca aeronautica italiana illustrata* (Florence, 1929); a supplement appeared in 1937. Boffito's work may be further supplemented with the *Bibliografia italiana di storia e studi militari 1960–1984* (Milan, 1987), published by the Centro interuniversitario di studi e ricerche storico-militari. For the British there is the Imperial War Museum's brief publication, *The Royal Flying Corps, Royal Naval Air Service and Royal Air Force, 1912–1918. A List of Selected References from the Reference Library* (London, 1962), which can be supplemented with Robin Higham's essay on "The Development of the Royal Air Force 1909–1945," in a collective work edited by Higham and entitled *A Guide to the Sources of British Military History* (Berkeley, 1971). Higham's work should in turn be supplemented by a volume in the Military History Bibliographies Series of the Garland Publishing

Company: Gerald Jordan, *British Military History: A Supplement to Robin Higham's "Guide to the Sources"* (New York and London, 1988). Two other volumes of the Garland bibliographical series are useful for materials on the French and German Air Services: Charles Christienne, Patrick Facon, Patrice Buffotot, and Lee Kennett, *French Military Aviation: A Bibliographical Guide* (1989); and Edward L. Homze, *German Military Aviation: A Guide to the Literature* (1987). Particularly useful for the U.S. Air Service is Kathleen Elizabeth Probrandt, "American Warbirds: An Annotated Bibliography," an M.A. thesis completed at San Angelo State University in 1986.

The vast majority of the "general" histories of the air war which one finds on the library shelves are of the "blazing skies" variety, centering on the most dramatic aspects of the conflict, the fighter war and the deeds of the aces. Most historians who have approached the air war with more scholarly intent have tended to fit it into the larger story of the development of air power; among the more successful of these surveys are Basil Collier's *A History of Air Power* (London, 1974) and Robin Higham's *Air Power: A Concise History* (New York, 1972). The East German historian Olaf Groehler has produced an ambitious *Geschichte des Luftkriegs 1910 bis 1970* (Berlin, 1971), which can be consulted with great profit.

Most of the belligerents launched "official" histories after the war; they were generally vast, collective works centering on the great land struggles, with air power figuring as a minor element, which in truth it was. But there were also plans for ambitious "air" histories, most of which never got off the ground. The Americans collected a vast amount of material that was to be used in writing the official history of the U.S. Air Service, but the history was never written. The research materials so diligently assembled are now housed in the National Archives, where they are known as the Gorrell Collection. After the war there was a spate of publications by individuals involved in the American air effort, but the Air Service still awaits its historian. It's operational history has been covered succinctly in James J. Hudson's *Hostile Skies: The Combat History of the Army Air Service in World War I* (Syracuse, N.Y., 1968). Among useful earlier works are Arthur Sweetser, *The American Air Service; A Record of its problems, its Difficulties, its Failures, and its Final Achievements* (New York and London, 1919); H.A. Toulmin, Jr., *Air Service, American Expeditionary Force* (New York, 1927), which stresses organizational matters; and Theodore McFarlane Knappen's exposition of the challenges in the field of matériel, entitled *Wings of War, An Account of the Important Contribution of the United States to Aircraft Invention, Engineering, Development and Production during the War* (New York and London, 1920). More recently a view of the American air service through its documents has been offered by Maurer Maurer in *The U.S. Air Service in World War I* (4 vols., Maxwell Air Force Base and Washington, 1978).

The Luftwaffe's Kriegswissenschaftliche Abteilung was hard at work on a multi-volumed history of the German air service when war broke out again in 1939; several volumes had been completed for the series entitled *Die deutschen Luftstreitkräfte von ihrer Entstehung bis zum Ende des Weltkrieges 1918*—most notably the three-volume *Die Militärluftfahrt bis zum Beginn des Weltkrieges 1914,* which appeared in 1941 and was republished in 1965–66. A number of other volumes in various stages of completion were lost in the war and cannot be reconstituted. The void can be filled at least in part with cooperative works done in the interwar period, such as that edited by Georg Paul Neumann, *Die deutschen Luftstreitkräfte im Weltkriege* (Berlin, 1920), and that of Generalleutnant Walter von Eberhardt, *Unsere Luftstreitkräfte, 1914–1918: Ein Denkmal deutschen Heldentums* (Berlin, 1930). Neumann's work, which proved especially valuable, was put together with the help of some 30 specialists in various aspects of aeronautics, and its 600-odd pages offer a panorama of the German Air Service, with sections dedicated to such various topics as flight training, parachutes, and campaigning in Macedonia. An English-language edition appeared under the title *The German Air Force in the Great War* (London, 1920). Also written in English was a well-reasoned history by John R. Cuneo, who systematically exploited the published materials for *The Winged Mars* (2 vols., Harrisburg, Pa., 1944–46); unfortunately Cuneo did not carry the story beyond 1916. More recently John H. Morrow, Jr. has enriched the literature with his *German Air Power in World War I* (Lincoln, Nebr., 1982). Morrow has exploited what archival records remain for a study that is particularly strong on organization and matériel. Finally, since Bavaria had her own air service during the Great War, and also her own archives, which survived the Second World War in somewhat better shape than those of Prussia and imperial Germany, Peter Pletschacher has written a very solidly researched history of the Bavarian Air Service: *Die königliche bayerischen Fliegertruppen, 1912–1919* (Stuttgart, 1978).

The British succeeded in producing the massive *The War in the Air: Being the Story of the Part Played in the Great War by the Royal Air Force* (six vols., Oxford, 1922–37); though the authors of record were Sir Walter Raleigh and H. A. Jones, in fact Raleigh died after contributing to the first volume. It has become the custom among historians to cite the work as indispensable, which it is, and to condemn it for its tendency to enhance the image of the air arm, a tendency that is undeniable. It can almost always be consulted with profit, and its documents and tables are particularly useful; in this latter connection there is an unnumbered appendix volume that is especially valuable, though all too often it is not to be found with the other six volumes. Two other official histories should be noted; those relating to Australian and Canadian participation. The first of these, F. M. Cutlack's *The Australian Flying Corps in the Western and Eastern Theatres of War 1914–1918* (Sydney, 1923), was part of the 12-volume *Official History of Australia in the War of 1914–1918*, edited by Robert O'Neill; it related the story of the Australian Flying Corps, Australia being the only dominion that created its own flying service during the war. More recent and more valuable is the volume *Canadian Airmen and the First World War* (Toronto, 1980), whose author of record was S. F. Wise. Since Canadian airmen were dispersed throughout the R.F.C./R.A.F., the team of researchers embarked on nothing less than a general history of the British air service, with analyses and conclusions that differed considerably from those of Raleigh and Jones; what is more, the book rests on solid statistical compilations that are lacking in earlier works. The 700 pages of this collective effort are a significant contribution to our knowledge of the first air war. At the same time academic historians have further clarified and modified the picture of British military aviation in its early years; among the most recent and most worthwhile is Malcolm Cooper's *The Birth of Independent Air Power: British Air Policy in the First World War* (London, 1986).

The historiography of French military aviation has also been considerably enriched in recent years by the publication of a massive work by General Charles Christienne, General Pierre Lissarague, Alain Degardin, Patrick Facon, Patrice Buffotot, and Marcellin Hodeir, *Histoire de l'aviation militaire française* (Paris and Limoges, 1980). A hundred and fifty of the book's 500 pages are dedicated to *la Grande Guerre*, making it the point of departure for all research in that era of French aviation. As a boon to British and American readers the Smithsonian Press has brought out an English-language edition under the title *A History of French Military Aviation* (Washington, 1986). General Christienne published another useful work on the era: *L'Aviation française 1890–1919: Un certain âge d'or* (Paris, 1988). A number of young academic historians have been drawn into the field of aviation history in recent years, and as a result there has been a series of useful theses and monographs. One older work on the French air service is especially worthy of mention: the massive volume edited by Maurice de Brunoff entitled *L'Aéronautique pendant la Guerre Mondiale* (Paris, 1919); similar in format to the Neumann volume on the German Air Service, the work of de Brunoff and his collaborators offers chapters on virtually every facet of French military aeronautics. For reference purposes it may still be the single most important work on the French Air Service.

The Italian air effort is still known largely through older works such as General Felice Porro's *La guerra nell'aria* (Milan, 1935), though within the past two decades historical research has been renewed with such works as Angelo Lodi's *Storia delle origini dell' aeronautica militare, 1884–1915* (2 vols., Rome, 1976–77). Most recently the doctrinal and conceptual aspects of air power in Italy have been reexamined in an important work published under the patronage of the Ufficio Storico, Stato Maggiore Aeronautico and authored by Ferrucio Botti and Mario Cermelli: *La teoria della guerra aerea in Italia delle origini alla seconda guerra mondiale* (Rome, 1989).

It is in eastern Europe that scholarship has lagged the most; whether it be doctrine, operations, matériel, or any other aspect, the air war in the east remains little known. The Austro-Hungarian Air Service has found a historian in Ernst Peter, whose *Die k.u.k. Luftschiffer-und Flieger-truppe Österreich-Ungarns 1794–1919* (Stuttgart, 1981), may be supplemented for the air war against Italy with Riccardo Caviglioli's *L'aviazione austro-ungarica sulla fronte italiana 1915–1918* (Milan, 1934). For the Russian air service the chief source remains P.D. Duz', *Istoria vozdukhoplavania i aviatsii v S.S.S.R. Period mirovoi voine 1914–1918 gg* (Moscow, 1960). The limitations of this work were noted in the text, and it is to be hoped that the rising generation of Soviet historians will extend our knowledge of this all too obscure subject.

One kind of information all too rarely encountered for any of the belligerents is hard and precise figures, and for lack of them much that has been written about the air war is of necessity impressionistic. Even when there are statistics, their reliability is often in doubt—witness the officially confirmed claims of enemy planes downed. The problem was not helped by the subsequent destruction of archives, but it seems to stem also from the simple failure to keep records, especially in the first half of the war. While statistical data for the R.F.C./R.A.F. is found *passim* in Raleigh and Jones' *War in the Air,* and especially in its many appendices, there is a very useful trove of figures in the *Synopsis of British Air Effort during the War,* published in April 1919 as No. 100 of the British Parliament's *Papers by Command* series. The most sophisticated statistics regarding flying personnel are contained in the "Statistical Analysis of Canadians in the British Flying Services," Appendix C of Wise, *Canadian Airmen,* cited above.

General Christienne and his co-authors have compiled several pages of statistics relating to French aircraft production, losses of planes and personnel, etc. (pp. 183–87) in their *Aviation militaire française,* cited above. The most comprehensive and most frequently cited figures regarding the German Air Service are in "Leistungen, Erfolge and Verluste der deutschen Luftstreitkräfte im Lichte der Statistik," in Neumann's *Luftstreitkräfte* (pp. 578–90), while John Morrow has collected figures on aircraft and motor production, which are included in Appendices 1–7 of his *German Air Power* cited earlier. A unique compilation of casualties is Wilhelm Zickerick's "Verlustliste der deutschen Luftstreitkräfte im Weltkrieg," appended to Walther von Eberhardt's *Unsere Luftstreitkräfte, 1914–1918: ein Denkmal deutschen Heldentums* (Berlin, 1930). It lists some 12,000 German airmen who lost their lives, along with the place and date. While incomplete, as the compiler admits, the list has been used in conjunction with Allied airmen's claims to try to determine who shot down whom, but it could be made to yield other information as well. An old Soviet statistical study of Russia's participation in the war has some useful references to aeronautics: U.S.S.R. Tsentral'noe statisticheskoe upravlenie, otdel voennoi statistiki, *Rossia v mirovoi voine (v tsiffrakh)* (Moscow, 1925).

If there is one topic in aviation history for which the sources have always been abundant it is the airplanes themselves. This is preeminently the case for World War I aircraft, some models of which have been the subject of entire monographs. Several books pulled from the sea of literature on the subject were particularly helpful: John M. Bruce, *British Airplanes 1914–1918* (London, 1957), W.M. Lamberton's *Fighter Aircraft of the 1914–1918 War* (London, 1960), and his *Reconnaissance and Bomber Aircraft of the 1914–1918 War* (Los Angeles, 1962); Peter Gray and Owen Thetford, *German Aircraft of the First World War* (London, 1962); Kenneth Munson, *Fighters, Attack and Training Craft 1914–1918* (London, 1968); and Heinz J. Novarra, *Marine Aircraft of the 1914–1918 War* (Letchworth, England, 1967). To these books, which are essentially repertories of types with production and performance data, should be added others that follow the planes' evolution, such as the two works of Peter M. H. Lewis, *The British Fighter since 1912: Fifty Years of Design and Development* (London, 1965), and *The British Bomber since 1914: Fifty Years of Design and Development* (London, 1967).

The airplanes can also be profitably viewed from the perspective of those who built them and maintained them. Three books that were profitable in this regard were Stepney Blakeney, *How an Aeroplane is Built* (London, 1918), Fred Herbert Colvin, *Aircraft Mechanics Handbook: a Collection of Facts and Suggestions from Factory and Flying Field to Assist in Caring for Modern Aircraft* (New York, 1918), and R. Borlase Matthews, *The Aviation Pocket Book for 1918: A Compendium of Modern Practice and a Collection of useful Notes, Formulae, Rules, Tables, and Data relating to Aeronautics* (Sixth Ed., London, 1918). The broader challenge that aircraft posed to belligerents who had to design and produce them is best laid out by I. B. Holley in *Ideas and Weapons: Exploitation of the Aerial Weapon by the United States during World War I: a Study in the Relationship of Technological Advance, Military Doctrine, and the Development of Weapons* (New Haven, 1953). It is also important to understand the limitations placed on the performance of early aircraft—and all aircraft, for that matter—by the laws of aerodynamics, and a most useful book in this regard is John G. Lee's *Fighter Facts and Fallacies* (New York, 1942).

As is the case with the machines, there is an abundant literature about the men who flew in 1914–18. They themselves left behind a large quantity of testimony in the form of letters, diaries, and memoirs.

These are almost always interesting and useful, and sometimes they achieve genuine literary distinction, as is the case with Cecil Lewis' superlative memoir *Sagittarius Rising* (New York, 1936). The best guide to biographical and autobiographical materials in English is Noffsinger's *World War I Aviation, Books in English* cited above, while sources of this nature in French, German, and Italian appear in the bibliographies of Christienne *et al.*, Homze, and Boffito, also listed above. Two collective biographies were particularly useful for this book. One is Walter Zuerl's *Pour le mérite Flieger* (Munich, 1938), which offers biographical sketches of the German airmen who won the coveted "Blue Max," and the other is Daniel Porret's *Les "As" français de la Grande Guerre* (2 vols., Vincennes, 1983). Comparative studies are few, and are chiefly concerned with isolating those qualities possessed by the best fighter pilots, the aces. Paul Robert Skawran spent much of the interwar period on this question, and then published his *Psychologie des Jagdfliegers: Berühmte Flieger des Weltkrieges* (Berlin, 1940). The book rests upon impressive research and contains valuable information on such things as the age factor in a fighter pilot's career; it also reflects the National Socialist approach to scholarship, classifying celebrated pilots by race using the Nazi-approved terminology (Billy Bishop, Oswald Boelcke, Georges Guynemer and Eddie Rickenbacker were all Nordic, while Manfred von Richthofen was of the "Fälisch-dalisch" type). Most recently Mike Spick has reviewed the records of the best World War I fighter pilots in *The Ace Factor* (Annapolis, 1988), to determine if they shared with the aces of later wars a mysterious quality called "situational awareness."

Spick's book also belongs on the list of useful works on aerial combat in the First World War, along with several others particularly helpful to this study. C. Massenet de Marancour's *La chasse en avion* (Paris, 1920) is an early work by a French ace who tried to isolate certain precepts and principles in aerial combat, while perhaps the best recent studies of aerial fighting in the Great War are Peter Simkins' brief *Air Fighting, 1914–1918* (London, 1978); and Richard P. Hallion, *Rise of the Fighter Aircraft 1914–1918* (Baltimore, 1984). The Great War is also treated in three works that trace the evolution of aerial combat: Pierre Belleroche, *Histoire du combat aérien* (Marseilles, 1943); Air Vice-Marshal J.E. Johnson, *Full Circle: The Story of Air Fighting* (London, 1968); and Edward H. Sims, *Fighter Tactics and Strategy 1914–1970* (New York, 1972).

If the reconnaissance function was first in importance, it has been last in the amount of literature dedicated to it since 1918. The best single work in English is Peter Mead's *The Eye in the Air, History of Aerial Observation and Reconnaissance for the Army, 1785–1945* (London, 1983), which has the weakness of presenting the British experience as though it were everyone's experience. An older but valuable French perspective is offered by General Armengaud in *Le renseignement aérien, sauvegarde des armées* (Paris, 1934), and the French have also produced an excellent general account of wartime aerial photography: André-H. Carlier, *La photographie aérienne pendant la guerre* (Paris, 1921). A worthwhile American survey is Harold E. Porter, *Aerial Observation* (New York and London, 1921). But it is the Italians who have published most comprehensively on aerial reconnaissance: Leonardo Crosara, *Gli aerostieri: notizie storiche degli aerostieri militari dal 1793 al 1919* (Rome, 1924); M. Molfese, *L'Aviazione da ricognizione italiana durante la guerra europea* (Rome, 1925); and F. Muscarà, *Storia dell'osservazione aerea dell' Esercito* (Rome, 1974).

British bombing activity was prominently featured in Raleigh and Jones' *War in the Air*, then reexamined by Neville Jones in *The Origins of Strategic Bombing: A Study of the Development of British Air Strategic Thought and Practice up to 1918* (London, 1973); and by Barry D. Powers, *Strategy without Slide Rule: British Air Strategy, 1914–1918* (London, 1976). The last two works are chiefly concerned with strategic bombardment, but the question of tactical bombing has been reexamined in Wise, *Canadian Airmen*, cited earlier. The French experience is still best related by René Martel, *L'Aviation française de bombardement (des origines au 11 novembre 1918* (Paris, 1939); on the other hand the older Italian general histories can be supplemented with Giorgio Apostolo and Rosario Abate, *Caproni nella prima guerra mondiale* (Milan, 1970), and by Domenico Lodovico, *Gli aviatori italiani da bombardamento nella guerra 1915–1918* (Rome, 1980).

The topic of naval aviation is often subsumed under naval history, and much of the writing about the naval air services appears in more general naval histories of the Great War; this is the case for Italy, for example, although Ferrucio Botti and Mario Cermelli have treated both military and naval aviation in their recent *Teoria della guerra aerea*, cited earlier. Admiral Pierre Barjot has produced a very general work on maritime aviation in his *Histoire de la guerre aéro-navale* (Paris, 1961), as has John Killen in *A History of Maritime Aviation 1911–1968* (London, 1969). Archibald D. Turnbull and Clifford L. Lord collaborated on a highly regarded *History of United States Naval Aviation* (New Haven, 1949); while Donald McIntyre has concentrated on the British experience in *Wings of Neptune: the Story of Naval Aviation* (London, 1963), as has Hugh Popham in his *Into Wind: The History of Naval Flying* (London, 1969). Albert Vulliez has written the story of French naval aviation in *Aéronavale (1915–1954)* (Paris, 1955). The German historian Karl Köhler began a work on the German naval air service in the First World War but it was unfinished at his death; the typescript is in the Bundesarchiv-Militär-archiv in Freiburg.

Finally, the whole burden and import of the first air war are subjects still imperfectly explored three-quarters of a century later. As for the impact of the airplane on warfare, we have fallen into the habit of thinking that this was best analyzed by postwar "prophets" such as Billy

Mitchell and Giulio Douhet. In fact neither of these prolific writers was much read in Europe in the decade following the Armistice. The works most cited on the past and future of air power were books completely forgotten today: Hans Ritter's *Der Luftkrieg* (Berlin and Leipzig, 1926) and Major Orthlieb's *L'Aéronautique hier-demain* (Paris, 1920). As for the broader cultural impact, only parts of the story have been told in John Corn's *The Winged Gospel. America's Romance with Aviation 1900–1950* (New York, 1983), and with Bùi Xuân Bào's *Aviation et littérature; naissance d'un héroïsme nouveau dans les lettres françaises de l'entre-deux-guerres* (Paris, 1961).

Index